GREAT DECISIONS 2014

W9-ARX-187

About the cover

The Pegasus, a Navy UAV, rests at sunsrise on China Lake Naval Air Station in China Lake, CA. Unmanned aerial vehicles have revolutionized aviation, providing more accurate tracking with little human intervention.

Photo Credit:
JOE MCNALLY/GETTY IMAGES

GREAT DECISIONS IS A TRADEMARK OF THE FOREIGN POLICY ASSOCIATION.

© COPYRIGHT 2014 BY FOREIGN POLICY ASSOCIATION, INC., 470 PARK AVENUE SOUTH, NEW YORK, NEW YORK 10016.

LIBRARY OF CONGRESS CONTROL NUMBER: 201395545
ISBN: 978-0-87124-244-0

FOREIGN POLICY ASSOCIATION 1918

Researched as of November 26, 2013. The authors are responsible for factual accuracy and for the views expressed.
FPA itself takes no position on issues of U.S. foreign policy.

Life can only be understood backwards; but it must be lived forwards —Søren Kierkegaard

FOR MANY YEARS our promotional materials at the FOREIGN POLICY ASSOCIATION featured a photograph of the Capitol with the caption: "If you knew what they know, would you do what they do?" I have always thought a powerful variation on that campaign might feature photographs of former presidents with the caption: "Knowing what you know now, what would you have done differently?"

If life could be lived and understood forward, how different would our actions be? And, more importantly, how would such prescience alter the course of history?

History is replete with conflicts that could have been avoided. Take, for example, World War I, which coincided with—indeed, inspired—the founding of the Foreign Policy Association. After seeing the far-reaching consequences of World War I, would the United Kingdom and Germany have reconsidered their decision to go to war? Henry Kissinger thinks so: "The turning point in European history has been World War I. Europe has never recovered from World War I. And yet if any of the leaders who went into World War I had known in 1914 what the world would look like in 1918, they would never have done it."

In statecraft, shortsightedness of policies and false assumptions can come with tragic costs. During the Civil War, Confederate military strategy was underpinned by the assumption that the North would not absorb for long the great sacrifices of an extended conflict. Harvard President Drew Gilpin Faust observes: "At the war's outset, it seemed almost unimaginable that the North would be willing to fight so long and hard to keep the Southern states in the Union….With the inevitability of hindsight, with the nation preserved and projected toward the global leadership we have come to take for granted, we rarely consider that the North might in the mid-19th century have made a different decision, might have let the South secede or perhaps have negotiated a peace in the face of Confederate military successes during the war's early years."

Today, few decisions are as important as the ones pertaining to relations between the U.S. and China. China is on track to become the world's largest economy by 2020. As it narrows the economic gap with the U.S., the overriding question will be whether cooperation or conflict will characterize the new world order.

The lazy Susan found in most eateries in China offers an apt metaphor for the cooperation that ideally would guide relations between the U.S. and China. The lazy Susan works best when diners are aware of each other's needs. If one party holds the rotating surface or, worse, if diners seek to turn it in opposite directions, the result is deadlock. On many vital issues, neither China nor the U.S. will advance national interests without viewing the world from a positive-sum perspective. Over the long haul, it is in the interests of both the U.S. and China to make and to adhere to wise global standards.

I commend to you the analysis of Chinese foreign policy and the many other timely essays that have been assembled in GREAT DECISIONS 2014.

Noel V. Lateef
President and CEO
Foreign Policy Association

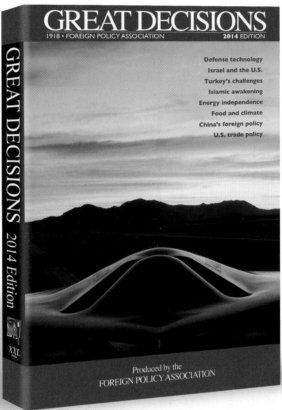

Defense technology
by P. W. Singer

An X-47B Unmanned Combat Air System (UCAS) demonstrator flies over the flight deck of the aircraft carrier USS George H.W. Bush in May 2013, the first aircraft carrier to successfully catapult launch an unmanned aircraft from its flight deck. (TIMOTHY WALTER/U.S. NAVY)

There's a famous line attributed to humorist Mark Twain that is often quoted as a guide for leaders. "History doesn't repeat itself but it does rhyme."

Throughout the past year, in meetings with every U.S. military service chief, as well as the Chairman of the Joint Chiefs of Staff, the writer made sure to ask the following simple but telling question of these men who are guiding the future of the U.S. military: What period of history do they believe is the best parallel to today?

Notably, every single one of them answered the same, comparing today's era to the early 1990s. All expressed their concern that the U.S. may be repeating the mistakes of the post-Cold War era they had lived through earlier in their careers, making painful budget and personnel cuts to their beloved services that could later prove too deep or injudicious.

The problem, though, is when looking for echoes of the past, we too often only see that with which we are most familiar, humming the songs of our youth. The chiefs have put their finger on how we are at a time of fundamental transition, but a better historic comparison may be much earlier, with a different nation.

P.W. SINGER *is Director of the Center for 21st Century Security and Intelligence at the Brookings Institution. For further information: www.pwsinger.com*

21st century issues, 20th century parallels

In many ways, today is more akin to the period surrounding World War I than the end of the Cold War. But our strategic parallel is not the U.S., which had just entered the world stage and then rapidly pulled back, but rather is closer to Great Britain's of that period.

Like the British Empire, today's U.S. military has global responsibilities but also global burdens that it must tackle alone. The U.S. military operates a system of roughly 600 bases and/or deployments in 156 countries and consumes just under half the world's military spending.

Like Great Britain and its colonial wars, the U.S. military has been engaged in a series of conflicts around the planet—what would have been called "small wars." The name is both true and at the same time misleading. The Boer wars and Afghanistans of the world are tough, painful and exhausting, but they do not constitute existential threats.

The U.S. is now what academics describe as a "status quo" power— it is not a rising power and instead is trying to figure out how to maintain dominance as the world shifts around it. The status quo description may not be politic, but it is the reality; Americans generally like the way the world system is structured today, largely because they designed much of it in the wake of World War II and once again after the end of the Cold War.

Emerging China

Yet, rather than a triumphant unipolar moment, the 21st-century world is far more competitive. Just as the United Kingdom had been the dominant global political, military and economic power throughout most of the 18th and 19th centuries, but then had to face the rise of new players like Germany and the U.S. in the 20th century, so too does the U.S. face the emergence of China onto the international stage. China has the second-largest gross domestic product (GDP) in the world, after that of the U.S. Its booming economy is accompanied by growth in military expenditures, and power. As the journal *Foreign Affairs* noted, "The rise of China will likely be the most important international relations story of the 21st century, but it remains unclear whether that story will have a happy ending."

China's rise raises a variety of questions, including issues of military tactics and doctrine. Will the Pentagon be able to counter China's new, extended-range ballistic missiles that might be able to sink the same U.S. aircraft carriers that once ruled the waves? Then there are the grand strategic questions posed by *Foreign Affairs* in its look at a not so "happy ending": "Will an era of U.S.-Chinese tension be as dangerous as the Cold War? Will it be even worse, because China, unlike the Soviet Union, will prove a serious economic competitor as well as a geopolitical one?" Questions such as these regarding the strategic implications of China's rise mirror those famously posed in *Foreign Affairs'* "Mr. X" article in 1947, in which State Department official George Kennan called for containment of the Soviet Union.

Debt crisis

At the same time that the U.S.' status as a global superpower is undergoing relative if not absolute decline (i.e., the U.S. isn't going to be a second-rate power, but its edge certainly is shrinking), just as happened in the UK, the nation is undergoing a fundamental period of political self-evaluation of its role in the world. Part of this re-evaluation, like the UK's back then, is driven by a growing debt and a broadening economic competitiveness challenge. In fall 2013, the U.S. national debt stood at close to $17 trillion. In other words, the U.S. debt could pay the rent for every American for the next half century or could finance NATO's entire defense budget for some 17 years. This burgeoning debt crisis, combined with domestic political dysfunction, created a series of generalized spending cuts, known as "sequestration" or the "se-

A Chinese Navy submarine takes part in an international fleet review to celebrate the 60th anniversary of the founding of the Peoples Liberation Army Navy in Qingdao, Shandong province, April 2009. (REUTERS/CORBIS)

quester," that will shrink U.S. spending for the next decade.

There is also a question of whether one "needs" the old commitments that guided U.S. strategy for the last several generations. Just as the UK started to change its view of colonies from assets to burdens, the U.S. is re-evaluating its relationship with once dear client states, particularly in the Middle East. U.S. dependence on foreign sources of oil, especially the Gulf States, has shifted with its domestic ramp-up of production. As a result, the nation is on its way to becoming the world's largest oil producer by 2020 and energy self-sufficient or "independent" by 2035. As Ian Bremmer, president of the risk consultancy Eurasia Group, writes, "That's a game changer," with resonance for everything from the future of the American economy to its outlook toward regions like the Middle East. The U.S. has played a role as a security provider for half a century in a region it no longer needs as it did in the past.

New isolationism

Yet, perhaps more important to the context surrounding U.S. strategic thinking moving forward is a growing strand of isolationism entering into U.S. politics, echoing back to the 1920s. President Barack Obama's difficulty in garnering a coalition to support intervention in Syria this past year was not a blip. Rather, it reflected an ongoing broader generational shift inside the U.S. body politic. One survey of over 1,100 young Generation X, or "millennial," leaders found that their worldviews were shaped by 9/11, the Iraq War, and domestic crises like Hurricane Katrina, with the end result that 57% thought the U.S. was "too involved in global affairs." To put this into context, it is double the level of isolationist sentiment among older generations of leaders and voters that presently shape the majority of U.S. policy. This shift is now playing out in the changing makeup, and the aging, shrinking influence of the internationalist wings of each political party, especially on the Republican side, much as a generation of war-weary Brits began to question the once unquestionable burdens of empire. ∎

Technology game changers

A remote control robot with the U.S. Army moves a pressure plate taken from an Improvised Explosive Device (IED) that was discovered during a day-long route clearance mission near Khakriz, Afghanistan, July 7, 2010. (JUSTIN SULLIVAN/GETTY IMAGES)

For military officers, though, perhaps the most important comparison to the last interwar years is the role of technology and its effects on war. Back in the early 20th century, a series of technologies emerged that had once been science fiction and then literally changed the nature of the game, both on and off the battlefield. These included strange things like Jules Verne's concept of boats that would travel under the water attacking civilian shipping, A.A. Milne's idea of using flying machines in war, H.G. Wells' "Land Ironclads," metal contraptions, impervious to rifle fire that would cross battlefields, or even the crazy concept Wells had of a bomb that would be powered not by chemistry but by radioactive materials. These once crazy concepts became the modern submarine, tank, airplane and atomic bomb that shaped the reality of war for the next century.

In the last decade, the unmanned system has proven to be one of these "killer applications"—indeed, literally giving a double meaning to the term. The U.S. military went into Afghanistan after 9/11 with just a handful of robotic systems—otherwise known as unmanned aerial systems, remotely pi-

loted aircraft or drones—in the air and zero unmanned systems on the ground, none of them armed. Today, there are over 8,000 drones in the U.S. inventory and another roughly 12,000 on the ground. It is not just the U.S.; the technology has gone global, with 87 other countries wrestling with questions like how one staffs units fighting remotely? What doctrine should guide them? What impact can and should they have on the choices of when and where to go to war? Take, for instance, the "drone wars" debate that emerged after the U.S. not only used unmanned systems in military operations in Afghanistan, but a series of covert campaigns in places like Pakistan and Yemen as well.

While the Predator drone still seems like science fiction to many in the public and the military, it is a technology that actually first went operational in the 1990s Balkans war. (It wasn't until it was armed in the opening months of the Afghanistan operation post 9/11 that it truly became a game changer.) The challenge for today's strategists is determining what comes next. That is, what are the technologies that the naysayers derisively describe as "science

experiments" that will be key to shaping the battlefield of tomorrow?

For the last year, a Pentagon project called "NeXTech" has explored the comparable game changers that loom for war and strategy. The project ranged from interviews with the scientists and investors who will create and pay for the tools to war games with soldiers from multiple countries who will use them to fight. The results are startling in their range:

■ Autonomous robotics, from large drones that fly themselves like the X-47 that recently landed on an aircraft carrier, to tiny systems the size of swarming insects, are not just moving the human role geographically from the point of action in war, but also chronologically, in that key decisions are being made by software developed months even years before.

■ Growing dependence on big data, cyberwarfare and the so-called "Internet of things," where devices undertake activities, and infrastructure such as power and transportation makes decisions without human instruction, creating a reactive battlefield terrain.

■ New directed energy systems (aka "lasers") are being deployed for use on Navy ships and missile defense. These are the first weapons to use something other than kinetic force (e.g., a fist, a bullet, etc.), meaning they are weapons that can modulate their power, focus and duration.

■ Direct Digital Manufacturing, so-called "3D" printing, allows a bit, a computer design, to be turned into an atom, a thing, be it a car part, a gun or even a drone. The ability to prototype at a pace more rapid than ever before,

but also to manufacture on site and on demand, is as big a disruption to the defense economy as the early assembly lines. For instance, one set of university students in the UK last year designed, constructed and flew a new drone in a week, a process that used to take major companies decades.

■ And finally, "Human Performance Modification" technologies are using hardware and chemical technology to change our physical or mental capabilities, from robotic limbs to implants that improve cognition, pushing past our very human limitations in everything from endurance to focus. Think Lance Armstrong crossed with Iron Man.

All these changes affect the underlying where, when, how and even who of war. It's heady stuff, but none of this new technology changes the why of war; human flaws and mistakes still drive war, whether it is fought with a stone or a drone. Nor does it mean that one can ignore the historic lessons of war. War will never be perfect. Indeed, when the airplane appeared on the battlefield in the last century, some claimed that war would end or that there would be no more need for ground armies. This was far from reality. Just as they were back then, the need for, and the consequences of, human "boots on the ground" will remain a reality, and risk, of any war.

That is not to say that the new technologies like the airplane were not game changers, however. The new technology forced leaders to rethink certain fundamental assumptions they had about war

A MQ-9 Reaper unmanned aerial vehicle prepares to land after an Operation Enduring Freedom mission in Afghanistan in December 2007. It has the ability to carry both precision-guided bombs and air-to-ground missiles. (BRIAN FERGUSON/LIGHTROOM PHOTOS/USAF/REDUX)

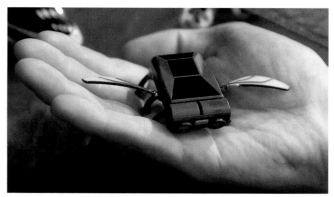

In July 2011, a model of an insect-sized U.S. Air Force drone is held by a member of the Air Force Research Laboratory, which is developing drones so small that they resemble small birds and insects, some even having moving wings. (REUTERS/CORBIS)

OK. Show of Hands. Who's For Drones?

DANZIGER
CartoonArts International / NYTimes Syndicate

A robot distributes promotional literature calling for a ban on fully autonomous weapons in Parliament Square in London, England, in April 2013. (OLI SCARFF/GETTY IMAGES)

and how to fight and win it. It was especially tough for those on top to make the changes that were needed to keep up with all that these new technologies disrupted, as they were less motivated to change. As the "mechanical cavalry" began to challenge the role of the horse, many British and U.S. officers were resistant, not just out of love for the old ways, but also because it would mean reorganizations of units and cultures they knew and loved. This same dynamic, for instance, has started to play out in the senior leaders in the U.S. Air Force, a fighter pilot-centric community that has witnessed unmanned systems become the fastest growing and most active portion of the force. Similarly, when the air opened up as a potential battle space with the early airplanes, it created a battle over whether there was

a need for an entire new part of the army to fight in it. After much resistance, it became its own service, the Air Force. This same may be in play with the opening up of cyberspace as a potential domain of war, with many seeing this as the future of the U.S. Cyber Command.

The 2020s, not the 1920s

No parallel is exact, hence Twain's notion of a "rhyme" rather than a "repeat." Yet, even the differences of today are instructive. Today's competition is much wider than it was a century ago. The number of states that could build or even utilize previously dominant battle platforms like the battleship or the strategic bomber plane could be counted on one hand. By comparison, today at least 87 nations' militaries have deployed unmanned aerial systems, and more

than 100 have cyberwarfare programs (roughly 20 have advanced capability).

Just focusing on states misses one of the key parts of the story. Nonstate actors are not only becoming more relevant and more powerful than traditional state militaries and agencies from international finance to cybersecurity and everywhere in between, but this new wave of game-changing technologies is often empowering them at a faster rate. For example, who matters more on cyber issues, the U.S. State Department and Chinese Foreign Ministry, presently holding cyber diplomatic talks, or companies like Google and Huwei that are literally making the future of cyberspace?

For the last 400 years, it was the state that could best mobilize the people and finances needed for prior game changers and organize their military forces

Call of Duty

I use my own unintentional role in the military-industrial complex as an illustration. Working as a consultant for the *Call of Duty* video game that sets players within a U.S. military unit circa 2025, we conceived of what the next generation of soldiers might want in a tactical level drone. The concept we developed took inspiration from the strengths and weaknesses of the current generation of military systems and what was becoming available on the civilian side of the market. It melded a nimble quadcopter that could move rapidly but also perch and stare in "urban canyons" of modern city battlefields, armed with a machine gun and explosives, taking on roles that ranged from scout to sniper. It had to be easily controlled by a single soldier with minimal training but also able to take on certain roles autonomously. It also had to be cheap enough to be distributed across the battlefield, able to be purchased in sufficient numbers such that they

could conceivably be deployed at the squad or platoon level.

The concept itself is appealing (and yet would be slowly chewed apart if anyone proposed it inside the traditional Pentagon acquisition system), but what happened next is fascinating. For a commercial for the video game release in 2012, Activision built "Charlene." It was a kind of prototype of the fictional vision—not the final version, but a working version of the system with the various key attributes. It cost less than $5,000. Notably, when video of Charlene went viral on YouTube, which showed a quadcopter controlled with a tablet computer shoot up various target equivalents and then take out a car in a fiery explosion, offices in the Pentagon began to wonder why some crazy Russian, who was actually an actor, had a better drone today than the U.S. military planned to have tomorrow. At the 2013 weapons trade shows, various defense contractors began to display their early knockoffs of Charlene, but always at a much higher price, as the government is a less savvy client than a video game maker. ■

best around them. From the cannon to the atomic bomb, these technologies required mass and scale. Other structures of governance like city-states and dukedoms simply could not compete and went the way of the knights. As Charles Tilly, the famous historian of war, wrote, "War made the state and the state made war."

Today, the new technologies are certainly ones that the state is able to gain, but they also come with low barriers to entry. The NeXTech war games looking at the future accessibility and business models behind the "game changers" of the future concluded that the parallels would be more like the GPS-enabled cell phone than the atomic bomb. The state may have played a core developmental role in both, but it does not have a monopoly. Moreover, the fear is not just one of lost monopoly but the benefits that come from having comparatively fluid organizations compared to the bureaucracy that once gave the state such power. As the U.S. Army general in charge of future force development put it, "The threat's ability to take the technology and innovate with it is higher than ours." ∎

Deeper questions

Patrick Bellinger, one of the first pilots in the history of U.S. Naval Aviation, sits in a 1920s biplane. (UNDERWOOD & UNDERWOOD/CORBIS)

Such shifts, from new technology to new political concerns, show the measure of the disruptions that loom. They require strategists to look beyond merely determining what size the force should be or the budget placeholders that have become the norm. If this parallel is to the more distant past rather than the 1990s, we cannot be consumed by worries of repeating mistakes of our youth. Instead, there are a series of essential questions that they should be posing back to the system. These questions are as much about looking inward, asking questions of ourselves, as they are towards the external environment. These questions are as much introspective as they are extroverted. They require not just navel-gazing, but also action. As Vint Cerf, a computer scientist credited as being one of the "fathers of the Internet," puts it, "What happens when you see bad stuff in the mirror? Well, you don't fix the mirror."

∎ **Are you changing by learning?**
Among the most important lessons from the last interwar years was the need to question traditional military concepts, tactics, and doctrines, and experiment with new ones. A tight budget is no excuse not to engage deeply in research, development, experimentation, wargaming and exercises. Our forebears who went through the Great Depression would laugh at the notion that sequestration's 8% budget cuts are preventing these activities. Indeed, despite needing to meet far tougher budget lines, they figured out everything from new uses for the new aircraft carrier to the development of an "Army Air Corps." Contrary to the current approach, they understood that many of these activities did not require waiting for the full purchases of an entire new suite of technology. In various British war games, cars with the word "tank" written on the side sufficed in mechanization studies. Meanwhile, the U.S. Marines did not have a single working modern landing craft, but still figured out the concepts of the amphibious warfare they would use to "island hop" across the Pacific in World War II.

In the rush to protect politically cherished programs today, the research and experimentation part of the budget is not being protected well. The importance of these activities was not just about generating new ideas and throwing away old ones, but also about identifying the types of leadership needed to succeed in future wars. Some aspects will stay the same, but some will change. The "Louisiana Maneuvers" of this period, for instance, were a set of excercises in the interwar years where the U.S. Army explored how a "horseless" force using trucks and tanks operated compared to a horse-borne operations. In many ways the culmination of the debate in the Army between mechanization and horse cavalry, but they were also used as a way to talent scout for the new type of officer needed in a future world war.

∎ **Are you protecting the new from the old?**
In any kind of transition, whether it was from horses to tanks or from manned to unmanned aircraft, there will be winners and losers. The aspect that leaders must be mindful of is that in military culture and bureaucracies, the old is not only more established but is often at an advantage in any internal battle.

The old is privileged by current

tribes and constituencies, who often see their careers as linked to a single system or specialty that may define their professional identity. Even today, you can meet U.S. Air Force pilots who have flown unmanned systems for years but will still introduce themselves as F-16 Viper pilots. Industry and politics reinforce this. The existing dominant systems come with current contracts to protect, current program officers to staff them, and current factories in political districts, with current armies of lobbyists fighting for them. Yesterday's contracts and today's constituent jobs do a better job of mobilizing Congress than any potential of tomorrow.

A look at the largest "programs of record," the systems that take up the most in the Pentagon budget, illustrates this dynamic. Among the top 25, there is not much that that would fit the category of truly new and disruptive. Some are decades old, like the C-130J "Super" Hercules, first flying in 1954, while others like the F-35 jet fighter are based on decades-old designs, improvements to be sure but not true game changers. Moreover, what the U.S. spends the most on today is what it still plans to spend a great deal on tomorrow. The F-35, literally the "most expensive weapon ever developed," tops the list of today's spending, but it still has more than a trillion dollars worth of spending on it yet to come.

What this means is that any new spending on something truly new and disruptive must either be in addition to the existing programs, or, in tough budget times at their expense. For the British back then, new aircraft carriers battled with old battleships, while U.S. Army horse cavalry officer General John K. Herr, argued that "Not one more horse will I give up for a tank."

Even more, the problem is that tough budget times also provide an excuse to use the narrative of "shared cuts" to pull out longer knives for the newcomers. For example, the overall U.S. military budget is being cut by about 8%. But when it came time to develop the upcoming year's budget, the Air Force requested a 33% *reduction* in spending on Unmanned Aerospace Systems (UAS),

U.S. Air Force Chief of Staff Gen. T. Michael Moseley speaks during the inauguration ceremony of the F-35 Joint Strike Fighter at Lockheed Martin Aeronautics Co. in Fort Worth, Texas, in July 2006. (REX C. CURRY/EPA/CORBIS)

about four times the size of the rest of the force's budget cuts. Similarly, just as the U.S. Navy met with success with its X-47 next-generation drone that took off from a carrier, potentially revolutionizing naval aviation, its budgeters requested a 24% reduction in UAS spending, again several times the size of the rest of the budget cuts. They even unsuccessfully tried to early retire the new drone, planning to send it off to a museum right after it pushed the frontiers of technology.

■ Are you spreading your bets and ignoring sunk costs?

In 1934, the British Air Ministry began to buy a new plane, which sought to advance past the World War I generation of planes. The Gloster Gladiator was made of metal, could fly almost 250 miles per hour and carried four machine guns. It was the best biplane ever built.

Unfortunately, it was already outdated. Faster single-winged monoplanes like the German Messerschmidt BF-109 were already starting to arrive in the air. And yet, having already invested in the project, the British still plowed ahead with the old model, ultimately building more than 700. The later pilots unlucky enough to be flying the best, last biplane when World War II started just a few years gave it a different nickname, the "Flying Coffin."

While militaries may not like it, they have to be prepared for cherished developmental programs to go out of date on

a rapid basis. Rather than holding on, they have to be prepared to treat them as sunk costs, past spending that is to be lamented but not to be weighed in setting future requirements. The challenge, though, is not to merely ignore lost bets like a good investor, but to recognize that a transition is taking place. Success depends not on merely taking risks but spreading risks. Another way of putting it is that if there is a danger of betting only on the best of the last generation, there is also a danger that comes from embracing the first generation of what is new too closely.

If the position of the U.S. and its allies today is comparable to that of the British almost a century back, the case of the *HMS Furious* is instructive. The British battleship fleet was dominant, but they still revolutionized a new capability called an "aircraft carrier," a ship that brought the airplane out to sea, and in turn created a whole new disruption. While the British may have pioneered the carrier, they were not able to move far enough past early designs and concepts of use. The first generation is never the best generation. Instead, the U.S. and Japanese figured out the fleet carrier. Bringing in the new requires asking whether you are locking in on the first generation of that technology's design or tactics.

■ Does your personnel system link in to your strategic priorities?

Personnel are often ignored in strategic

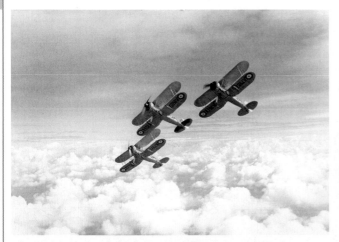

Gloster Gladiator I aircraft from the 87 Squadron RAF in formation, in 1938. (CHARLES E. BROWN/ROYAL AIR FORCE MUSEUM/GETTY IMAGES)

The aircraft carrier HMS Furious *of the English Navy performs maneuvers near North Africa in 1936.* (HULTON ARCHIVE/GETTY IMAGES)

reviews and technology discussions. It comes down to a fundamental question of whether a military's personnel processes and incentives are working for or against its goals. Right now, in every military, there is a new generation of young officers debating in what direction to take their careers. In many ways, they may be compared to a young officer originally commissioned in the horse cavalry just over a century ago. That officer loved his craft and, indeed, was so good at its key skills of horsemanship, fencing, and pistol shooting that he competed at the 1912 Olympics in the pentathlon. Fortunately, after being mentored by a colonel with a knack for both talent scouting and strategic forecasting, a young George S. Patton

George Patton on horseback, circa 1910. (PHOTO BY LAKE COUNTY MUSEUM/GETTY IMAGES)

joined the nascent tank corps. (The same Colonel Fox Connor would also mentor a young Dwight Eisenhower, showing the importance not just of the choices young officers make, but also the role of mentors in times of great change.)

Today's U.S. military officers face similar questions of whether to transition into new fields and what will be the accompanying risks and rewards. While some will be "true believers," many will take their guidance both from mentors and the tone and results of the personnel system. For instance, if the future goal of the Air Force is to maintain its leadership in unmanned/remotely piloted aircraft, what signal does it send when only 43 out of 4,500 of its colonels have experience in the area? Or even worse, a young officer in this community is roughly 13% less likely to be promoted than his/her peers, a figure that has actually dropped in the last several years.

What kind of leaders do we need?

The conclusions that can be drawn from such parallels and questions are that technological shifts are not about easy new solutions or silver bullets there for the taking. Another repeating pattern, affecting everyone from Giulio Douhet, the Italian air officer in the 1920s who triumphantly claimed bombers had ended the era of ground wars, to the Pentagon acolytes of so-called "network-centric warfare" in

the 1990s drawdown who claimed the same, is the error of thinking that some new technology will somehow solve all problems, or in their words, "lifting the fog of war." Shifts are about new problems and new questions that must be accepted even if all the answers are not available. Whether it was the 1920s or today, success or failure in these dynamic environments most of all depends on what kind of leaders today's strategists decide to be.

One leadership model is that of the aforementioned John K. Herr. Like horse cavalry officer Patton, Herr was offered the chance to join the nascent U.S. Tank Corps during World War I. He turned the opportunity down and like the rest of the cavalry did not see any active combat as a cavalaryman. This did not dissuade him of the continuing value of the horse.

After the war, he rose up the ranks to become a general, notably while Patton and others languished by comparison. In 1938, General Herr became chief of cavalry. His description by Lucian Truscott, then a young officer at Fort Leavenworth in Kansas, is telling, perhaps because the type may exist today. "A magnetic and pleasing personality…unfortunately he was impatient with those who might hold contrary views, and he did not hesitate to make his opinions of such persons known on any and all occasions." He created a command climate where only officers who agreed with him were heard, and his staff would only send him news articles that buttressed his ideas.

Herr made many efforts not just to fight the future but also to roll back reforms, especially in what he considered to be the folly of mechanization. This meant that as late as 1939, just as the blitzkrieg was poised to strike, he argued to Congress that "We must not be led to our own detriment to assume that the untried machine can displace the proved and tried horse."

Another path is that of the visionary. As early as 1906, a young Billy Mitchell was predicting that new technologies like the airplane would allow future conflicts to take place in different domains, and require new organizations. Savvy, smart, and with a strong personality, Mitchell was one of the first people to realize the potential of air power, and he rose to command all American air combat units in World War I.

In the interwar years, Mitchell became an advocate for an independent air force. He recognized that the age of previously dominant battle platforms had passed, and, through tests like the controversial bombing of the captured German battleship *Ostfriesland*, made the case that continued investment in the old was a waste of both money and ultimately lives.

The problem was that Mitchell was too much of a visionary for his own and his own causes' good. He threw out good ideas but also rhetorical rocks. He was a master thinker but also a master at creating more enemies than allies. In 1925, he was court-martialed after accusing senior leaders in the Army and Navy of incompetence and "almost treasonable administration of the national defense." Whether Mitchell was right or wrong did not matter anymore; he was wrong in his means.

The final model is that of William Moffett. A naval surface officer, Moffett was awarded the Congressional Medal of Honor for his role in a daring 1914 raid on Veracruz. Subsequently, he took command of a battleship, once the peak of a naval surface officer's career.

Moffett is remembered in history for none of this. Instead, it is for his interwar years role as the "air admiral."

U.S. and Philippine Navy servicemen launch an Unmanned Aerial Vehicle (UAV) while aboard a patrol boat during a joint annual military exercise at a former U.S. military base in the Philippines in June 2013. (ERIK DE CASTRO/REUTERS/CORBIS)

In 1921, Moffett took command of the newly formed U.S. Navy Bureau of Aeronautics (BuAer). In many ways, it was an odd choice, as unlike his frequent sparring partner Billy Mitchell, Moffett was not a flier himself. However, he combined key skills. He was a visionary but also a pragmatist, and most of all, a master politician.

Through his career, Moffett worked the internal bureaucracy, driving it toward change, but in ways it could accept. He also built and maintained relationships with key civilians thinkers and leaders, most notably Franklin D. Roosevelt, the Assistant Secretary of the Navy who would go on to become president. Under Moffett's leadership, aviator training programs were established and an aviator culture took hold; new technologies like aircraft carriers were developed and deployed; and new war tactics and doctrines experimented with. Of particular importance to the transition of new technologies and industries today, BuAer made a point to diversify production, in order to encourage a nascent and nonmonopolized aircraft industry. This surface fleet officer would ironically die in an aviation accident, but the U.S. Navy that won the looming war in the Pacific was his legacy.

Facing change

The swirl of change in U.S. defense means that the same old approaches are simply not enough. In this time of strategic and technologic shift, what budget line item to tweak to mitigate sequestration or how many hundred staff jobs to cut to shave personnel costs should not consume bigger, more strategic concerns.

Instead, the best way to succeed, and the most important lesson of the past, is that thinking must take into account not just the interplay of technology and strategy, but the people behind it. Such past leader models are important as they guide us in how to face the trends that may shape our future world.

If Twain advised us to look to the past to avoid repeating mistakes, thinkers like Martin Luther King also advised us to keep another eye on the future horizon, if our goal was to "bend the arc of history" in our direction. For those who work in the realm of national security and war, it means facing the kind of challenging tasks of self-examination and change that armed forces have not gone through for generations. If instead we ignore the big questions of today, there is the danger of setting up our military for failure on the battlefields of tomorrow. ■

 Don't forget to vote! www.greatdecisions.org/ballot

discussion questions

1. Recent military engagements in the Middle East have made combat dispersed and improvised enemy forces a priority. At the same time, the military continues to invest in conventional military programs originating in the Cold War era that are more fit for fighting large unified enemy forces. How should the U.S. balance its strategic policies between these two different priorities?

2. The nature of today's technological advances threaten the state's monopoly on it and simultaneously empower non-state actors. Assuming the state can quickly adapt, how should it adapt? Should it invest in regaining a monopoly on strategic military-relevant technology? Should it place restrictions on civilian uses of these technologies? Should it make alliances with non-state actors? What risks do these strategies pose?

3. How well have U.S. defense priorities adjusted to a changing technological landscape? Is U.S. technological superiority seriously at risk of being overtaken by countries like China? What technological areas should the U.S. most actively target for rapid development?

4. How has the development of unmanned vehicles like the Predator drones impacted the way in which military operations are conducted? As evolving technology cheapens the human cost of war, should increased measures be taken to prevent a corresponding escalation in military operations? What are such measures?

5. When the U.S. Cyber Command (USCYBERCOM), the agency responsible for offensive cyber operations, became fully operational in 2010, it was placed under the command of General Keith B. Alexander, also the head of the National Security Agency (NSA). Is this an unnecessary blurring of the lines between a national spy agency and a military command, as critics have alleged, or is this an efficient organization of highly overlapping organizations, as General Alexander and his supporters have argued? Should USCYBERCOM be an independent command?

suggested readings

Gentile, Colonel Gian. **Wrong Turn: America's Deadly Embrace of Counterinsurgency.** New York: The New Press, 2013. 208 pp. $24.95 (hardcover). Colonel Gian Gentile draws upon his extensive experience as a combat battalion commander in the Iraq War to describe what he views as the tremendous failure of the current U.S. doctrine of counterinsurgency (COIN) in Afghanistan.

Mazetti, Mark. **The Way of the Knife: The CIA, a Secret Army and a War at the Ends of the Earth.** New York: Penguin Press, 2013. 400 pp. $29.95 (hardcover). Mark Mazzetti, a Pulitzer Prize-winning reporter, chronicles how the CIA and America's special operations forces have transformed into lethal machines extending to the remotest regions of world.

Nagl, John A. **Learning to Eat Soup with a Knife: Counterinsurgency Lessons from Malaya and Vietnam.** Westport, CT: Praeger Publishers, 2002. 280 pp. $17.00 (paper). Lieutenant Colonel John A. Nagle, a veteran of both American missions in Iraq, dissects the Malaya and Vietnam experiences to understand how armies adapt to circumstances they are unprepared for.

Ricks, Thomas E. **The Generals: American Military Command from World War II to Today.** New York: Penguin Books, 2012. 576 pp. $18.00 (paper) .Thomas E. Ricks gathers meaning from the stories of this century's best and worst American generals about what constitutes great leadership.

Singer. P.W. **Wired for War: The Robotics Revolution and Conflict in the 21st Century.** New York: Penguin Books, 2009. 512 pp. $18.00 (paper). P.W. Singer, author of the GREAT DECISIONS 2014 chapter on "Defense Technology," examines how robotic warfare is revolutionizing military warfare, as well as the politics, economics, laws, and ethics that accompany it.

Singer. P.W., and Friedman, Allan. **Cybersecurity and Cyberwar: What Everyone Needs to Know.** New York: Oxford University Press, USA, 2014. 320 pp. $12.79 (paper). Primer on cyberspace and its security issues, including discussion of new Chinese and U.S. military cyber units.

Wheeler, Winslow T. and Lawrence T. Korb. **Military Reform: A Reference Handbook.** Westport, CT: Praeger, 2007. 256 pp. $55.00 (hardcover). Korb, a guest on GREAT DECISIONS IN FOREIGN POLICY 2014, and Wheeler ground their assessment of the fundamental strengths and weaknesses in thoughtful research and deliver a deep understanding of what genuine military reform ought to entail.

TO LEARN MORE ABOUT THIS TOPIC AND TO ACCESS WEB LINKS TO RESOURCES GO TO www.greatdecisions.org

Israel and the U.S.
by Seth Anziska

U.S. President Barack Obama shakes hands with Israel's Prime Minister Benjamin Netanyahu during their press conference in Jerusalem, part of Obama's official state visit to Israel and the Palestinian Territories in March 2013. (KOBI GIDEON/GPO/FLASH90/REDUX)

The depth of emotion that surrounds public and private conversations about the relationship between Israel and the U.S. can be staggering. From college campuses to church groups, think tanks to synagogues, and op-ed pages to congressional hearings, few issues are as contentious as America's relationship with the State of Israel.

Supporters of Israel in the U.S. stress shared values and a friendship that is crucial for securing U.S. interests in the Middle East. Despite the turmoil of the Arab Spring and the instability that increasingly marks U.S. relations with longstanding allies like Egypt and Saudi Arabia, backers of a strong U.S.-Israel partnership highlight the benefits of maintaining close ties and continuing to provide extensive economic and military aid to Israel.

For critics of the U.S.-Israel relationship, it is this close friendship that has fueled hostility toward the U.S. in the Arab world. Critics point to the lack of even-handedness that characterizes U.S.-Israeli relations, citing Washington's acquiescence to settlement expansion in the West Bank, the lack of movement in the peace talks with the Palestinian Authority, and strategic differences over relations with Iran and regional allies.

Why is it so difficult to openly debate these matters? For many, Israel's place in the U.S. is not simply a question of how to best secure foreign policy goals in the Middle East. For domestic supporters of Israel—Jewish and non-Jewish alike—the country's fate and America's role in protecting its future raises an existential question of national survival. To question support for Israel or its foreign policy is perceived by some as casting doubt on the broader trajectory of political Zionism and Israel's right to exist. Conversely, domestic defenders of Palestinian rights—whether Muslim, Christian or Jewish—feel that valid concerns about the roots of the Palestinian refugee problem, the occupation of the West Bank and Gaza Strip after 1967, and Israel's treatment of its

SETH ANZISKA *is a doctoral candidate in international history at Columbia University, focusing on Israeli and Palestinian history, U.S.-Middle East relations and modern Jewish politics. A recipient of the Boren, FLAS and Wexner Fellowships, he has written for* The New York Times, Foreign Policy, *and* Ha'aretz *and is currently completing his dissertation,* Camp David's Shadow: The United States, Lebanon and the Israeli-Palestinian Conflict, 1977–88.

non-Jewish citizens are overlooked in the mainstream media and political discourse. Vocalizing this unease, by raising genuine concern about the fate of Palestinian rights or Israel's viability as a self-defined "Jewish and Democratic state," is often portrayed as exhibiting an anti-Jewish prejudice, a dangerous conflation of criticism toward Israel's domestic and foreign policy agenda with anti-Semitism. In light of the passion and polemics such debate engenders, how can a more constructive conversation take place?

No matter one's take on U.S.-Israeli relations, it is clear that the nature of this relationship and its future prospects will continue to be a central concern for policymakers and citizens in the coming years. There is a need to think historically about how the U.S.-Israel relationship has developed, and its attendant complexities over the last six and a half decades. The course of this relationship has never been a clear-cut tale of abiding friendship or persistent antagonism; there has always been a fair amount of both. In revisiting this history, it is helpful to examine Israel's recurring Palestinian question, which remains at the heart of regional conflicts and related policy debates. Israel's own strategic position in the Middle East requires attention as well, particularly in light of the way in which revolutions and counterrevolutions in the Arab world have transformed the region.

Where are U.S.-Israeli relations heading? What are the challenges these two countries are facing, and how can the recent past offer guidance on the choices that lie ahead? No one could argue that these decisions are clear-cut. Perhaps identifying the origins and milestones that have characterized Israeli-American relations since Israel's establishment in 1948 can delineate a tenable path forward. There is too much at stake—for the U.S., Israel, Palestine and the greater Middle East—to ignore the difficult questions along the way. ∎

Historical backdrop

In the aftermath of World War II, the U.S. assumed a position of prominence in the Middle East, filling the vacuum left by departing colonial powers. The guiding motivation behind U.S. involvement in the region after 1945 shifted from the rhetoric defending self-determination, which characterized President Woodrow Wilson's 14 Points, to a more strategic interest in securing access to oil resources and containing the U.S.S.R. Yet ideological support for Zionism, a modern national movement seeking the establishment of a Jewish state in Palestine, could be found in the White House and Congress. It came into conflict with more pragmatic attitudes in the departments of State and Defense and the Central Intelligence Agency (CIA). President Harry S. Truman, much to the consternation of some of his advisers, was the first foreign leader to recognize the newly created state of Israel in 1948.

Over 700,000 Palestinians were expelled or fled from territories that became Israel in the course of the 1948 Arab-Israeli War (an event Palestinians describe as the *nakba*, or "catastrophe"). American policymakers focused exclusively on the humanitarian needs of these refugees rather than the political dimension of their dispossession. This approach was reflected in the extensive support for the refugee resettlement work of the United Nations Relief Works Agency (UNRWA). It also shaped the course of American relations with Israel and the Palestinians in the ensuing decades, as the burgeoning refugee population in the neighboring Arab states of Lebanon, Jordan and Syria grappled with the consequences of prolonged statelessness.

U.S. support for Israel was not inevitable or historically consistent in the early years of Israel's existence. Rather, it only took on its "special" characteristics later on. In the wake of 1948, for example, the U.S. generally displayed an even-handed stance toward Israel and the Arab world as part of a broader Cold War containment strategy. During the administration of President Dwight D. Eisenhower, this approach dovetailed with the Eisenhower Doctrine, a strategy aimed at wresting individual Arab countries away from the U.S.S.R.

Eisenhower's approach to the Middle East culminated with his forceful opposition to the British, French and Israeli action during the Suez Crisis of 1956. The president's critical stance was a result of persistent concerns that Israeli actions were undermining U.S. interests in the Middle East. The U.S. threatened to impose economic sanctions against Israel, even threatening to expel the country from the United Nations (UN) and disassociate from it politically. An explicit alliance with Israel was viewed as undermining relations with Arab states. As Secretary of State John Foster Dulles noted, "backing Israel might be very costly to vital United States national interests." Although Eisenhower forced Israel to withdraw from the Sinai during the Suez campaign, he also acknowledged the legitimacy of Israeli security concerns.

John F. Kennedy's ascendancy to the White House heralded a shift in U.S. policy aims and methods toward the Middle East, with the new president taking bold steps to engage with adversaries like Gamal Abdel Nasser in Egypt in a bid to promote regional stability. Yet the shifting reality of the Cold War also pushed the U.S. much closer to Israel, and Kennedy began to treat the young country as a bulwark against growing Soviet interests in the Middle East. To this end, U.S. policymakers stressed shared values with the Jewish state and offered military and economic aid to assert regional influence. Kennedy, according to the scholar Yaakov Bar-Simon Tov "was the first president to define US-Israeli relations as special, to take seriously Israel's security problems, and to provide Israel with major defensive arms." As Warren

Bass details in his aptly named study of U.S.-Israel relations in this period, *Support Any Friend: Kennedy's Middle East and the Making of the US-Israel Alliance*, Israel managed to introduce a nuclear program despite Kennedy's deep concern with proliferation.

1967 war and aftermath

The replacement of Israeli Prime Minister David Ben-Gurion with Levi Eshkol in 1963 and the onset of Lyndon B. Johnson's presidency further strengthened U.S.-Israeli relations. Eshkol gave way on nuclear development and allowed periodic U.S. inspection of the Dimona Reactor in return for greater military coordination and aid. Johnson, who was personally "warm and admiring" toward Israel in the view of one expert, decided to supply the country with direct arms shipments, including Skyhawk aircraft with strike capability. Having supplied arms to Saudi Arabia and Jordan as well, Johnson's alignment with Israel was seen as a move to counter Soviet regional influence.

Johnson's focus on Vietnam may have shifted the Middle East to a lower priority, but the outbreak of a full scale Arab-Israeli war in June 1967 (also known as the Six Day War) moved the region and the fate of U.S.-Israeli relations to center stage. America's political backing "enabled Israel to realize its military aims free of the threat of Soviet intervention." Israel's swift victory in the Six Day War was a watershed moment, not least because it secured control of Arab territory in the Sinai Peninsula, the West Bank, the Gaza Strip and the Golan Heights. Johnson decided there should not be a return to the status quo, supporting Eshkol's bid to retain the territories until the Arab states recognized Israel and made peace. This stance was codified in November 1967 in UN Security Council Resolution 242, which was understood internationally as a guideline for pursuing an exchange of "land for peace," but by many accounts did not call for a full withdrawal from all the territories. The resolution also did not refer to the Palestinians directly, calling for a "just settlement to the refugee problem," without mentioning the fate of the West Bank and Gaza Strip.

Israel's territorial expansion in these areas raised profound political and demographic questions for the country's leadership. Weeks after the war ended, the question of how to manage the Palestinian population took on central importance. A "decision not to decide," in the words of Israeli historian Avi Raz, ensured control over the territories themselves while avoiding a political resolution of the Palestinian question in national or territorial terms. The creation of the first West Bank settlements in the aftermath of the 1967 War marked the start of a ongoing occupation that has indelibly marked U.S. involvement in the region.

Even with its expansive territorial aspirations, Israel was seen as a regional ally capable of defending U.S. interests in the Middle East. The election of President Richard M. Nixon challenged this new reality. Nixon was suspicious of Washington's tilt toward Jerusalem, and equally apprehensive that missteps in the Arab world had undermined U.S. strategic interests in the Middle East. Soon after he entered office in 1969, he told Secretary of State William Rogers that he sought an "even-handed policy,"

U.N. Partition, 1947
- ☐ Israel
- ▨ Palestinian land

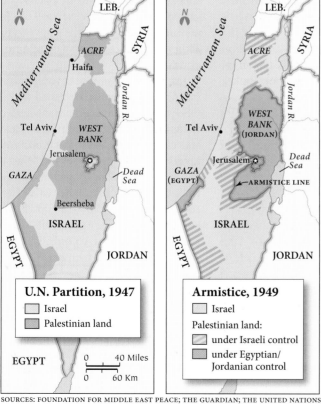

Armistice, 1949
- ☐ Israel

Palestinian land:
- ▧ under Israeli control
- ▨ under Egyptian/ Jordanian control

Six-Day War, 1967
- ☐ Israel
- ▧ Israeli occupied

(SINAI)

Intifada to 2013
- • Israeli settlement
- — Israeli security fence
- ☐ Israel
- ▧ Israeli occupied

SOURCES: FOUNDATION FOR MIDDLE EAST PEACE; THE GUARDIAN; THE UNITED NATIONS — LUCIDITY INFORMATION DESIGN, LLC

Note: Israeli settlements in Gaza were evacuated in 2005.

including Israel's return of the territories occupied in 1967, but he faced opposition both from Israel and some of his advisers. National Security Adviser Henry Kissinger, who opposed Nixon's settlement plan, stated, "the longer Israel holds its conquered Arab territory, the longer the Soviets cannot deliver what the Arabs want."

A crucial development in U.S.-Israeli relations followed after Egyptian President Nasser's death in September 1970. The new Egyptian president, Anwar al-Sadat, pivoted his country to the west, seeking to align with the U.S. rather than the Soviet Union. In a bid to force a settlement to the Arab-Israeli conflict, Sadat launched the 1973 October War against Israel. As historian Craig Daigle has recently argued, Sadat wanted to create a "crisis of detente" so as to break the region's status quo. Following an Arab attack on the morning of Yom Kippur, the holiest day in the Jewish religious calendar, Israel's leadership sought out U.S. aid to turn the tide of the fighting. A massive U.S. airlift of tanks and airplanes reversed the Egyptian and Syrian advances, and further solidified close U.S.-Israeli relations.

With Nixon distracted by the Watergate scandal, Kissinger negotiated the terms of agreement to end the war. They were passed as UN Security Council Resolution 338, which called for a "just and durable peace in the Middle East" along the lines of UN Security Council Resolution 242 after the 1967 War. Kissinger, as Nixon's envoy and later as Secretary of State to President Gerald Ford, pursued a step-by-step approach to achieve a diplomatic solution between Israel and her neighbors. But these attempts at negotiating a comprehensive solution favored a piecemeal approach that separated the Israeli-Palestinian issue from broader regional concerns. Palestinian national aspirations, which were emerging as a central point of contention between Israel and the Arab states, were ignored by Kissinger's diplomatic initiatives, such as reaching a cease-fire between Israel, Syria and Egypt. The consequences of 1973, therefore, may have strengthened U.S.-Egyptian and U.S.-Israeli relations, but postwar diplomacy also prolonged regional conflict indefinitely.

Reemergence of the Palestinian question

By the late 1970s, a small number of American officials began to recognize the necessity of limited Palestinian rights, fueled by the broader wave of decolonization around the globe. The election of President Jimmy Carter in 1976 helped crystallize this paradigm shift. Carter's administration took a regional rather than strictly Cold War approach to Israel and the Middle East, marked by a concern with localized political dynamics and awareness of the need to deal with the Palestinian issue head on. Carter asserted that the Israel-Palestine dispute was at the heart of the Arab-Israeli conflict and should be tackled directly. He also spoke openly of the need for a "Palestinian homeland," making him the first U.S. president to use that term. Carter's critics bitterly opposed such an approach, fearful about the emergence of a Palestinian state. The military activity of the Palestine Liberation Organization (PLO) and other Palestinian nationalist groups had raised the global profile of the Palestinian struggle, but also generated widespread condemnation given the Palestinian use of violent tactics to achieve nationalist ends. Nevertheless, by singling out the Palestinian question for substantive consideration while engaging Israel on the need for permanent territorial borders, the Carter administration helped reshape the parameters of any eventual settlement.

The election of Israeli Prime Minister Menachem Begin in 1977 represented a decisive challenge to U.S.-Israeli relations. Begin was a revisionist Zionist with deep-seated ideological opposition to Palestinian territorial rights. He was also a believer in settlement expansion in the occupied territories, which he pursued with the help of Ariel Sharon, his agriculture minister and later Israel's 11th prime minister. Roughly 5,000 Jewish settlers lived in the West Bank when Begin entered office; however, the number of settlers continued to rise, to over 80,000 by the late 1980s, even after the signing of the historic Camp David Accords. These accords, reached on September 17, 1978, led to a formal Egypt-Israel peace treaty signed by Sadat and Begin on March 26, 1979. The treaty ensured the return of the Sinai Peninsula to Egypt, but Begin's price was the retention of the West Bank, which he referred to by the biblical name of "Judea and Samaria." The peace treaty also included more military and economic aid to Israel than had been given under any previous administra-

U.S. Secretary of State Henry Kissinger in the cabin of his aircraft in September 1975, as he flew from Alexandria, Egypt, to Tel Aviv, Israel, during negotiations to return the Sinai, which was captured by Israel during the 1967 War, back to Egypt. (DAVID HUME KENNERLY/ GETTY IMAGES)

tion: $10.2 billion over four years, a little less than half in grants. Egypt and Saudi Arabia also received military aid and security guarantees, highlighting the spectrum of U.S. allies in the Middle East.

Strategic relationship

Ronald Reagan's election victory in 1980 signaled a return to global Cold War geopolitics, reconstituting the Middle East as a site of contestation between the U.S. and the U.S.S.R. Given this new reality, relations with Israel were granted strategic priority. General Alexander Haig, Reagan's hawkish secretary of state, articulated a policy of "strategic consensus" between the U.S., Israel and pro-American Arab governments. Given the limits of regional cooperation, the Reagan administration signed a Memorandum of Understanding enshrining bilateral cooperation with Israel on November 30, 1981. This strategic alliance included military cooperation between the U.S. and Israel, and U.S. policymakers afforded Israel the special status of an ally for the first time. As William Quandt, a leading scholar of U.S. foreign policy has written, "the entire relationship was given a strategic rationale that had previously been missing."

Despite this alliance, divergent interests emerged in the 1980s, beginning with Reagan's decision to sell AWACS and F-15 aircraft to Saudi Arabia. The limits of the Israeli-American relationship emerged most visibly during Israel's 1982 war in Lebanon (the "First Lebanon War"). The invasion was initially an attempt by Israel to contain Palestinian attacks on its northern border towns, but it quickly escalated into a full-scale effort to remake Lebanon as Israel's Christian ally. Secretary Haig was informed of Israel's war plans by Israeli Defense Minister Ariel Sharon in the spring of 1982. Israel's unprecedented siege of Beirut that summer disturbed Reagan deeply and led to a confrontation with Prime Minister Begin. After Reagan and his advisers realized that Israel's actions posed serious challenges to their broader Middle East strategy, the president remarked to Begin that "Your actions in Lebanon have seriously undermined our relationship with those Arab

President Jimmy Carter, Egyptian President Anwar Sadat (left) and Israeli Prime Minister Menachem Begin (right) stand during the playing of national anthems on the north lawn of the White House during ceremonies for the Camp David Peace Accords in March 1979. (WALLY MCNAMEE/CORBIS)

governments whose cooperation is essential to protect the Middle East from external threats and to counter forces of Soviet-sponsored radicalism and Islamic fundamentalism now growing in the region.... U.S. influence in the Arab world, our ability to achieve our strategic objectives, has been seriously damaged by Israel's actions."

The PLO's evacuation from Beirut at the end of August seemed to provide a window of stability for diplomatic action. Reagan unveiled his administration's new peace plan, dubbed the Reagan Plan, in a primetime address on September 1, 1982. Building on Carter's Camp David framework, he acknowledged that implementation of the Camp David Accords had been slow. "Israel exists; it has a right to exist in peace behind secure and defensible borders; and it has a right to demand of its neighbors that they recognize those facts," the president remarked. Reagan continued: "[W]e must also move to resolve the root causes of conflict between Arabs and Israelis." The central question, he said, was "how to reconcile Israel's legitimate security concerns with the legitimate rights of the Palestinians." For Reagan, this meant "self-government by the Palestinians in the West Bank and Gaza in association with Jordan," as well as "the immediate adoption of a settlement freeze by Israel." The Reagan Plan reflected a return to the notion of

comprehensive peace; however, it did not support outright the creation of a Palestinian state, opting instead for Palestinian self-government in association with Jordan. Begin was incensed with the new plan issued by the White House. He and his cabinet issued a swift rejection, and the Reagan Plan became the last serious attempt to broker a solution to the Arab-Israeli conflict in the 1980s.

U.S. involvement with Lebanon increased in the wake of Israeli military action. Reagan redeployed U.S. Marines to Beirut out of guilt over the failure to protect Palestinian civilians slaughtered in the Sabra and Shatila massacre of September 1982, paving the way for further bloodshed. In October 1983, the bombing of the U.S. Marine barracks by Syrian and Iranian proxies led to the death of 241 U.S. servicemen, the highest number of American military deaths in one day since the Vietnam War. Having grown resentful of the Israeli and American presence in their country, local opposition militias metastasized into the birth of Hezbollah, an Iranian-backed paramilitary organization that emerged as a key player in the region during the early 1980s. "American Cold War naiveté opened the door for Iran in Lebanon," said one scholar of the period. In this regard, U.S.-Israeli relations are meaningful beyond debates over military or economic aid, having precipitated transformations in the Middle East in a

An Israeli soldier restrains another from manhandling an arrested Palestinian who lies on a Nablus street with his hands tied together, during anti-Israeli demonstrations in the first intifada in February 1988. (ERIC FEFERBERG/AFP/GETTY IMAGES)

manner that has affected both countries well into the 21st century.

Palestinian agitation continued to grow in the occupied territories in the wake of the PLO's evacuation from Beirut. By December 1987 Israel's control over the Palestinian territories was seen as intolerable, and spontaneous protests erupted in the Gaza Strip and spread to the West Bank. The first *Intifada* ("shaking off") exploded, demonstrating that Isra-

el's subjugation of the Palestinians could not be ignored. Israeli Defense Minister and future Prime Minister Yitzhak Rabin publicly sanctioned "a policy of beatings and breaking of bones." Before long, as Quandt notes, "images of savage Israeli beatings of Palestinian youngsters were a part of the American evening television news." Israel's image in the mind of the U.S., long informed by cultural assumptions of a biblical David (Israel) fighting

Goliath (the Arab states), had been overturned.

The PLO, which was based in exile in Tunis, was "more surprised than the Israelis" by the uprising, which was entirely generated from within the territories, and was a spontaneous eruption. Seeing an opportunity to capitalize on popular discontent in order to secure political clout, the PLO began to play a leadership role in the *Intifada*—as did the Muslim Brotherhood's Palestinian off-shoot Hamas, the Islamic Resistance Movement. However, it was the PLO, long maligned by Israel and the U.S. as a terrorist organization, that would gradually emerge as the sole representative of the Palestinian people.

In one of President Reagan's final acts in office, the U.S. agreed to begin a dialogue with the PLO. Its longstanding leader, Yasser Arafat, formally accepted UN Resolution 242 in December 1988, acknowledging Israel's right to exist and renouncing terrorism. The PLO's recognition of Israel and acceptance of the "two state solution" had begun to emerge in the mid-1970s, and was implicitly endorsed as part of the November 1988 Palestinian Declaration of Independence. Arafat's accompanying public statement in Geneva ended on a triumphal note: "Victory is at hand. I see the homeland in your holy stones. I see the flag of our independent Palestine fluttering over the hills of our beloved homeland." ■

The peace process

The election of George H. W. Bush precipitated new opportunities and challenges for U.S. diplomatic relations with Israel. During Bush's tenure and with the help of Secretary of State James Baker, the peace process was revitalized as a key foreign policy goal for the U.S. The context for this reemergence was the end of the Cold War, which had removed the Soviet threat, and the outbreak of the first Gulf War in 1990. Israel's special relationship with the U.S. suffered as its strategic value in the region was undermined by international events, and Reagan's personal warmth toward Israel gave

way to the tougher stance of Bush and Baker. The two men did not appreciate the obstinacy of Israeli Prime Minister Yitzhak Shamir, and viewed his settlement policy as "a deliberate attempt to foil US peacemaking." One particularly bitter debate erupted around the U.S. refusal to grant Israel loan guarantees of $10 billion in light of ongoing settlement expansion. Baker publicly recited the number of the White House switchboard at a press conference, telling the Israelis, "When you are serious about peace, call us!"

Bush and Baker launched the Madrid Conference in October 1991. It was

the first official face-to-face gathering that included representatives from Israel, Lebanon, Syria, Jordan and the Palestinian Territories. The Palestinians were part of a joint Jordanian delegation coordinating closely with the PLO leadership in Tunis, who were prevented from attending the conference by Israel. President Bush and Soviet President Mikhael Gorbachev co-chaired these direct multilateral negotiations, which were significant but short-lived; more symbolic than substantive. Among the most important procedural legacies of Madrid was the idea of an interim agreement between Israel and the Palestinians, a move that deferred final status issues like the refugee question and the fate of Jerusalem.

This pattern of negotiating would persist following the Oslo Accords, which were signed on the South Lawn of the White House on September 13, 1993. The Accords, which resulted from secret talks in Norway's capital, were considered a breakthrough in the Israeli-Palestinian conflict as they formally launched a multi-year peace process between the parties. President William Jefferson Clinton, the former governor from Arkansas who had developed close ties with Israeli Prime Minister Yitzhak Rabin, took an active role as a full partner in these negotiations. Clinton's close cooperation with the Israelis fostered Rabin's confidence, who famously shook hands with Yasser Arafat as their deputies signed the Declaration of Principals. As Clinton's first term ended, the U.S.-Israeli partnership had become a cornerstone of American foreign policy. In the words of Vice President Albert Gore, this convergence was "the closest we have with any of our friends and allies anywhere in the world."

But the peace process launched by the Oslo Accords was nowhere near as picture perfect as the famous handshake suggested. In September 1995, Arafat and Rabin signed the Interim Agreement on the West Bank and Gaza Strip, or Oslo II, establishing the Palestinian Authority (PA) and dividing the West Bank into three separate zones of control. There was enormous skepticism of Arafat's move in the Arab world, where he was seen as selling out meaningful Palestinian sovereignty for the sake of his own return to the West Bank, where he was to be appointed as president of the PA. Oslo II granted the PA limited self-government, for an interim period of time, providing the vestiges of statehood without actual content. The process around Oslo lulled its proponents into the false belief that real issues like Jerusalem, refugees' right of return, settlements and security were being dealt with. Oslo II became the basis of the Wye River Memorandum in 1998 and President George W. Bush's Roadmap for Peace in 2002.

U.S. President Bill Clinton watches as PLO leader Yasser Arafat shakes hands with Israeli Prime Minister Yitzahk Rabin, September 13, 1993. Rabin and Arafat shook hands for the first time after Israel and the PLO signed a historic agreement on Palestinian self-government in the occupied territories. (J. DAVID AKE/AFP/GETTY IMAGES)

Extremists on both sides of the conflict detested Oslo and its consequences and attempted to undermine the interim milestones it aimed to secure. In Israel, Rabin's concessions in negotiating with the Palestinians set off denunciations by right-wing politicians and incitement against the prime minister. On November 4, 1995, after a rally to support Oslo, Rabin was assassinated.

Collapse

Benjamin Netanyahu, a fierce critic of the Oslo process and leader of the Likud party, defeated Labor leader Shimon Peres in the 1996 elections to replace Rabin. A spate of suicide bombings by Hamas inside Israel prompted support of a hardline politician who was outspoken against terrorism. Clinton worked to revive the floundering Oslo process, and he brought Netanyahu and Arafat together in Maryland at the Wye River Plantation in October 1998. The memorandum that resulted advanced the interim steps of Oslo and signaled an agreement to resume permanent status negotiations.

Yet despite the U.S.' best efforts, the Oslo Accords were beset by structural deficiencies and the erosion of trust between the parties. The PA never got control of more than 18% of the territory in the West Bank, and settlements continued to expand at a rapid pace, with

the number of Israeli settlers doubling between 1993 and 2000. Daily life for Palestinians did not improve, given the ongoing restrictions of movement and the limited Israeli military redeployment in the territories. Hamas, which rejected the concessions of Oslo, was increasingly seen as a counterweight to the corruption-prone environment developing around Arafat and his advisers.

Determined to overcome these shortcomings, Clinton hastily launched a summit at Camp David in July 2000. Ehud Barak, a Labor leader with more moderate views than Netanyahu, had been elected prime minister in May 1999 with a mandate to carry on with Rabin's pursuit of peace. Clinton invited Barak and Arafat to join him at Camp David in an effort to break the logjam around the negotiations, but it was a piecemeal attempt that left key issues unresolved. There would not be a full return to the 1967 borders, and issues such as sovereignty over Jerusalem and the right of return for Palestinian refugees remained unresolved. The debate over Barak's final offer and Arafat's refusal is a fierce one, yet blame for the collapse of the summit was pinned entirely on the Palestinians by Clinton and his advisers. In a final attempt to revive the failed talks before leaving office, Clinton crafted a set of parameters in December that led to the Taba Summit

Rescue crews remove body bags from the site of a Palestinian suicide bomb attack on a Jerusalem bus in June 2002. (RICKI ROSEN/CORBIS)

A Palestinian hands his I.D. to an Israeli solider at a Jerusalem checkpoint in 1991. (DAVID H. WELLS/CORBIS)

in January 2001, by which point the *Al-Aqsa Intifada,* or the second *Intifada,* had erupted.

The second *Intifada* lasted for five years and took the lives of over 1,000 Israelis and 4,000 Palestinians, including military and civilian casualties. According to some accounts, it began with Ariel Sharon's provocative visit to the Temple Mount in Jerusalem on September 28, 2000. Sharon, a Likud party candidate running for prime minister, ascended the *Al-Haram Al-Sharif* with over 1,000 bodyguards. After his visit, which infuriated Palestinian bystanders, he declared, "the Temple Mount is in our hands and will remain in our hands. It is the holiest site in Judaism and it is the right of every Jew to visit the Temple Mount." Other accounts of the period blame Yasser Arafat and Palestinian factions for pre-organizing the violence or not doing more to stop it when it erupted.

The unrest extended to general strikes like the first *Intifada,* but also armed attacks on soldiers and civilians, assassination attempts against Israeli and Palestinian leaders, and a manifold increase in suicide bombing. These attacks, which often targeted civilians, shook Israeli society to the core, and engendered a rightward shift in domestic politics. The psychological trauma of recurring violence was no less intense for Palestinians. In both West Bank cities and the Gaza Strip, the PA was targeted, urban centers were re-occupied by Israeli soldiers, and an expanded network of checkpoints controlled dai-

ly movement. There was a marked increase in Israel's use of targeted assassinations against Palestinian militants in densely packed urban areas, resulting in civilian deaths as well.

For many Americans, the attacks of September 11, 2001, emerged as a primary reference point for understanding the violence in the Middle East. Israeli Prime Minister Ariel Sharon, who defeated Ehud Barak in the elections of February 2001, encouraged such a strong link. He found a stalwart ally in U.S. President George W. Bush, whose rubric of fighting the War on Terror resonated with Sharon's own tactics at home. Sharon refused to meet with Yasser Arafat; Bush made it clear that he would not deal with Arafat either. The Israelis launched "Operation Defensive Shield" in March 2002, the largest post-Oslo incursion into the Palestinian territories, to "rout out…terrorist infrastructure." The destruction of the PA infrastructure in tandem with Sharon's isolation of Arafat exacerbated divisions between the ruling Fatah faction of Palestinian nationalists and Hamas, which would extend to a violent rupture several years later.

U.S. foreign policy during the Bush years had a formative impact on events in the Middle East, from the launching of two wars in Afghanistan and Iraq to a sweeping policy of democracy promotion in the Arab world. Bush had a vision for addressing the Israeli-Palestinian conflict that he unveiled in his Roadmap for Peace. In a speech on June 24, 2002, Bush remarked, "the current

situation offers no prospect that life will improve. Israeli citizens will continue to be victimized by terrorists, and so Israel will continue to defend herself, and the situation of the Palestinian people will grow more and more miserable. My vision is two states, living side by side, in peace and security." This vision was conditioned on the removal of Arafat. Bush continued, "I call on the Palestinian people to elect new leaders, leaders not compromised by terror."

Arafat died in France on November 11, 2004, having been flown to a hospital outside of Paris with a publicly unknown condition. In the 2005 Palestinian presidential elections, Palestinians in the West Bank and Gaza chose Mahmoud Abbas as his successor. Abbas has remained in the post ever since. In January 2006, Palestinian Legislative Council (PLC) elections brought Hamas to power, but the international community rejected the results. The U.S. opted for a policy of boycotting Hamas, which it viewed exclusively as a terrorist organization. The Quartet (EU, Russia, UN and U.S.) cut funding to the PA, and Israel withheld tax revenues it had collected. In June 2006, Hamas leader Ismail Haniyeh sent President Bush a letter by way of an American professor asking for the boycott to be lifted, and de facto recognizing Israel. As Haniyeh wrote, "We are so concerned about stability and security in the area that we don't mind having a Palestinian state in the 1967 borders and offering a truce for many years…. We are not warmongers, we are peace

WHY?

makers and we call on the American government to have direct negotiations with the elected government." Bush did not answer, maintaining his boycott of the movement.

In Israel, Sharon's retrenchment had led to a unilateral plan for withdrawal from the Gaza Strip settlements by fall 2005. Rather than negotiations, the prime minister believed that Israel had to pursue an alternative path. In the words of his chief adviser, Dov Weisglass, the disengagement plan was part of a broader diplomatic agenda for Israel vis-à-vis the Palestinians.

The significance of the disengagement plan is the freezing of the peace process...When you freeze that process, you prevent the establishment of a Palestinian state, and you prevent a discussion on the refugees, the borders and Jerusalem. Effectively, this whole package called the Palestinian state, with all that it entails, has been removed indefinitely from our agenda. And all this with authority and permission. All with a presidential blessing and the ratification of both houses of Congress.

As Weisglass suggested, the U.S. played a crucial role in facilitating this move, a clear sign that the pattern of U.S. mediation between the Israelis and Palestinians had fully evolved into active alignment with the agenda of one side during the Bush years.

Alongside the disengagement plan, Sharon launched the construction of what the Israeli's refer to as the security barrier between Israel and the West Bank. The barrier consisted of large sections of fencing and a massive fortified wall in various locations. It was seen as a necessary counterterrorism measure by the Israeli public, but also signaled that the wall was a mechanism to annex sections of Palestinian territory and ensure Israel's retention of major settlements. The Israeli Supreme Court, which was besieged with petitions by Palestinian farmers and families cut off from their land and homes as a result of the barrier, ordered several modifications but largely supported the endeavor. The debate over the wall reverberated abroad; many of Israel's

supporters viewed the fortification as a necessity for security, while critics condemned the wall for uprooting Palestinian families, cutting homes from agricultural land, and marring the landscape of the West Bank. Many believed that the barrier would mark Israel's future border with a Palestinian state. In July 2004, the International Court of Justice deemed the wall illegal, arguing that it was in violation of international law.

Sharon suffered a massive stroke in January 2006. Ehud Olmert, the former mayor of Jerusalem, succeeded him. Olmert promised to continue with Sharon's disengagement plan, and extend it to the West Bank. The outbreak of the Second Lebanon War on July 12, 2006, shifted Olmert's plans, as he responded with overwhelming force to Hezbollah's abduction of two Israeli soldiers along the northern border. The ensuing 34-day war, during which Israel targeted Hezbollah as well as Lebanese civilian infrastructure, and Hezbollah launched Katyusha rockets into Israel, led to the death of over 1,000 Lebanese and 163 Israelis. In the wake of the 2006 war, which also served as a proxy battle between Israel and Iran, Hezbollah claimed a victory by dint of its staying power despite the Israeli bombardment. President Bush disagreed at the time, but in his memoir, *Decision Points*, he remarked that Israel's "shaky military performance" had compromised its international credibility. In

2007, the Winograd Commission, an Israeli commission of inquiry, accused Prime Minister Olmert of mishandling the war, and thousands of Israelis protested and demanded his resignation.

For the Palestinian national movement, the international boycott on Hamas sowed internal divisions with the secular Fatah faction, whose militias were being funded and trained by the U.S. and Arab states like Egypt, Jordan and Saudi Arabia. A civil war erupted between the factions, and Hamas took over the Gaza Strip with Fatah remaining entrenched in the West Bank. The Palestinian unity government, which had preserved joint Hamas and Fatah rule, was disbanded, and an "emergency cabinet" was set up with Salam Fayyad as the new technocratic prime minister. The U.S., taking a heightened interest in reviving peace efforts between Israel and the Palestinians now that Hamas was out of the picture, encouraged Israel's siege of Gaza and the lifting of sanctions in the West Bank. Despite this move, Hamas remains a key constituent in the Palestinian national movement.

Secretary of State Condoleezza Rice led the Bush administration's revival of U.S. efforts to mediate peace, and invited Israelis, Palestinians and other Arab representatives to a conference in Annapolis, MD, in November 2007. The Annapolis Conference was intended to restart the peace process and boost international support for a negotiated settle-

A Palestinian man walks along the Israeli-constructed barrier wall separating Jerusalem from Abu Dis, a village in the West Bank. (WENDY SUE LAMM/CONTRASTO/REDUX)

Hamas militia members take position after they evacuated Gaza streets in May 2006. The Hamas-led Palestinian government ordered its militia off Gaza's streets in the wake of clashes with President Mahmoud Abbas's rival Fatah movement that stirred fears of civil war. (MOHAMMED SALEM/REUTERS/CORBIS)

ment between Israel and the Palestinians. Once again, the U.S. had come to the realization that peace between Israel and its neighbors was a necessity for securing U.S. interests in the region, and that by ignoring the urgency of the issue, the conflict had only been exacerbated.

At the beginning of the conference, Bush read from a joint statement signed by the Israelis and the Palestinians supporting a two-state solution.

We agreed to immediately launch good faith, bilateral negotiations in order to conclude a peace treaty resolving all outstanding issues, including core issues, without exception…. The final peace settlement will establish Palestine as a homeland for the Palestinian people just as Israel is the homeland for the Jewish people.

The parties agreed to meet regularly after Annapolis in order to implement Bush's Roadmap and conclude a peace treaty by the end of 2008. On the day the conference ended, Olmert warned of the consequences of not reaching a solution with the Palestinians in an interview with the Israeli newspaper *Ha'aretz*.

If the day comes when the two-state solution collapses, and we face a South African-style struggle for equal voting rights (also for the Palestinians in the territories), then, as soon as that happens, the State of Israel is finished…. The Jewish organizations, which were our power base in America, will be the first to come out

against us…because they will say they cannot support a state that does not support democracy and equal voting rights for all its residents.

It was a startling and frank admission by the prime minister, who continued negotiating with Abbas over the most contentious issues, including the division of Jerusalem and the Palestinian right of return. Observers claim that the two leaders came very close to a resolution, meeting 26 times between Annapolis and the outbreak of the Gaza War on December 27, 2008.

The number of rocket attacks from the Hamas-governed Gaza Strip increased throughout 2008, until a ceasefire was brokered between Israel and Hamas in June. An Israeli raid in Gaza was followed by airstrikes targeting Hamas

members and further rocket attacks. Olmert then launched "Operation Cast Lead," a 22-day air campaign and ground invasion that pounded Gaza, resulting in the death of over 1,100 Palestinians and 13 Israelis. Olmert intended to rout out rocket attacks and weapons smuggling into Gaza, with an undeclared goal of removing Hamas from power, but attacks from the movement intensified during the confrontation. A unilateral Israeli ceasefire was declared on January 18, 2009. The UN Fact Finding Mission on the Gaza Conflict, led by South African Justice Richard Goldstone, investigated the war and found both Palestinian militants and the Israeli army guilty of potential war crimes. Goldstone, coming under pressure by Israel, would later retract his claim that the Israelis deliberately targeted Palestinian civilians in the attack, having been unable to corroborate evidence without Israel's cooperation or to gather evidence in Gaza without Hamas' full cooperation. But the legacy of the Gaza War remained a troubling one, given the humanitarian catastrophe that confronted the population of the Strip and Israel's deepening isolation globally. As *The New York Times* reported on the war's impact, Israel faced its "worst diplomatic crisis in two decades." Ehud Olmert, besieged by corruption charges, announced his intention to resign, and Israeli elections in February 2009 elections brought Benjamin Netanyahu back to office. There was little hope that the negotiations Olmert and Abbas had been pursuing would continue. ∎

Obama and Israel

In the U.S., the transformative 2008 presidential elections brought Barack Obama to the White House. It was a heady time for supporters of a new American role around the globe, given the widespread disillusionment with the 43rd President. Bush's approval rating—which was over 80% in the aftermath of 9/11—stood at 34% upon leaving office in January 2009. Obama's victory spurred hopes in the Middle East that the U.S. would return to a more evenhanded policy when it

came to the Arab world and Israel. In his first few weeks in office, the President appointed former U.S. Senator George Mitchell as his Special Envoy for Middle East Peace, a position intended to demonstrate the importance the Obama administration placed on a resolution to the Israeli-Palestinian conflict. Mitchell, who had overseen negotiations for peace in Northern Ireland as the architect of the Good Friday Agreement and who had authored the Mitchell Report on the Arab-Israeli conflict, was seen as a serious diplomat capable of achieving progress. More broadly, Obama wanted to change the image of the U.S. in the Middle East. "My job to the Muslim world is to communicate that the Americans are not your enemy," Obama said in a January interview with *Al-Arabiya*, "We sometimes make mistakes. We have not been perfect."

This theme would be expanded in Obama's historic speech at Cairo University on June 4, 2009. In front of a large audience of Egyptian students, Obama charted a new path for U.S. engagement in the region, and singled out Israel and the Palestinians as a primary concern. As Obama explained to his audience, "America's strong bonds with Israel are well known. This bond is unbreakable. It is based upon cultural and historical ties, and the recognition that the aspiration for a Jewish homeland is rooted in a tragic history that cannot be denied." Obama continued, turning to the Palestinians.

It is also undeniable that the Palestinian people—Muslims and Christians— have suffered in pursuit of a homeland. … America will not turn our backs on the legitimate Palestinian aspiration for dignity, opportunity, and a state of their own.

In the President's view, "the only resolution is for the aspirations of both sides to be met through two states, where Israelis and Palestinians each live in peace and security." How to achieve this goal remained a difficult task. Obama stressed an end to Palestinian violence, telling his audience that it would not resolve the conflict, and that Hamas would have to put an end to their tactics. As for Israel's responsibility, Obama implored Israelis to "acknowledge that just as Israel's right to exist cannot be denied, neither can Palestine's. The United States does not accept the legitimacy of continued Israeli settlements. This construction violates previous agreements and undermines efforts to achieve peace. It is time for these settlements to stop."

As it had been for Carter and Begin 30 years earlier, Obama's disagreement with Netanyahu over the settlements would derail his ambitious first term

agenda for a resolution to the conflict. Ten days after Obama's Cairo speech, Netanyahu delivered his own address at Bar-Ilan University, where he formally accepted the principle of two states living side by side.

We must also tell the truth in its entirety: within this homeland lives a large Palestinian community. We do not want to rule over them, we do not want to govern their lives, we do not want to impose either our flag or our culture on them. In my vision of peace, in this small land of ours, two peoples live freely, side-by-side, in amity and mutual respect. Each will have its own flag, its own national anthem, its own government. Neither will threaten the security or survival of the other.

For Netanyahu, however, the content of that Palestinian state was far less than they would be willing to accept: It was to be "demilitarized," with Jerusalem remaining the capital of Israel, and the Palestinians giving up on the right of return. Netanyahu also argued that natural growth for existing Jewish settlements on the West Bank would be permissible.

This position, which was enacted via a 10-month settlement freeze, did not include East Jerusalem or apply to the 3,000 housing units already under construction. During a visit by U.S. Vice President Joseph Biden to Israel in March 2010, Netanyahu's government announced the construction of 1,600 further units in the East Jerusalem

neighborhood of Ramat Shlomo. Secretary of State Hillary Clinton called the move "deeply negative," and Obama was reportedly "livid." General David Petraeus, testifying in front of the Senate Armed Services Committee shortly after Biden's visit, remarked that tensions over Israel-Palestine have "an enormous effect on the strategic context in which we operate." Netanyahu, acknowledging the bad timing, still defended the building in a Jerusalem neighborhood as part of long-standing Israeli policy. "Our policy on Jerusalem is the same policy followed by all Israeli governments for 42 years, and it has not changed. As far as we are concerned, building in Jerusalem is the same as building in Tel Aviv," Netanyahu remarked. The President met with Netanyahu at the White House on March 26, in an encounter that by most accounts was unpleasant. Obama asked for written guarantees that the freeze would be extended, but Netanyahu refused to give them. Reports about U.S.-Israeli relations were filled with recrimination and anger in the media, having hit the lowest point in years.

In September 2010, Obama hosted Netanyahu, Abbas, Jordan's King Abdullah and Special Envoy Mitchell for the restart of negotiations to reach a final status settlement. As Israel's settlement moratorium lapsed, the talks broke down, and Mitchell eventually resigned from the office of the Special Envoy in May 2011.

Palestinian protesters throw stones at Israeli vehicles during an October 2013 protest against the expanding of Jewish settlements in Kufr Qadoom village, near the West Bank city of Nablus. (NIDAL ESHTAVEH/XINHUA/EYEVINE/REDUX)

After his own resignation as secretary of defense some months later, Robert Gates reportedly remarked that Netanyahu was "ungrateful" to the U.S., who received "nothing in return" for ensuing Israel's security. Sentiments like those from Gates seeped down into public discourse, with more vocal criticism and frustration mounting with the policies of the right-wing Likud-led government. Even within the American pro-Israel community there were signs of fracturing, as the growth of a more centrist political action group, J Street, mounted a challenge to the rightward leaning lobby powerhouse, the American-Israel Public Affairs Committee (AIPAC).

Obama publically declared his support for the demarcation of an Israeli-Palestinian border along the 1967 lines in the spring of 2011. He clarified that this included mutually agreed land swaps after his speech elicited criticism from Republican officials. The political costs of the President's involvement in Israeli-Palestinian peacemaking had become abundantly clear ahead of the 2012 elections. The upheaval in the Arab world, which had begun in Tunisia at the end of 2010, had also shaken the U.S. position in the region. The "Arab Spring"—a contested term used to describe events as disparate as the Egyptians overthrow of the long-standing President Hosni Mubarak to the protests in Syria that turned into a full-scale civil war—nonetheless left an indelible mark on Israel and the Palestinians. It also shaped the degree of U.S. involvement in resolving the conflict given the proliferation of other regional crises. As Obama won reelection in 2012, and Netanyahu emerged with a third term as prime minister in early 2013, the complexities and tensions affecting the U.S.-Israeli relationship had not at all subsided.

In an effort to reset his relations with Israel, Obama's first trip abroad in his second term was to Israel and the West Bank. He delivered a major speech directly to Israeli students in Jerusalem's International Convention Center on March 21, 2013. In his speech, Obama displayed a close identification with the Jewish state:

I believe that Israel is rooted not just in history and tradition, but also in a simple and profound idea: the idea that people deserve to be free in a land of their own…. And Israel has achieved this even as it has overcome relentless threats to its security— through the courage of the Israel Defense Forces, and a citizenry that is resilient in the face of terror.

Observers noted the change in tone from Obama's Cairo speech, which had put many Israelis on edge. Here was an American leader in the heart of Jerusalem, speaking directly to young people (rather than their political leaders in the Knesset), signaling that he identified with their success and empathized with the challenges they faced. At the same time, Obama turned to the fate of the Palestinians, and the underlying tension that animates Israeli political reality.

The Palestinian people's right to self-determination and justice must also be recognized. …Neither occupation nor expulsion is the answer. Just as Israelis built a state in their homeland, Palestinians have a right to be a free people in their own land.

It was a bracing assessment by Obama, who had compelled his audience to acknowledge the untenable nature of the occupation, and the degree to which it was compromising the core of Israel's identity as a democracy.

Obama put forth his own set of principles that could guide the parties back to negotiations. "Now is the time for the Arab World to take steps toward normalized relations with Israel. Meanwhile, Palestinians must recognize that Israel will be a Jewish state, and that Israelis have the right to insist upon their security. Israelis must recognize that continued settlement activity is counterproductive to the cause of peace, and that an independent Palestine must be viable with real borders that have to be drawn." The statement on borders echoed Obama's earlier calls for the return to the 1967 lines, but the insistence that Palestinians recognize Israel as a "Jewish state" was a nod to the demands of Prime Minister Netanyahu. Critics dismissed the speech as a wholesale adoption of Israel's posi-

tion, having pinned their hopes on an American president who might restore balance to American involvement in the region.

Yet Obama, like so many of his predecessors, faced a crush of domestic and foreign policy crises, and could not expend the political capital that would result from entangling himself in the intricacies of Israeli-Palestinian peacemaking. On July 29, 2013, the president appeared alongside former U.S. Ambassador to Israel, Martin Indyk, appointing him as the new Special Envoy for Middle East Peace. Indyk, who had extensive government experience and went on to head the Saban Center for Middle East Policy at the Brookings Institution in Washington, DC, would shoulder the burden of U.S. involvement along with the new secretary of state, John Kerry. A passionate voice for American engagement in Arab-Israeli peacemaking from his time in the Senate, Kerry had signaled this issue as a top priority after taking office in early 2013. During his UN General Assembly speech in September, Obama announced the pursuit of Israeli-Palestinian peace as a priority alongside the negotiation of a nuclear deal with Iran and addressing the civil war in Syria.

The scaling back of U.S. engagement with Egypt and the broader unrest in the Arab world signaled a more modest agenda for American foreign policy in the Middle East, one that recognized the limits of military intervention. Opponents of this new agenda voiced concern that it also revealed American weakness in the region, a similar criticism that surfaced when Reagan defeated Carter in 1980. Behind the scenes, the Israelis and the Palestinians conducted several rounds of negotiations, excluding Indyk from some of the meetings. They set a nine-month timetable to reach an agreement. At the time of this writing, the negotiations have failed to produce a viable framework for a political solution. Netanyahu's detractors have argued that his demands are unreasonable and the prime minister is proceeding with bad faith.

On November 7, 2013, Kerry criticized the Israelis for their actions on settlements during a press conference with Netanyahu in Jerusalem. The latest Israeli moves, which included the surprise announcement of more than 20,000 planned settlement units by Housing Minister Uri Ariel, went even further than previous building in bisecting a possible Palestinian state. In the view of some observers, the announcement revealed an internal power struggle between Netanyahu and the more intransigent right-wing members of his coalition government who hope to scuttle any possible deal. Regardless of the reason, this action elicited the resignation letters of the chief Palestinian negotiators, Saeb Erekat and Mohammed Shtayyeh, who vocally opposed Israeli settlement activity. Erekat, who has attempted to resign several times before, criticized Israel's "government of settlers, for settlers and by settlers." Mahmoud Abbas suggested that the PA might consider pursuing the UN Security Council as a venue to discuss the settlements, despite having promised Kerry not to go to the international community for the duration of the negotiations.

Relations today

2014 is poised to be a decisive year for U.S.-Israeli relations in light of ongoing international attempts to broker a deal with Iran on the nuclear issue and the narrowing timetable for an agreement with the Palestinians. Israeli strategic thinkers may not countenance a nuclear equipped Iran, but they also recognize the constraints under which their government can act. The recent diplomatic solution brokered by the P5 +1 (the five permanent members of the UN Security Council and Germany) in Geneva in November undermines Israel's international legitimacy in the event of a unilateral attack on Iranian soil. Some of Israel's staunchest allies in Congress worry that American diplomacy is compromising Israel's window of immunity. During a congressional briefing against new Iranian sanctions in November, Secretary Kerry's statements were brandished as "anti-Israeli" by Republican senators, a reminder that

(KICHKA/CARTOONARTS/NYTS)

U.S.-Israeli relations remain fraught. But while Netanyahu's repeated calls for swift action may resonate in some parts of Washington, the leadership in Jerusalem knows that the relationship between the two countries and their mutual security interests are too intertwined to countenance unilateral action in the face of a red light from President Obama.

In his Jerusalem speech, Obama acknowledged these tensions and spoke forcefully about the dangers posed to Israel and the U.S. in the event of a nuclear-armed Iran. "When I consider Israel's security, I also think about a people who have a living memory of the Holocaust, faced with the prospect of a nuclear-armed Iranian government that has called for Israel's destruction. It's no wonder Israelis view this as an existential threat. But this is not simply a challenge for Israel – it is a danger for the entire world, including the United States…As President, I have said to the world that all options are on the table for achieving our objectives. America will do what we must to prevent a nuclear-armed Iran." It is a promise that continues to mitigate Israeli concerns about the diplomatic breakthrough in Geneva, but for how long? There are reports of joint Israeli-Saudi Arabian planning for a military option against Iran in the wake of a diplomatic agreement, a further sign of shifting alliances in the Middle East. As the U.S. tries to manage

these competing tensions in the region, in addition to the upheaval in Egypt and the civil war in Syria, Iran's nuclear issue will continue to shape relations with Israel in the coming year.

Whether or not the successive rounds of talks between Israel and the Palestinians amount to an agreement, the persistent lack of a resolution profoundly shapes American—and global—opinions of Israel. From the birth of the Palestinian refugee problem in 1948 through the onset of Israel's occupation in 1967 and the more recent attempts to reach a two-state solution, the question of equality and civil rights has taken center stage. Israel's conflicting identity as both a proud democracy and a definitively Jewish state continue to clash with one another. The country's staunchest supporters have grown uncomfortable with the structural inequality that is manifest in the political status quo, both inside Israel and in its relationship to the Palestinians. Of all Israel's allies, perhaps no country is as well equipped as the U.S. to recognize the risks of this imbalance, and to support a resolution. But given the track record of American involvement in the peace process, and the longer history of relations with Israel, there is no guarantee that the U.S. can play a constructive role. So it may be up to Israel—the most powerful player in this conflict, albeit an anxious and beleaguered one—to reckon with what the future might hold. ∎

 Don't forget to vote! www.greatdecisions.org/ballot

[handwritten: UN PARTITON plan for Palestine]

discussion questions

1. Israel has grown as a democratic government that has developed key institutional strengths through freedom of the press, civil society and fair elections. It has also pursued settlement expansion programs and the construction of the West Bank wall. Do such policies and actions curtail the democratic potential of Israel?

2. Leaders have dealt with various strategies for negotiations regarding the Israeli-Palestinian conflict. With past mediation efforts in mind, is the piecemeal approach a viable path toward peace deals? Is success dependent on the political administration and the individual leaders that are involved in the negotiation efforts?

3. How has the Arab Spring impacted U.S. relations with Israel? How has the tumultuous political environment of the Middle East influenced Israeli-Palestinian negotiations?

4. To what extent are there similarities between U.S. foreign policy in the Middle East and Israel's national interest in the region? Did a special relationship between the United States and Israel evolve from coinciding foreign policy interests in the Middle East or did such a special relationship exist prior to coinciding foreign policy agendas?

5. In September 2013, President Barack Obama and President Hassan Rouhani held the first telephone conversation between high officials of the two countries since 1979; in November 2013, the U.S. and five countries struck a deal to temporarily freeze Iran's nuclear program. What do such efforts signal to Israel, and how do U.S. negotiations with Iran shape Israeli foreign policy in the region?

6. Each United States president has assigned varying degrees of attention to the Israeli-Palestinian conflict in the larger context of Arab-Israeli issues. Would it be more advantageous for the Obama administration to view other regional powers as partners in mediation efforts or has the Israeli-Palestinian issue developed into a conflict solely between two entities?

[handwritten: 850K Jews + Christians pushed out of Arab Countries]
[handwritten: 250K - 300K Arabs left in 47-48 June]
[handwritten: 200K - 250K " " Bo stage to Mar '49]

suggested readings

Avishai, Bernard. **The Tragedy of Zionism: How Its Revolutionary Past Haunts Israeli Democracy.** New York: Helios Press, 2002. 389pp. $16.95 (paper). From a leading writer and analyst of Israel, a critical study of Zionism's impact on the emergence of the Israeli state and relations with the Palestinians.

Einsenberg, Laura Zittrain and Neil Caplan. **Negotiating Arab-Israeli Peace, Second Edition: Patterns, Problems, Possibilities.** Bloomington: Indiana University Press, 2010. 452pp. $35.00 (paper). Eisenberg and Caplan coherently link over sixty years of Arab-Israeli negotiations and identify a pattern of negative behavior that has continually prevented the emergence of a sustainable peace.

Hertzberg, Arthur. **The Zionist Idea: A Historical Analysis and Reader.** Philadephia: The Jewish Publication Society, 1997. 648pp. $34.00 (paper). An indispensible anthology of writings by leading Zionist thinkers, with brief biographies of each figure.

Gorenberg, Gershom. **The Accidental Empire: Israel and the Birth of the Settlements, 1967-1977**. New York: Times Books, 2006. 480pp. $30.00 (paper). A groundbreaking account of Israel's settlement project in the occupied territories, focusing on the early years of Labor led efforts.

Khalidi, Rashid. **The Iron Cage: The Story of the Palestinian Struggle for Statehood**. Boston: Beacon Press, 2007. 288pp. $17.00 (paper). From a leading scholar of the Middle East, an extended treatment of the Palestinian attempts to achieve independence and the reasons for their ongoing failure.

Kimmerling, Baruch and Joel Migdal. **The Palestinian People: A History**. Cambridge: Harvard University Press, 2003. 608pp. $25.50 (paper). A comprehensive history of the Palestinian people, with a focus on Palestinians in Israel and identity formation, from the 19th century through the peace process.

LeVine, Mark and Gershon Shafir, eds. **Struggle and Survival in Palestine/Israel**. Berkeley: University of California Press, 2012. 472pp. $34.95 (paper). A social history that examines personal narratives to provide a human dimension to the history of the region.

Morris, Benny. **The Birth of the Palestinian Refugee Problem Revisited**. Cambridge: Cambridge University Press, 2004. 666pp. $62.00 (paper). A pioneering study of the Palestinian exodus during the 1948 Arab-Israeli war by a leading Israeli revisionist historian.

Ross, Dennis. **The Missing Peace: The Inside Story for the Fight for Middle East Peace.** Farrar, Straus & Giroux, 2005. 880pp. $25.00 (paper). Ross, chief U.S. negotiator under Bush and Clinton, details the highs and lows of the Israeli-Palestinian negotiations from 1988 to 2001 in this exhaustive insider's account.

Shlaim, Avi. **The Iron Wall: Israel and the Arab World.** New York: Norton, 2001. 704pp. $24.95 (paper). A critical study of Israel's foreign relations with its Arab neighbors by a leading historian of the conflict.

Quandt, William B. **Peace Process: American Diplomacy and the Arab-Israeli Conflict Since 1967**. Third ed. Washington, DC: Brookings Institution; Berkeley and Los Angeles: University of California Press, 2005. 535pp. $24.95 (paper). Authoritative account of U.S. involvement in Arab-Israeli peacemaking by scholar and former NSC official in the Nixon and Carter administrations.

TO LEARN MORE ABOUT THIS TOPIC AND TO ACCESS WEB LINKS TO RESOURCES GO TO www.greatdecisions.org

Turkey's challenges
by Lenore G. Martin

Supporters of modern Turkey's secular foundations wave flags and portraits of Ataturk during a demonstration on June 19, 2008. (KEREM UZEL/NARPHOTOS/REDUX)

The demonstrations that erupted on Istanbul's streets at the end of May 2013 and spread to 79 of Turkey's 81 provinces point to fissures in the republic that have smoldered since its founding. The modern Turkish republic was born out of the end of World War I, which had proved disastrous for the Ottoman Empire. At the end of the war, Sultan Mehmed VI's agreement to the Treaty of Sèvres of 1920, stripped the empire of much of its territory, forcing it to cede large swaths of land in the east, west and south to Greece, the United Kingdom, France and Armenia. These cessions left the Ottomans with an indelible fear of the dissolution of the state as the Sèvres syndrome. Mustafa Kemal, later known as Atatürk, rejected the Treaty of Sèvres and led the Turkish War of Independence (1919–22). The Lausanne Treaty of 1923 replaced the Treaty of Sèvres and established the boundaries of modern Turkey.

As the first president of the new republic, Atatürk used his forceful style of leadership to try to integrate Turkey's many ethnic groups into a unitary nation and to fulfill his dream of modernizing the Turkish state. Atatürk's goal was for Turkey to "catch up to contemporary civilization." By this he meant moving Turkey toward becoming a European power and away from what he saw as a "backward" Middle East. Atatürk's modern state was founded on the six "arrows": republicanism, populism, statism, revolutionism, nationalism and secularism. These six "arrows" subsequently became known as Kemalism.

LENORE G. MARTIN *is Professor of Political Science at Emmanuel College. She is Associate of the Weatherhead Center for International Affairs and the Center for Middle Eastern Studies both at Harvard University where she co-chairs the Seminar on Turkey in the Modern World.She is on the editorial board of Turkish Studies and has received three Fulbright Scholarships for work and study in Turkey. She has published widely on Turkey and the Middle East and is the co-editor with Dimitris Keridis of* The Future of Turkish Foreign Policy, *MIT Press, 2004.*

After difficult debates between conservative nationalists and proponents of a sweeping reform agenda, the Constitution of 1924 was adopted, officially making Turkey a republic. Over the next several years, laws were passed to try to ensure Turkey's transformation to a modern nation-state. Latin print rapidly replaced Arabic script. Ankara replaced Istanbul, the former seat of the caliphate, as the nation's capital. Women were discouraged from wearing Islamic dress, and wearing the fez and religious dress by men outside of mosques was outlawed. Religious schools were abolished, and Sufi religious orders *(tarikats)* were closed. By 1934 women were granted the vote in national elections and were able to stand for election and be seated in Parliament.

Atatürk understood that an integrated nation was essential to building the new state. As religion was no longer the main unifying element, Atatürk and his followers sought to mold a uniquely "Turkish" identity. The Turkish language was given great importance, and scholars wrote Turkish histories and textbooks. The new constitution read: "The people of Turkey, regardless of religion and race were, in terms of their citizenship, Turkish." Turkish civil identity, in theory, included every religious and ethnic group. In reality many critics would argue Turkey has operated more through ethnic nationalism, where the Sunni Muslim Turks are seen as the true Turks.

Atatürk employed the institutions of state to transform Turkish society. Primarily among them was the Turkish military, who were seen as the heroes of the War of Independence. After Atatürk died, the military saw itself as the guardian of the republic, upholding his ideology. This led to a military intimately involved in government and the three coups of 1960, 1971 and 1980. The military was also accused of leading a "soft coup" (or "postmodern coup") in 1997 and of plotting the overthrow of the Islamist-rooted Justice and Development Party (AKP) after its election in 2002.

Turkish leader Mustafa Kemal Atatürk and his wife Latife Hanm, who is unveiled in 1923. (MANSELL/MANSELL/TIME & LIFE PICTURES/ GETTY IMAGES)

Challenges to Kemalism

Atatürk's transformative agenda has not been an easy one to implement and gave rise to the challenges that Turkey is facing today:

■ Increasing Islamic religiosity in the public sphere supported by the government and opposed by a secular minority that demands clearer separation of mosque and state.

■ Increasing demands for the rule of law and democratization.

■ An alienated Kurdish minority demanding political, cultural and economic equality that at times uses violence to accomplish its goals.

■ A foreign policy that tries to keep Turkey's feet in Europe while wading, some might say swimming, into Middle East politics and getting caught up in its murky waters.

Under the AKP

Though Atatürk and his followers had employed an energetic program to secularize Turkish society, many citizens remained wedded to Sunni Islam and a conservative mindset. They kept forming political parties, though the courts continued to outlaw them, claiming that they were undermining the secular nature of the state and therefore unconstitutional. Despite these barriers, the AKP was formed in 2001 by a reformist core of members from the Virtue Party, an Islamist party forcibly disbanded in 2001. The AKP intended to get elected by appealing to the conservative populace while avoiding being shut down by working within the "system." Soon after its formation, the AKP won its first election gaining a majority of parliamentary seats in November 2002. Much of the AKP's first electoral victory is credited to the fact that the previous coalition government was seen as particularly corrupt and presided over a failing economy. Since 2002, the AKP has gone on to win two parliamentary elections in 2007 and in 2011, increasing its popular vote each time.

Yet because of Turkey's electoral system, the AKP held fewer seats in parliament after each national election. Turkey's electoral system requires a uniquely high threshold of 10% of the national vote for a party to be seated in parliament, which eliminated minority parties that had garnered votes but were below the threshold. Those parties that had passed the threshold split the votes of the parties that did not get seated. Thus, in 2002 the AKP received 34.43% of the popular vote but held 365 of the 500 parliamentary seats, a two-thirds majority. Once minority parties began to pass the 10% threshold, they gained parliamentary seats and reduced the size of the AKP's parliamentary majority. While the AKP received 46.47% of the vote in 2007, its parliamentary majority was reduced to 341 seats. In 2011 it received 49.95% of the vote but only held 326 seats.

Religion and the AKP

After coming to power, the AKP began enacting laws to appease a more religious constituency. Prime Minister Recep Tayyip Erdoğan has been outspoken on religious and social issues. In a number of these situations, however, he has had to back down. For example, his attempt to criminalize adultery produced a great uproar, and he revoked

High school students, some in headscarves, attend class in Diyarbakir on October 1, 2013. (MEHMET ENGIN/AFP/GETTY IMAGES)

Turkish activists hold placards protesting jailing of journalists in Istanbul on November 5, 2013. (SEDAT SUNA/EPA/CORBIS)

the proposal. He also withdrew his proposal to criminalize abortion in the face of strong criticism from the secular opposition, women's groups who feared unequal application of the law and increased honor killings, and the European Union (EU). The AKP has had more success in three religiously oriented areas: the use of alcohol, the education system and the wearing of headscarves.

■ Availability of Alcohol

Drinking alcohol is prohibited in orthodox Islam; therefore, the AKP has done its best to limit its sale and consumption in Turkey without outlawing it. It has doubled the tax on alcohol and allowed local communities to limit the sale of alcohol in many areas outside of the major cities and even in some sections of the major cities. Besides this legal campaign, the AKP has engaged in a cultural one, pressuring television executives to remove alcohol consumption from television programs; if alcohol consumption does appear, it is what the "bad guys" do, not the "good guys." A round of three new laws intended to limit alcohol sales and consumption went into effect in 2013: Advertisements for all alcoholic drinks were banned; alcohol retail sales were banned between 10 p.m. and 6 a.m.; new licenses for the sale of alcohol cannot be given to establishments near a school or mosque, and now require the approval of the local municipality and the Ministry of Culture and Tourism.

■ Changing the Education System

The AKP has also made major changes to Turkey's education system. In 2012 it increased the number of years of required education from eight to 12 years. However, it also increased the opportunity for parents to opt for a more religious education for their children by adopting a "4-4-4 system." Here, the first four years of primary school are required of all students; the second four years of primary school are also required, but students can choose to attend a vocational school—including religious schools—during this period; and in the last four years a student can choose to be homeschooled. The secularist community disagrees with the "4-4-4 system" and says that it permits students to enter religious schools at a very young age. The critics of the homeschool option say that it may limit education for girls and also open up the possibility of child labor. The AKP responded by stating that parents choosing homeschool will have to seek permission to do so. Additionally, in November 2013, the AKP Deputy Speaker of Parliament criticized co-ed education and promised to abolish it in the future.

On the university level, the AKP has allowed those graduating from religious schools to compete for places in universities on an equal basis with those from secular schools. University entrance exams have begun including a section on religion as one of the optional exam sections.

■ Lifting the Ban on Headscarves

The wearing of headscarves has been the most visible issue challenging secularism in Turkey. For secularists the headscarf is a symbol of political Islam; for the more religious in Turkey it is an act of piety. Atatürk encouraged women to remove the headscarf, and a 1982 regulation prohibited women working in the public sector, such as teachers, from wearing headscarves. In 1997 the military went further and forced the coalition government and Erbakan to outlaw the wearing of the headscarf in universities.

The 1997 headscarf law was part of what is referred to as the February 28 process or the "postmodern coup." where the military acted as guardians of the Kemalist state. From the military to the president of the country, many were concerned about the increasing Islamic activity by Erbakan's Islamist Refah Party and its call for sharia law at a Jerusalem Day celebration in February 1997. While there were no tanks on the street, the military convened large meetings in support of secularism and forced Erbakan to resign from power on June 30, 1997. In 2013, the AKP proposed a lift of the headscarf ban in public spaces. The only women unable to wear the headscarf in the public sector would be those who wear uniforms, namely prosecutors, judges, the military and police. It has been posited that this new law may bring more Turkish women into the workplace.

Role of the military

In recent years, Turkey's push to join the EU has limited the power of the military. In 2003, the Turkish military leadership was supportive of EU accession as part of Turkey's Westernization project. It was also fearful that standing in the way of EU membership would cost them popular support. Thus, the military relinquished its dominant position on the National Security Council (MGK). This was the first of a number of steps leading towards bringing the military under the control of the civilian government, including control over the military budget. These changes came to the fore in 2007 as Erdoğan prepared to nominate then Foreign Minister Abdullah Gül, a founder of the AKP, as president of the republic. The military issued a memorandum on its website implicitly threatening to overthrow the government. Erdoğan took his chances and called an election, winning even more votes for the AKP. That was a message to the military that the public no longer would support direct interference by the military in Turkish politics.

The victory gave the AKP confidence to take further steps to suppress the Kemalist military leadership. In 2007 the government began investigating a case that culminated in the arrests of generals, academics, scientists, journalists, physicians and leaders of non-governmental organizations for an alleged conspiracy to overthrow the government, many of whom were outspoken critics of the AKP's policies. The case was dubbed "Ergenekorn," a reference to a mythical place in the Altai mountains. In August 2013 the court handed down verdicts on 300 defendants, including General Ilker Basburg, the military's former chief of the general staff. Twenty-one of the defendants were found not guilty; the others, including General Basburg, were found guilty and handed sentences all the way up to life imprisonment. It also brought two other cases against the military, alleging a conspiracy to overthrow the government—one case named "Sledgehammer" and the other "February 28." The Sledgehammer

Tayyip Erdoğan waves in front of a portrait of Mustafa Kemal Atatürk on June 24, 2003. (STRINGER/REUTERS/CORBIS)

case also included two civilians and the February 28 case included one civilian.

For AKP supporters these cases have come to represent freedom from the fear of future military coups. For many of the secular members of Turkish society, these cases represent retribution against those with whom the AKP strongly disagrees on political and social policy, particularly on secularism.

Economy

Notwithstanding the challenge to democratization and the rule of law, the AKP government has maintained substantial popular support. In addition to the party's appeal to conservatives, a relatively strong economy has contributed to its domestic popularity. By following the International Monetary Fund's (IMF) Dervish plan that was de-

veloped to address Turkey's desperate economic situation in 2001, the AKP has presided over a period of strong growth. The "Anatolian Tigers," the conservative businessmen who have benefitted from the economic growth are an important source of the AKP's political strength. They have branched out wherever they can, leading Turkey into new markets in places such as the Middle East and Africa.

Over the last 10 years Turkey has managed to survive the two global downturns relatively well. Nevertheless, Turkey faces large current account deficits especially due to the increasing energy imports that it needs to fuel its economic growth and the imported intermediate inputs needed for its manufacturing sector. Turkey imports almost all of its oil and gas: 44% of its crude oil comes from Iran, 58% of its gas comes from Russia. It is trying to reduce its dependency on imported energy by developing hydropower and building nuclear reactors. Since the 1960s Turkey has been working on the Southeastern Anatolian Project (GAP), seeking to harness the hydropower of the Tigris and Euphrates that could provide up to 25% of Turkey's energy needs. The GAP project also aims at improving the agriculture through better irrigation and the economy generally of the Southeast region that is the home of a large percentage of Turkey's Kurdish population. Turkey also aims at becoming an energy hub, increasing the number of pipelines bringing oil and gas from Central Asia and the Middle East through Turkey, and on to Europe. As a hub, Turkey increases its own access to energy resources and receives revenue derived from transit fees. ■

The Alevis

Turkey has an Alevi community with an estimated number of from 13–25 million people. Alevis have faced persecution throughout the years and suffered through recent massacres in 1978, 1980 and 1993. In 2010, the Alevis appealed to the European Court of Human Rights (ECHR), requesting state funds for their religious activities. According to the Turkey's Religious Directorate, Alevis are considered Muslims; therefore, because Muslims worship in mosques, Alevis' religious places of worship, *cemevis*,

are not recognized by the state. Alevis also requested their children be exempt from required religious instruction in schools, for which they have received support from the ECHR. To the community's disappointment, Prime Minister Erdoğan's 2013 democratization package failed to address these demands. The government further disappointed the Alevi community with its decision to name a new bridge across the Bosphorus in Istanbul the Yavuz Sultan Selim Bridge, after the Ottoman sultan, Selim I, who is believed to have carried out the largest massacre of Alevis. ■

The Kurdish challenge

Atatürk's formation of Turkish national identity triggered resistance from a number of Kurds who saw themselves as a separate nation. The Kurdistan Workers' Party (PKK), formed in 1978, has become the hallmark today of more persistent pressure on the Turkish state for recognition of separate identity for Turkey's Kurds. At some points this has meant seeking independence, at other points autonomy, but at all times it has included cultural and political rights for the Kurds.

Though there were periodic outbreaks of violence from Turkey's Kurds, beginning with the 1925 Sheikh Said rebellion, a shift in 1984 under the leadership of Abdullah Öcalan brought more sustained violence to southeastern Turkey. In 1982 the PKK made a deal with Massoud Barzani, the Kurdish leader in northern Iraq, to allow the PKK access to the Turkish border. In 1984 the PKK began their armed struggle within Turkey with attacks against the Turkish military. Since then the Kurdish insurgency is estimated to have cost more than 30,000 lives. Its first phase ended with Öcalan's capture in Nairobi in 1999.

Ceasefires, 1999–2013

After his capture, Öcalan called for the withdrawal of Kurdish fighters from Turkey. Responding to his call for a ceasefire, the coalition government of Bulent Ecevit began to discuss increasing cultural rights for Kurds in 1999. No changes resulted from these discussions. Almost immediately upon coming to power in 2002, the AKP, anxious to meet the EU accession criteria, increased the cultural rights of Kurds. The AKP's reforms in 2002 provided the Kurds with limited broadcasting rights in Kurdish, allowed them to give their children Kurdish names and to teach Kurdish in private schools. Although the changes ultimately did take place, the PKK remained unsatisfied and the violence continued.

Though there have been alternative Kurdish voices, it is the PKK and

A Kurdish child flashes a victory sign while demonstrators wave a flag picture jailed PKK leader Abdullah Öcalan on September 22, 2013, during a demonstration in Istanbul. OZAN KOSE/AFP/GETTY IMAGES

Öcalan that have been the principal representatives of the Kurds of Turkey, in part because the PKK would not allow any other organizational challenge. However, successive Turkish governments have made political activity difficult for the Kurds by closing most political parties organized by the PKK. Today's Kurdish Peace and Democracy Party (BDP) is considered the political arm of the PKK. BDP members have served as intermediaries between Öcalan, whom they have been able to visit in jail, and the rest of the PKK, as well as the Kurdish people. In October 2013 Öcalan sanctioned a new party to exist along with the BDP, the People's Democratic Party (HDP). It will include a number of leftist parties and is intended to appeal to voters beyond southeastern Turkey.

The government has arrested thousands of Kurdish politicians, elected officials, activists and even children. Many are still in jail pursuant to a case brought against members of the outlawed Kurdish Community Unions (KCK), the urban wing of the PKK. Their incarceration is based on Turkey's anti-terrorism laws, which were enacted by the military during a state of emergency in response to Kurdish violence

in 1991, that have been broadly interpreted by successive Turkish governments. The AKP government widened these anti-terrorism laws in 2006.

At the heart of these laws is Article 102 of Turkey's Penal Code. Under this article, the court can detain a person without a trial for two years and extend detention for another three years. If a person is accused of terrorism or organized crime, the detention time can be doubled. That means the accused can be detained for up to ten years before being brought to trial. These laws have been applied in the massive arrests in the major cases involving the KCK and Ergenekorn, Sledgehammer and February 28th cases. Even students demonstrating on campuses have been charged under these anti-terrorist laws.

Peace process 2013

Shortly after publicly disclosing talks with Öcalan, the Turkish government reached an agreement with the PKK in 2013 on a three-phased peace process. In the first phase, the PKK militants would withdraw from Turkey; the second phase would implement a democratization package; the third phase would include complete disarmament and a repatriation process permitting the return of disarmed PKK members to Turkey. Some PKK fighters did leave Turkey, many going to northern Iraq and taking their weapons with them, much to the disappointment of the government.

The BDP made it clear that for them to move forward with the peace process, the government must meet their demands for constitutional changes as part of what Erdoğan has called a "democratization process." The Kurds' most important demands were: the complete abolition of Turkey's anti-terrorism laws and sections of the penal code used to imprison Kurdish political activists and

mayors; education in a student's mother tongue; a lower threshold for electing members of parliament, enabling them to have sufficient voting power to elect a Kurdish party to parliament; and more robust local governance.

On September 30, 2013, Erdoğan announced a democratization and human rights package that he is taking to parliament. It was a disappointment for the Kurds. The package allowed for education in the mother tongue in private schools but not in public schools. (The average income in the predominantly Kurdish southeast is far below the average income in Turkey; therefore, paying for private school would be prohibi-

tive.) It also failed to abolish the anti-terrorism law under which many Kurds are imprisoned. Though the package did offer two possible options to lower the electoral threshold, both options would limit the election of Kurdish representatives to the southeast. According to one Kurdish representative, the options in the package were "an attempt to jail the BDP in a specific region." As a result, there have been hints from the Kurds that the ceasefire may end, threatening the relative quiet in the southeast. The unsolved Kurdish issue has clear security implications within Turkey and leaves it vulnerable to interference from its neighbors Syria, Iran and Iraq. ∎

Gezi Park and rule of law

A protestor is knocked back by a police water cannon as riot police advance toward Gezi Park from Taksim Square in Istanbul on June 11, 2013. Protestors had occupied the square to save a nearby park from redevelopment. (ED OU/NEW YORK TIMES/REDUX)

In the summer of 2013 the societal divisions that have been plaguing Turkey came to a head. The spark that ignited the demonstrations was the government's plans to destroy Gezi Park's open space by recreating Ottoman barracks and building a shopping mall. Gezi Park is one of the busiest areas in the heart of Istanbul, and has served as the site of numerous demonstrations and commemorations over the years. The government cracked down on the peaceful demonstrators

began with the use of tear gas and pressurized water. What started as a protest over use of public park space became a protest over what demonstrators called the authoritarian nature of Erdoğan's leadership style. The protests spread tthroughout most of Turkey's, eliciting the same extreme reaction from government forces.

The widespread demonstrations brought Turkey's serious need for increased democratization to the attention of the Turkish public and the

international community. An earlier example of the AKP's repression of freedom of assembly occurred in October 2012, when members of opposition groups were denied a permit to celebrate Republic Day after the government claimed they received intelligence that the demonstration could become violent. The protesters went ahead with their rally, and the police used tear gas and pressurized water to disperse them.

The protests highlighted the need for a free press as well. Infringements on the freedom of the Turkish press have plagued the republic throughout its history. The fact that many of Turkey's media outlets are owned by holding companies has traditionally made them vulnerable to business and government pressure. Under the AKP, Turkey now has the dubious distinction of having more journalists in jail than either China or Russia. In August of 2013 there were 64 journalists in prison and 123 on trial. Nearly all were imprisoned on terrorism or anti-state charges.

One method used by the AKP government to repress criticism in the press has been a tax evasion case for $2.5 billion dollars against the owner of the main opposition press, the Doğan Group. The Doğan Group owned approximately 50% of Turkey's media outlets. Many of the media assets of the

Doğan Group are now run by supporters of the AKP. Even those newspapers that the Doğan Group continues to own and the rest of the opposition press are reluctant to criticize the government, fearing that could trigger a call from government officials for the firing of a journalist. The effect has been pervasive self- censorship. The extent of the self-censorship became undeniable when media outlets showed a film on penguins at the beginning of the Gezi Park protests rather than covering the demonstrations.

Closely linked to restrictions on the freedom of the press are restrictions on the freedom of speech that are embedded in the Turkish Penal Code. Article 301 of the Penal Code, for example, bans "insulting Turkishness." In 2008 the government reworded this provision to "insulting the Turkish state" and decreased the punishment from three to two years in prison. Not all those convicted of violating Article 301 have been incarcerated, however. Orhan Pamuk, 2006 winner of the Nobel Prize in Literature, was tried and convicted under Article 301 but did not serve prison time. ∎

Foreign policy dilemmas

Following Atatürk's vision, Turkey has sought to join the European community. It first joined the Organisation for Economic Co-operation and Development (1948), the Council of Europe (1949), the North Atlantic Treaty Organization (1952) and became an associate member of the European Economic Community (1963). Turkey applied to become a full member of the EEC in 1987.

After 18 years of discussions and disappointments, EU accession negotiations began in 2005. Since then, Turkey has provisionally completed only one chapter, or policy area, namely Chapter 25 on Science and Research. The continued stalemate over the reunification of Cyprus, which has been partitioned since 1974, has been one of the greatest hurdles for Turkey's EU membership, as have human rights concerns. Fourteen of the 35 EU chapters were taken off the negotiating table until the Cyprus issue is solved.

The Turks have occupied the northeastern portion of Cyprus following invasions in July and August 1974, which were in response to an Athens-administered attempted coup d'état by pro-unification Greek Cypriot nationalists. In 2004 Turkish Cypriots accepted the Annan Plan, which proposed the creation of a United Cyprus Republic. The decision by the EU to accept the Republic of Cyprus into the EU even if it voted against the plan gave the Greek Cypriots little reason to compromise. With little to lose, they rejected the plan.

The Republic of Cyprus joined the EU on May 1, 2004. In response, Turkey has refused to recognize the Republic of Cyprus even after it became an EU member. It has continued to block Greek Cypriot vessels access to its ports—a response to the EU's 30-plus year trade embargo on the northern portion of the island that has yet to be lifted.

After almost no movement on Turkey's EU membership, negotiations restarted in November 2013 with discussion on a new policy area, regional policy. The negotiations, which had been planned for June 2013, were delayed by five months due to what the EU believed was an overly harsh reaction by the Turkish government to the peaceful protests that began in Gezi Park.

How important is EU membership to the Turks? Turkey has pursued an independent foreign policy in Iran, Egypt, Syria and Israel, and even with Hamas and Hezbollah. Were Turkey a member of the EU, there would undoubtedly be strong pressure to conform to EU foreign policy. Although Turkey's trade with the EU was negatively affected by the euro zone crisis, Turkey did not suffer the enormous financial upheavals like those in the euro zone suffered. Additionally, some Turks are tired of the accession process and feel a sense of rejection, resulting in less political pressure within the country to join the union.

On the other hand, EU membership could be tremendously beneficial for Turkey. Both Turkey and the EU share common interests in the Mediterranean, North Africa and the Middle East. Turkey and the West could be a positive force if they work together. The accession process could strengthen the push for more democratization and human rights protection in Turkey. Furthermore, there are many Turks and Europeans who believe that the EU accession process is vital to keep Turkey working on expanding press and speech freedoms, rule of law and judicial reforms. While there are some in the EU who raise concerns over cultural dif-

Paratroopers fall from Turkish Air Force transport planes on the first day, June 22, 1974, of the invasion of Cyprus by Turkey.
(BETTMANN/AP/CORBIS)

LUCIDITY INFORMATION DESIGN, LLC

ferences between Turkey and Europe, the accession process continues. However, EU and Turkish authorities are far from identifying a decade, let alone a set date, when Turkey can become part of the union.

■ Middle East Policy Pre-AKP

Though Atatürk's vision was of a Turkey that faced westward, the last ten years have seen Turkey become increasingly intertwined in Middle East politics. Even before the AKP came to power in 2002, there were brief periods in which Turkey looked east rather than west. Throughout the 1970s, Turkey grew closer to the region in response to the West's negative reaction to its invasion of Cyprus and to ease credit funding for its energy supplies following the 1973 oil embargo. When Turkey received little Arab support for its Cyprus policy, it soon returned to the Western fold. As the Cold War ended, Turkey began to fret that it would not be as essential to the West since it would no longer be needed on the front line to block an aggressive Soviet Union. Therefore, when the U.S. organized an

international force to eject Iraqi President Saddam Hussein in 1990, President Turgut Özal agreed to join the coalition, permitting the use of Incirlik air base and closing the oil pipeline from Iraq that passed through Turkey to Syria. President Özal's decision prompted the military's chief of the general staff to resign in protest over a policy that brought Turkey directly into Middle East politics. Ankara estimated that this foray into Middle Eastern politics cost Turkey about $40 billion dollars.

Perhaps more problematic for Turkey was the flow of Iraqi Kurdish refugees across the border into Turkey at the end of the war. At Turkey's request the U.S., Britain and France created a no-fly zone so that the Kurds could return to Iraq, enabling the formation of the Kurdish Regional Government (KRG). The development of an autonomous Kurdistan in northern Iraq was a major step toward fulfilling the Kurdish dream of a state of its own. Yet in Turkey there was also fear that a Kurdish state or autonomous region could foster Kurdish irredentism and

threaten Turkey's territorial integrity.

The Kurdish issue also brought Turkey to the brink of invading Syria in 1998. Damascus had been harboring Öcalan and his PKK troops during their insurgency in southeast Anatolia since 1984. "Playing the PKK card" was Syria's attempt to pressure Turkey to negotiate about the GAP that Damascus feared would limit their access to the Euphrates. After Turkey massed troops at the border in 1998, Damascus expelled Öcalan from Syria, leading to his capture in Nairobi. Afterwards, Turkey's relations with Syria began to improve in economic areas such as trade and tourism, and the two states held discussions on energy and transportation links. In this friendlier atmosphere the long-standing territorial dispute dating back to 1939 over Hatay/Alexandretta was allowed to fade into the background.

The PKK issue also strained the Iranian-Turkish relationship, as did the 1979 Iranian Revolution, which was based on an Islamist ideology diametrically opposed to the secular tenets of the Kemalist state. During the 1990s and into the early 2000s, Turkey accused Tehran of giving the PKK and radical Islamists shelter, as well as arms and training, at the Iranian border. This tension ultimately led to a diplomatic rupture in 1997 after the Iranian ambassador called for the adoption of sharia law in Turkey.

Despite this low-level conflict, the two states worked on increasing trade and, importantly for Turkey, increasing energy imports. This included the opening of a new gas pipeline in 2001, much to the chagrin of the U.S. In 2003 during the U.S.-led invasion of Iraq, the Turkish-Iranian relationship improved significantly. Both states were concerned about the possible formation of an independent Kurdish state and began to work together to contain the PKK and its Iranian offshoot, the Free Life Party of Kurdistan (PJAK).

Finally, although Turkey recognized Israel in 1949, their relationship waxed and waned in parallel with the changing course of the Arab-Israel and Palestinian-Israeli disputes. The signing of Oslo Peace Accords in 1993 gave the green light for a huge boost to Israel-Turkish relations. The two states' military and business communities forged strong ties and their diplomatic revival had important political implications for Turkey's domestic and international policies. Their two militaries exchanged information and held joint training exercises. Israeli pilots even trained in Turkish airspace. The two states also concluded a number of important defense contracts. These very public agreements sent a strong signal of a new alignment that could be a threat to Syria, Iraq and Iran. It also gave Ankara another source of arms if the Armenian and Greek lobbies sought to block U.S. arms sales to Turkey, as had happened in the past. On the domestic front, the relationship with Israel sent a tacit message to the Islamist Welfare Party, then leading the coalition government in Ankara, that Turkey's military leadership would oppose attempts to build close relationships with other Islamist governments in the Middle East.

■ *The AKP and the Middle East*

With the coming to power of the AKP, Turkey's vision of its place in the region took a 180-degree turn. The president, prime minister and chief foreign policy adviser all had ties to the Islamic world and were at ease in the Middle East. In his book, *Strategic Depth*, Turkey's foreign minister Dr. Ahmet Davutoğlu explains that Turkey's geography and history give it a unique role in the region. Davutoğlu has advocated a policy of "no problems with neighbors" and for taking a more active role in its region to assure Turkey's security. In effect, Davutoğlu developed a foreign policy independent of the West, bringing Turkey diplomatically closer to Syria, Iran and Hamas. The AKP fostered strong economic ties, eliminated visas, organized joint cabinet meetings and in 2010 held joint military exercises with Syria—all this while the U.S. and Europe were trying to isolate the regime of Bashar al Assad. In Iran, Davutoğlu partnered with Brazil to try to mediate a UN deal to stop the UN Security Council from passing sanctions in response to Iran's ongoing nuclear program. Finally, Turkey invited the Hamas leader Khaled Meshal to Ankara within a month of the party's parliamentary election victory in 2006. Meanwhile, Western powers were trying to pressure Hamas to renounce violence before normalizing contacts. Turkey also has worked to develop a role as a mediator in disputes between Syria and Israel, and between Hamas and Fatah.

Turkey's Foreign Minister Ahmet Davutoğlu and his Iranian counterpart Ali Akbar Saleh attend a news conference in Ankara on January 19, 2012. (UMIT BEKTAS/REUTERS/CORBIS)

Though Ankara was not always successful in these efforts, the AKP government felt that the good working relationships it had achieved with its neighbors afforded Turkey the ability and respect for these diplomatic undertakings. Nevertheless, Turkey's relationship with Israel blew up as a result of Israeli Prime Minister Ehud Olmert ordering an invasion of Gaza just after returning home from discussions in Ankara. Feeling betrayed, Erdoğan publicly attacked Israeli President Peres in Davos, Switzerland in 2009. Following this verbal attack on the Israeli President, Erdoğan's popularity shot up by 19% at home and the AKP's popularity went up 10%. A similar jump in his popularity took place in the region. In a 2010 survey of the most popular leader in the Middle East, not including the respondent's own leader, Erdoğan jumped from number four in 2009 to the top of the list, number 20.

The worst incident between the two former allies developed in 2010 out of a Turkish non-government organization's decision to send ships with humanitarian supplies as part of an international flotilla, including the Mavi Marmara, to break the Israeli blockade of Gaza. In its attempt to stop the aid ships from reaching Gaza, the Israeli military killed eight Turkish citizens and one Turkish American. Turkey has since demanded an apology, compensation for the victims and the end of the blockade of Gaza. Though President Obama was able to orchestrate an apology by Netanyahu and an acceptance of that apology by Erdoğan in 2013, negotiations have stalled.

To add salt to the wound, a *Washington Post* article in October 2013 reported that the Turkish Intelligence Agency gave the names of ten Iranians who were spying for Israel to Teheran. This was particularly damaging to the restoration of trust between these two regional players. If trust were restored, it might allow the Turks to play a mediating role between the Israelis and the Palestinians. Although Turkey does not have a close relationship with the leadership on the West Bank, it does have a close relation-

Prime Minister Recep Tayyip Erdogan and Israeli President Shimon Peres participate in a debate on the Gaza strip hosted by the World Economic Forum in Davos on January 29, 2009. (FABRICE COFFRIN/AFP/GETTY IMAGES)

ship with Hamas. Notwithstanding the very strained diplomatic relations between Turkey and Israel, trade between the two states has continued. Their trade today has reached approximately $4 billion dollars.

■ The Arab Uprisings

The Arab uprisings, later known as the Arab Spring, that began at the end of 2010 surprised Turkish policymakers. Although Turkey was supportive of the rebels in Tunisia, Bahrain and Egypt, it was much slower to support the rebels in Libya and Syria. Turkey had a large number of workers in Libya and a good working relationship with Muammar Qaddafi. Furthermore, the AKP government believed its close relationship with Syria and Assad would enable it to convince the regime to make political concessions to the insurgents. When they failed, the Turks not only condemned Assad, but also allowed the Syrian political and military opposition to organize on the Turkish border. The Turks were betting that Assad would fall, as did Hosni Mubarak in Egypt, and that the Syrian Muslim Brotherhood, with whom the AKP had a good relationship, would come to power. The Arab uprisings have created a new reality in the Middle East, and with it new challenges for the leadership role in the region that Foreign Minister Davutoglu had sought for Turkey.

■ The KRG and Iraq

Turkey has greatly improved its relationship with the Kurdistan Regional Government (KRG) since 2007. They reached an agreement on how to limit the movement of the PKK ensconced in the Qandil mountains of northern Iraq, developed a booming cross-border trade, and built a new pipeline carrying oil and gas from the KRG to Turkey's port of Ceyhan, with another in the works. Turkey's friendly relations with the KRG has raised the hackles of the Iraqi central government. Baghdad protests against separate energy deals with the KRG out of concern over financial losses for the central government and the increased independence the energy deal could provide for the KRG. In a new twist arising from mutual concerns over spillover from the Syrian uprising, the Iraqi central government and Turkey have been holding meetings to address the threat they both feel from the Sunni Islamists who are flocking to Syria to challenge Assad, and who could later pose a threat to the region.

■ The Syrian Civil War

Turkey has good cause to be worried about the consequences arising from the civil war in Syria. Of major concern to Ankara is the role Syria's Kurds will play in the war and the implications for Turkish territorial integrity in the future. The Democratic Union Party

(PYD), the largest Kurdish group in Syria, is closely allied with the PKK. It now controls some of the Kurdish areas along the Turkish-Syrian border. Turkey is concerned that if there is an autonomous area carved out of northern Syria, it will support a renewed separatist fight in southeastern Turkey. Turkey has been suspected of allowing Sunni extremists to cross into Syria and challenge both the Assad regime and the Syrian Kurdish PYD. Turkey is now concerned about the spillover of Sunni extremist violence into the country and is denying that it has supported them.

Additionally, the Syrian uprising has given rise to new tensions between Iran and Turkey over Tehran's support for Assad, which has included supplying his forces with arms, fighters and training. Still, there has been no indication that aligning on opposite sides over Syria will rupture Turkey's relations with Iran. Turkey still needs large energy imports from Iran and Iran needs to continue to export its oil and gas to Turkey, because of the economic sanctions imposed by the West.

Policy options

Turkey borders the most serious hot spots in the Middle East today: Syria, Iraq and Iran. Turkey's responses to national security threats arising from the instability in the region, and its more independent and activist approach in the Middle East have created challenges for U.S. policy in the region. There are four salient issue areas for the Turkey-U.S. relationship that raise questions as to what policy options the U.S. should adopt on: Syria, Israel, Turkey's air defense, and Iran.

■ Turkey and the Syrian Uprising

Turkey has taken a very strong policy stand against the Assad regime out of concerns about refugees, terrorist activity and border security. It has welcomed the Syrian political and military opposition headquarters on the Turkish side of the Syrian border, and it is believed to have allowed arms and fighters to flow from Iraq into Syria. Ankara has also been frustrated with the U.S. policy of sending non-lethal aid to only some rebel groups, training carefully selected rebel groups in Jordan, and supporting diplomatic negotiations to end the war. Prime Minister Erdoğan would have preferred a military strike in response to Bashar al Assad's use of chemical weapons, as President Obama indicated he would do early in the civil war, rather than Washington's agreement to an internationally supervised program to remove all chemical weapons from Syria. A missile attack on Syria at the time was the least the Turks had requested. Moreover, Ankara has been pushing the U.S. in vain to create a no-fly zone to help secure the hundreds of thousands of refugees and sections of the Turkish border as well. For its part, Washington from the beginning has been concerned not to repeat the mistakes of Afghanistan and Iraq, and it does not want to get involved in another Middle Eastern war whose end is not clear. The question for the U.S. is how to respond to these Turkish concerns.

■ *Turkey and Israel*

Turkey's policy towards Israel remains very problematic for the U.S. Even after President Obama's success in May 2013 in coaxing President Netanyahu to apologize to Erdoğan for the deaths of the eight Turks on the Mavi Marmara, negotiations between Israel and Turkey quickly bogged down over the issue of compensation to the Turkish families of the victims and the issue of improvement of the humanitarian situation in Gaza. Both of these issues are considered extremely important to Ankara. Members of the families of those hurt and deceased are demanding the right to bring criminal and civil suits in a Turkish court, something Israel is vehemently opposing.

■ *Turkey and NATO*

NATO provided Turkey with six Patriot missile batteries to help protect it from Syrian missiles. It was therefore a great shock to Turkey's NATO allies when Ankara announced that it was accepting a Chinese bid to build a Turkish air defense system. U.S. Ambassador to Turkey Francis Ricciardone and NATO

KAL/CARTOONARTS/NYTS

Secretary General Anders Rasmussen have both reminded Turkey that it would be impossible to integrate the Chinese system with NATO's defense system. Ambassador Ricciardone also reminded Turkey that the Chinese company that made the bid was under U.S. sanctions for violations of the Iran, North Korea and Syria Non-Proliferation Act. Therefore, Turkish defense companies that work with the U.S. could be hit if the Chinese deal is implemented. The Turkish and Western press have raised questions as to what this move would mean for Turkey's longer-term relationship with Europe and the U.S.

■ *Turkey and Iran*

Turkey seeks to play a mediating role between Iran and the U.S. over Syria. But despite the West's sanctions against Iran, the Turks and the Iranians are talking about ways to increase trade opportunities, and Turkey continues to import large amounts of oil from Iran. Even so, the Turkish-Iranian relationship has been strained by the Syria conflict, and the Turks have even accused Tehran of once again aiding the PKK. Both Turkey and Iran share concerns about al Qaeda's increasing power in Syria, but differ over Turkey's insistence that Iran's ally Assad must go.

Conclusion

Some of the persistent challenges to Turkey's Kemalist agenda have significant implications for Turkey's relationship with the West. That relationship has gone through numerous ups and downs since Turkey's decision to join NATO in the face of the Cold War. Turkey's progress on the difficult path to membership in the European Union still has a long away to go if it is ever to reach a conclusion. Turkey's unresolved dispute over Cyprus, periodic tensions with Greece and multiple disagreements over policies in the Middle East, all underscore the difficulties Turkey faces in maintaining close relations the West. Foreign Minister Davutoglu's response to these foreign policy challenges is very different from that contained in the message of Atatürk. For the foreign minister, Turkey's Ottoman history and geography are to be embraced and used to propel it to a leadership position in its multiregional neighborhood and from there as an important global player in the international arena. Atatürk's goal was for Turkey to modernize by joining the West and to avoid political entanglements in the Middle East. He spoke of "peace at home, peace abroad." Turkey today continues to be challenged both at home and abroad. ■

 Don't forget to vote! www.greatdecisions.org/ballot

discussion questions

1. Should the U.S. exert more pressure on Turkey to diversify its sources of oil imports so as to be less reliant upon Iran? Should the U.S. encourage Turkey to play a mediating role between Iran and the West on Syria?

2. Will the proposed Chinese air defense system affect possible military coordination and trust between the U.S. and Turkey, two NATO members? If so, how?

3. As Turkish-Israeli relations continue to suffer, what could or should the U.S. do to improve the relations between Israel and Turkey, two of its strategic allies in the Middle East?

4. Should the U.S. be more accommodating to Turkish concerns and increase non-lethal aid to the Syrian rebels, add lethal aid to the package, institute a no-fly zone, while pushing for a peace conference? Is accommodating Turkey's concerns in the U.S.' interests or not?

5. How can the U.S. and Turkey further their cooperation, perhaps as NATO members, in combatting and preventing the radicalization and growth of militant groups in neighboring war-torn countries like Syria?

6. How can the U.S. address concerns about democratization and human rights in Turkey without sacrificing its relationship with a critical ally in the Middle East? What tools can the U.S. use to push the AKP to address these concerns without coming across as a threat to the AKP's power?

7. Is in Turkey's interest to join the EU? Indeed, is it in U.S. interests for Turkey to join the EU? Why or why not?

---

suggested readings

Altunisik, Meliha Benli and Lenore G. Martin, "Making Sense of Turkish Foreign Policy in the Middle East under the AKP," **Turkish Studies**, Vol 12 No. 4, 2011, 569–587. The authors analyze the interplay between Turkey's domestic and international policies in the Middle East and the impact those policies have had throughout the region.

Cagaptay, Soner. **The Rise of Turkey: The Twenty-First Century's First Muslim Power**. Dulles: Potomac Books, 2014. 192 pp. $25.95 (hardcover). Available February 2014. Soner Cagatpay carefully outlines the challenges facing a modern Turkey struggling to balance its Eastern and Western desires and expectations.

Findley, Carter Vaughn. **Turkey, Islam, Nationalism, and Modernity: A History**. New Haven: Yale University Press, 2011. 544 pp. $32.50 (paper). Findley's comprehensive examination of the last two centuries of Turkish history reveals how the modern Turkish state came to be.

Hale, William. **Turkish Foreign Policy Since 1774**. London: Routledge Press, 2013. 360 pp. $48.95 (paper) This is an updated version of Willam Hale's book, considered the most comprehensive text by a single author on Turkish foreign policy.

Kinzer, Stephen. **Crescent and Star: Turkey Between Two Worlds.** New York: Farrar, Straus & Giroux, 2008. 288 pp. $17.00 (paper). Kinzer details Turkey's potential to be a bridge between the West and the East, and the steps its taken to meet its potential.

Heper, Metin and Sabri Sayari, eds. **The Routledge Handbook of Modern Turkey**. London: Routledge Press, 2012. 400 pp. $225.00 (hardcover). An especially fine collection of studies on Turkish culture, history, politics, society and economics by some of the most accomplished scholars in each area presented.

Lewis, Bernard. **The Emergence of Modern Turkey.** London: Oxford University Press, 2002. 568 pp. $49.95 (paper). Bernard Lewis' book grounds itself in history's turbulent past but looks forward to modern issues like Turkey's Western orientation, its struggles to join the EU, and its struggles with Islamic fundamentalists.

Mango, Andrew. **Ataturk: The Biography of the founder of Modern Turkey.** Woodstock: The Overlook Press, 2002. 539 pp. $24.95 (paper). Mango, a former BBC expert on Turkey, details the public life of Mustafa Kemal Ataturk, from his early days to his rise to power and finally his death. Mango's biography provides one of the most concise English-language portraits of the founder of modern Turkey.

Pamuk, Orhan. **Istanbul: Memories and the City**. New York: Vintage Books, 2006. 400 pp. $16.95 (paper). Orhan, a Nobel Prize in Literature winner, details in this highly-personalized account the ever-changing face of Istanbul, exploring the changes in lifestyle, society and architecture throughout the years while providing insight into the strains and challenges the country faces today.

Pope, Nicole and Hugh Pope. **Turkey Unveiled: A History of Modern Turkey.** Woodstock: The Overlook Press, 1997. 432 pp. $16.95 (paper) A good history of modern Turkey that is also very readable.

TO LEARN MORE ABOUT THIS TOPIC AND TO ACCESS WEB LINKS TO RESOURCES GO TO www.greatdecisions.org

Islamic awakening
by John P. Entelis

Tunisian protesters break windows as they wave Islamic flags above the gate of U.S. embassy in Tunis September 14, 2012, during a protest against a film mocking Islam. Protesters broke through into the compound of the embassy, undeterred by volleys of tear gas and warning shots fired by security forces. (FETHI BELAID/AFP/GETTY IMAGES)

The five countries of North Africa, also known as the Maghreb, have many commonalities, including their indigenous cultures, history of colonialism and religious heritage. But they also possess distinctive historical experiences, linguistic variations, subcultural identities and economic resources. Although the region was fully Islamicized long ago, a Berber identity continues to challenge the Arab-dominated character of each country. Until the Arab Spring in 2010–11, North Africa's political profile remained relatively uniform despite the different official designations attached to each country—the Kingdom of Morocco, the Republic of Tunisia, the Popular and Democratic Republic of Algeria, the Islamic Republic of Mauritania and the Great Socialist People's Libyan Arab Jamahiriya. These contrasting labels could not hide the essentially authoritarian manner in which power was assumed, controlled and applied. Each Maghrebi state was in the hands of relatively small elites whose legitimacy remained forever in doubt even if achieved through putatively competitive elections. Economically, the Maghrebi states possessed broadly different sources of wealth and exploited them in a similar parasitic manner. Given the fusion of economic, political and coercive powers in the hands of repressive state elites, many assumed that fundamental change could never occur.

Yet change has indeed occurred, beginning in Tunisia in 2010 and Libya in 2011, but impacting Algeria, Morocco and Mauritania as well. What began as a populist, non-ideological, non-organized, leaderless and spontaneous Arab revolt against long-enduring oppressive regimes has turned into an Islamist awakening whose political impact has yet to

JOHN P. ENTELIS *is a Professor and Chair, Department of Political Science, Fordham University and the President of the American Institute for Maghrib Studies (AIMS).*

be fully measured or understood. Indeed, North Africa is currently experiencing a precarious transition from a long-established system of secular authoritarianism to a more democratic order dominated, if not controlled, by Islamist forces. The ultimate outcome remains uncertain given the relatively brief period of the transition and also the enormous influence that external actors are having on the transition process itself.

Turn toward Islamism

Contemporary North African states and societies are deeply penetrated by and fully immersed in Islam—as religion, as belief system, as social movement, as political organization. Both state and society compete for control of the Islamic idiom. The former legitimizes its otherwise authoritarian rule; the latter opposes such rule and seeks to impose an alternative regime.

Half a century ago this was not the case. The post-independence regimes of the Maghreb pursued distinctly secular, nationalist and/or socialist policies intended to achieve socioeconomic development and to institutionalize their systems of rule. Even more secular and left-wing groups dominated those opposing regime incumbents. Today, both liberal and socialist ideological tendencies have virtually disappeared from the North African political landscape, replaced by differing versions of an Islamist identity.

In the immediate post-independence period, the North African secular state pursued two diametrically opposed policies that were instrumental in creating and fostering an Islamist environment in the subsequent decades. In all five countries of the Maghreb ruling elites promoted modernization policies. These countries intended to house, educate, employ and provide adequate medical care to their respective populations as part of a larger strategy of creating powerful new nation-states. While the record of accomplishments was uneven within and across the five countries, a new middle class did emerge with expectations of greater future opportunities and rewards. These included aspirations to

political power and access to the decisionmaking structures of authority from which further socioeconomic opportunities would flow.

The new aspirational elite began to express independent political views, usually framed in the language of the left with strong neo-Marxist overtones. Ruling regimes responded by propping up once politically impotent Islamist groups to counter the secular left. Thus the contradictory forces that were eventually to supplant secularism with sectarianism were put into place.

One unintended consequence of a government strategy of pitting Islamists against secularists was the rise of autonomous religiously based social movements. These movements challenged state authority, which in turn led incumbent regimes to co-opt, preempt and routinize the Islamist idiom as an alternative to the growing appeal of political Islam. The overall consequence of this process has been the formation of a political environment in which both incumbents and opponents frame their discourse in the language of Islam, all at the expense of secularism and liberal democracy.

It was within such a divisive environment that Islamism in North Africa emerged as the language of self-assertion. Islamism mobilized those largely middle-class high achievers created by the state-led modernization project, who felt ostracized by their society's dominant economic and political forces. For them, the perceived failure of both capitalist modernity and socialist utopianism made the language of morality, by way of religion, a substitute for politics. It was the disenfranchised middle class' way of saying no to what they considered their excluders—their national elites, secular governments and those governments' Western allies.

Thus, two simultaneous but contradictory processes precipitated Islamism's emergence and political domination from the 1970s until the present: opportunity and suppression. The opportunity for massive educational expansion, economic development and social mobility went hand in hand with suppression by way of continuous polit-

ical repression, socioeconomic marginalization, a sense of cultural alienation and growing inequality.

Can Islamists govern democratically?

In the immediate post-authoritarian period following the Arab Spring, Islamic political parties have performed exceptionally well once given the opportunity to participate in genuinely democratic elections that are free, fair and transparent. (The case of the Islamist party Ennahda in Tunisia is a noticeable example of such success.) In Morocco, where elections are relatively free and contested, the moderate Islamic movement, the Party of Justice and Development (PJD), managed to win a plurality in parliamentary elections in November 2012. PJD's premiership is the first time ever that a so-called Islamist party has headed a Moroccan government. In elections in Algeria, Libya and Mauritania, Islamist parties did not do as well, but still managed to make their political presence felt.

The rise of Islamism as a political force in North Africa has reflected a broader regional trend. Islamist movements have gained considerable power either as heads of government or as central players in the political process as the examples of Hamas in Gaza, Hezbollah in Lebanon, the AKP in Turkey and the Muslim Brotherhood in Egypt clearly demonstrate.

Yet in both the Middle East and North Africa, serious questions have arisen about the efficacy of Islamist rule and the ability of Islamist parties to craft broad-based coalitions that incorporate diverse political and ideological tendencies, particularly ones that reassure the public that effective, responsible and accountable governance and not ideological purity serve as their party's guiding principles. Even in Tunisia, where Ennahda came to power in partnership with two secular parties, transition to democracy has been erratic at best and dysfunctional at worst. As one informed analyst observed, "political consensus has remained elusive, economic grievances have continued to stir social unrest and tensions between Islamists and

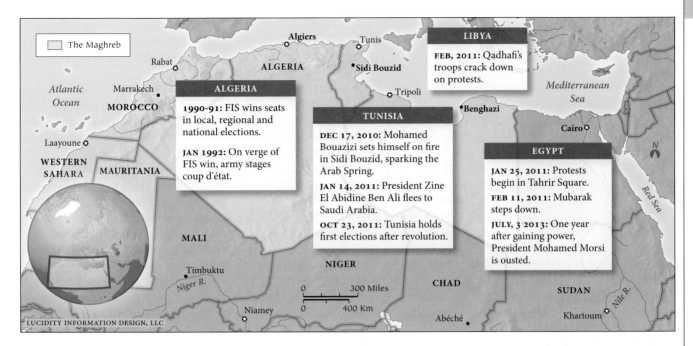

The Maghreb

LIBYA
FEB, 2011: Qadhafi's troops crack down on protests.

ALGERIA
1990-91: FIS wins seats in local, regional and national elections.
JAN 1992: On verge of FIS win, army stages coup d'état.

TUNISIA
DEC 17, 2010: Mohamed Bouazizi sets himself on fire in Sidi Bouzid, sparking the Arab Spring.
JAN 14, 2011: President Zine El Abidine Ben Ali flees to Saudi Arabia.
OCT 23, 2011: Tunisia holds first elections after revolution.

EGYPT
JAN 25, 2011: Protests begin in Tahrir Square.
FEB 11, 2011: Mubarak steps down.
JULY, 3 2013: One year after gaining power, President Mohamed Morsi is ousted.

LUCIDITY INFORMATION DESIGN, LLC

secularists have escalated." Neither a new constitution nor electoral law is in place, complicating an already fragile political order that faces multiple challenges, including security sector reform, fighting corruption, administrative reorganization and economic reform.

While nothing as dramatic as the Egyptian military's coup d'état on July 3, 2013, has occurred in the Maghreb, there is a clear counter-Islamist trend. Such a trend raises more fundamental questions about the ability of Islamism to fully integrate within a democratic political order. Indeed, the same factors that long inhibited Islamic political parties from participating seem to have equal relevance in the present day. ∎

Islam and democracy: Algeria's experience

The emergence of Islamic political power in the post-authoritarian era can be best understood by re-analyzing the first such experience in North Africa, that of Algeria. It is this experience that overhangs the political thinking and behavior of current Islamist political movements, whether in power (Tunisia, Morocco), at its doorstep (Algeria, Libya, Mauritania), or beyond (Egypt, Syria). In the media and across the Web, repeated references have been made to the Algerian experience following the overthrow of Egypt's democratically elected Islamist (Muslim Brotherhood) government in 2013.

Algeria comes close to representing the metamorphosis enabled by hydrocarbon-generated wealth serving as the springboard for a state-led developmental strategy intended to rapidly and thoroughly modernize the country more effectively than its neighbors. The Algerian state achieved considerable social progress with the help of oil rent: It created jobs, increased purchasing power, lowered the prices for consumer goods through government subsidies, and promoted universal health care and an education system that ensured the schooling and training of many young Algerians. Thus emerged a broad middle class in the 1960s and '70s, along with a strong public sector providing access to the ranks of the state class. Welfare benefits were being assured at the expense of political freedoms, a condition most Algerians accepted in the name of institutionalizing "the revolution for the people and by the people."

In the mid-1980s, oil prices collapsed and the socialist experiment came crashing down. The crisis of the rentier state put an end to the wealth distribution strategy that Algeria had relied heavily on in order to maintain loyalty among its citizens. The number of socially marginalized youth was growing rapidly, and the demands of the middle class for more economic and political freedoms became more insistent. These conflicting trends culminated in the nationwide riots of October 1988 that opened the gates for Islamism's formal entry into politics. Such an entrance represented the institutionalization of a process of re-Islamization that had long been under way but remained of secondary significance in an environment of relative economic well-being.

The principle beneficiary of the political opening up was the Islamic Salvation Front (FIS). Nearly 60 other parties were legalized when the Al-

For villagers in Algeria frightened by the Islamist threat in 1998, there were only two options: arm themselves and face what may come or flee from their homes. (NACERDINE ZEBAR/ GAMMA-RAPHO/GETTY IMAGES)

gerian constitution was amended in 1989. Notably, the amendment formally abolished the one-party state that had been under the control of the National Liberation Front (FLN) since independence in 1962. In the local, regional and national elections in 1990 and 1991, the FIS far outperformed its competitors, es-

Commandos reinforced with an armored vehicle take position in the Bab El Oued area in Algiers in January 1992 to dissuade supporters of the Islamic Salvation Front party from attending Friday prayer. (ANDRE DURAND/AFP/GETTY IMAGES)

pecially the now disgraced FLN.

The FIS attracted a wide range of followers, but especially present were members of the blocked middle class and groups representing the marginalized urban lower class. The movement's Islamist credentials appealed to both social groups long disillusioned by the rampant corruption, opaqueness and manipulation of the governing class, but it was the opportunity to advance economic interests that most attracted followers to the FIS. While the middle classes hoped to wrench reforms from the government by joining the FIS, lower class groups had a more radical agenda of altogether eliminating the ruling class.

Inevitably, these diverse social classes with opposing political agendas hindered the FIS' ability to develop a coherent party structure. Yet when it appeared that the FIS was on the verge of a decisive electoral victory at the polls in January 1992, the Algerian army high command staged a coup d'état, cancelled the election results, banned the FIS, imprisoned thousands of its followers, suspended the constitution and imposed martial law. (Martial law was only lifted in the aftermath of the Arab Spring on February 22, 2011.) The more radical wing of the FIS regrouped in the countryside to

begin an insurgency struggle, resulting in several different stages of violence and terrorism that has left over 200,000 dead.

The Algerian experience served as an exemplar of what authoritarian regimes must never allow to happen if they value their incumbency and all the power, perks and privileges associated with it. It is a lesson that leaders in Cairo learned belatedly but those in the Maghreb have long recognized.

The alternative to a purely coercive response to an Islamist challenge has been a policy of co-optation of the Islamist idiom and the incorporation of "moderate" (i.e., pliable) Islamist groups within the existing political system but outside the regime structure. This has been the case in Algeria, where alternative Islamist groups have been propped up to serve as visible alternatives to the FIS. The best known of these groups is the Movement for a Society of Peace (MSP). The MSP has been the most visible partner in the regime's efforts to pacify and integrate the Islamist current. By offering the MSP's middle class base remunerative economic options, the regime fostered MSP's political ambitions through active participation in electoral politics and parliamentary life. The overall result has been an "Islamist" party that differs little from its secular competitors—all requesting access to the rent-seeking activities of the state. The MSP and its middle class base show little interest in democratic development. It is, however, more interested in a state-run capitalization to enhance its economic status.

For its part, the regime has continued its policy of promoting a more religious society. It has constructed more mosques, certified more imams, expanded the powers and responsibilities of the ministry of religious affairs, broadcast more religious programming on television and radio and generally permeated Algerian society with an Islamic identity. If its policy of "out-terrorizing the terrorists" directed against the Islamic insurgency in the 1990s succeeded, so could "out-Islamizing the Islamists." ∎

Inhibiting Islamist expansion

Like the Algerian experience, past and present Islamist participation in North African politics reveals a series of common challenges for any Islamic movement seeking to participate legally in a political process transitioning from authoritarianism to democracy. Given the presence of a modicum of political freedom in a country that has a majority Muslim population, can explicitly political Islamist movements satisfy the structural requirements within and without their organizations needed to meet the norms and practices of democratic rule?

Organizational factors

The single greatest obstacle to democratic inclusion and effective democratic governance rests within the Islamist movements themselves—a lack of participatory experience. Whether inspired to action by deep socioeconomic grievances, cultural alienation, spiritual aridity and/or political oppression, Islamist organizations have emerged as spontaneous expressions of mass discontent. Such expression has been channeled into existing or para-institutional religious structures where problems have been diagnosed and solutions proffered. The intimacy of those experiences has personalized the response procedures, making it almost unnecessary to worry about organization, discipline, strategy,

tactics and leadership. Self-appointed leaders can gain respect, if not the admiration, of their followers on the basis of personal conduct and ideological vision with greater ease than creating political organization. Supporters have paradoxically viewed the lack of practical organizational experience as evidence of ideological purity, in contrast to the manipulative practices of those in power. Thus, even where incentives may exist for organizational effort, the initial stage of populist enthusiasm makes such effort seem counterproductive if not counterintuitive. The overall result has been high levels of political mobilization based on broadly articulated Islamic principles, all operating within loose or almost nonexistent political structures.

Civil society

The FIS experience in Algeria informs the broader challenge Islamists confront within civil society. One unintended consequence of the FIS electoral victories, both in the local and regional elections of 1990, as well as the first round of parliamentary elections of December 1991, was the anxiety and concern it created among groups in civil society. While mostly democratic themselves and sharing in the FIS's deep opposition to the existing authoritarian order,

there was a growing concern among these groups that a secular dictatorship would soon be replaced by a theocratic one. However inaccurate or misleading such categorization may have been, the FIS failed to appreciate the deeply contested nature of an Algerian civil society operating within a pluralistic environment. Berberists, feminists, Marxists and Westernized intellectuals, among others, were unnecessarily excluded from those dialogues needed to pursue a democratic agenda rooted in Islamic principles.

In retrospect, the Algerian Islamists might not have realized the full meaning of their accomplishments, constituting as it did the first ever truly democratic process in the Arab world in which an opposition party, in this case an Islamist one, was on the verge of assuming national power. Those not sharing this vision had only revolutionary Iran, militarized Sudan and anarchic Afghanistan as their points of reference. As these concerns, anxieties and fears began to accumulate among a minority of Algerians, the FIS became increasingly defensive. One result was the creation of an artificial polarity that had so-called "democrats" challenging the validity of the Islamist project however democratically arrived at. To be sure, it would be unfair and unreal-

A supporter of the Islamic Ennahda party holds a Salafist flag at a large gathering by party supporters August 3, 2013, at the Kasbah in Tunis, Tunisia, to support the transitional government. (GHASSEN CHRAIFA/DEMOTIX/CORBIS)

A Tunisian demonstrator holds a sign during a demonstration August 24, 2013, against the country's Islamist-led government in Tunis on the first day of a planned week-long campaign. (SALAH HABIBI/AFP/GETTY IMAGES)

istic to assume that given the newness of the whole democratic experience and the relative naïveté if not amateurism of the FIS's organizational efforts, that "community outreach" would be given political priority.

The Algerian experience mirrors that of Tunisia today. Although the country is becoming increasingly polarized between "secularists" and "Islamists," much formal governance is shared by a coalition of liberal and religious parties. Ultimately, however, it has been the actions of the state, exploiting the artificial divisions in civil society, which constitute one of the insurmountable obstacles to effective Islamist democratic participation.

The state

Islamist participation is challenged the most in the Arab-Islamic world by the actions and reactions of the state, no matter how liberal or semi-democratic its political credentials. It is no surprise that the Islamist effort at inclusion in a pluralist process should find it so difficult both to enter the political process in otherwise closed or semi-closed systems or to effectively govern in fully open ones.

The example of Algeria brings home the difficulties Islamist political parties have in gaining acceptance, even if they disavow violence, play by the rules, commit themselves to democratic principles and abide by existing treaty arrangements and other aspects of international diplomacy and behavior. Whether overtly or covertly, the place of the army in civilian political orders undermines Islamist efforts at democratic participation. The greater tragedy of this process is that in denying Islamist participation, army-led or -influenced regimes are constraining the rights of opposition groups and other organizations from participating. This speaks to a broader concern in democratic participation in the Islamic world. For instance, can there ever be a full democracy if Islamist political movements are denied the right to participate or, once in power, threatened with removal? Evidence to date seems to indicate no. Denying such movements the opportunity to contest elections and participate

freely—the twin foundations of procedural democracy—leaves the way open for any groups perceived as lacking the requisite attributes of "democracy" as defined by the class least qualified to give such guidance—the military.

To their misfortune, the FIS in Algeria and the Muslim Brotherhood in Egypt have learned that democratic commitments, both in theory and practice, are insufficient to satiate the predatory instincts of authoritarian regimes. There remains one last area of opportunity, and risk, for such movements if they are to gain acceptance within democratizing political orders, namely the international community.

Global environment

In the post-Cold War era, the role of international actors in influencing and determining states' domestic policy has increased significantly. Especially in the case of Third World systems, fragile polities and dependent economies have made societies open to outside influence and intervention. In the Arab-Islamic world, such interference has been contingent on the agendas of domestic elites, who have supported expanding their countries' foreign economic activities but have been resistant to political "meddling" from outside. The addition of human rights and democracy to the foreign policy goals of Western countries to whom many Arab-Islamic regimes look has the potential for influencing political calculations of incumbent regimes in ways that would be reassuring for opposition movements, Islamic or otherwise.

Given the developments in other formerly authoritarian regions in the last decade or so, it was natural that democratically minded Islamist movements would find comfort in the direction that, say, the U.S. and France took with regard to human rights, democracy and pluralism. Perhaps innocently and naïvely, such movements expected not only support for their efforts to promote democratic change, albeit in an Islamic context, but firm responses in instances when such change was undermined or usurped. The hard reality, as in the experiences of Algeria and Egypt, has

proven otherwise. Neither France nor the U.S. conditioned greater bilateral and multilateral engagements on democratic change. Indeed, the opposite seems to have been the case. Washington and Paris have either remained silent or encouraged regime intervention in democratic processes where Islamist parties were in power (Egypt) or on the verge of acquiring it (Algeria).

Other global actors have followed in the footsteps of the big powers. International business, the International Monetary Fund and the World Bank, the United Nations, the Organization of African Unity and the Arab League, for example, have been consistent supporters of the status quo, even at the expense of genuine democratic change. As long as there is a commitment to prop up a new world order that ensconces finance capital, opens markets to global capitalism and faithfully follows the foreign policy of the U.S. in its willingness to recognize Israel, stop terrorism and intercept drug trafficking, these institutions have been willing to accept the pseudo-democracies in Algeria, Morocco and Mauritania. Even in the newly formed incipient democracies in Tunis and Tripoli, it is unclear how resolved external actors will be in supporting the democratic process should Islamists become increasingly radicalized.

Women, Islamism and democracy

After the Arab Spring, the status of women has served as the ideological battleground, both symbolically and politically, for Islamism and secularism. Women have always faced major challenges to political advancement, economic opportunity and social recognition. Embedded within this contestation over women's rights is a deeper cleavage separating women's social groups defined by education, language use, professional attainment and residence. Simply put, women with advanced degrees who speak one or more European languages and live in well-to-do neighborhoods in major cities hold profoundly different world views than rural women of modest means and basic education who are strongly attached to traditional Islamic values. The rise of Islamic parties has accentuated this divide, creating a "clash of cultures" that has hindered advancement of women's rights and, in the process, the establishment of a consensual democracy.

The situation appeared radically different during North Africa's authoritarian phase, when countries like Tunisia and Morocco were heralded as progressive on women's rights, albeit imposed from above. Tunisia in particular has long been applauded for its "enlightened" family code promulgated at the time of independence in 1956. As one respected international report has stated: "One of Tunisia's greatest achievements since independence is the body of laws which gave women rights not enjoyed anywhere else in the Arab world." Such an effusive appraisal derives from the country's adoption of a "modern" family code, one that focuses on individual rights and obligations within a nuclear family system. This contrasts with Islamic family law that has served as the building block of kin-based solidarities within tribal groups in countries like Algeria, Mauritania and Libya.

Has the Arab Spring advanced, neutralized or gutted the legal protections embodied in progressive family codes? Similarly, has the Islamist awakening made women more or less reluctant to occupy public spaces, thereby forcing fundamental behavioral change independent of whatever legal protections accorded them? More directly, can an Islamicized social order provide greater or fewer freedoms for women regardless of class or social standing? The case of Tunisia best illustrates both the opportunities and challenges confronting Maghrebi women. As women seek to protect rights that are already guaranteed, there is a push to extend them to those who have historically felt excluded, all within a politically open environment predominated by Islamism.

Tunisia: Nahdawis vs. Laïcistes

In 1956, the year of independence, Tunisia promulgated a Code of Personal Status (PCS) that reformed family law radically, constituting a sharp break

Deputies of the Ennahda party attend an assembly in Tunis, August 8, 2012, in which the Islamist-dominated government was asked about the social tensions in Tunisia on the eve of a strike in hospitals and the state's key tourism sector. (FETHI BELAID/AFP/GETTY IMAGES)

from preexisting Islamic law. It outlawed polygamy, abolished repudiation, entitled women to divorce on the same grounds as men, increased mothers' custody rights and expanded inheritance rights for daughters and granddaughters. Compared to other countries in the region at the time, Tunisia's PCS represented a significant advance in the protection and promotion of women's rights. Yet this accomplishment was the result of a top-down process initiated by Tunisia's first president, Habib Bourguiba (1957–87), and his like-minded Western-inspired ruling elite, who made little effort to incorporate the traditional interests and opinions of Tunisia's majority female population living in small towns and villages. It should have come as no surprise, therefore, that when Ennahda assumed power after the Arab Spring it upset Tunisian secularists but gave hope to more Islamically oriented females.

In the cultural clash that ensued after Ennahda's political victory in 2011, competing narratives have emerged that cloud the reality of the Tunisian situation. Not surprisingly, hard core secularists or *laïcistes* (those identifying with a French-inspired secularism) painted *Nahdawis'* (supporters of

Ennahda) "rise as a dramatic fall from grace—the tragic descent of a once secular, pro-women's rights country into a backwater regime run by Islamist misogynists." While the nostalgic appeal of this narrative remains powerful for many of Ennahda's critics, "it oversimplifies a more complex historical reality in which Tunisia's post independence presidents manipulated women's rights in conjunction with religious discourse to maintain one-party rule." Under both Bourguiba and Zine El Abidine Ben Ali (Tunisia's second president, 1987–2011), only secularly oriented women's organizations were allowed to form and operate in Tunisia. It is unclear whether both men had any personal commitments to egalitarian gender relations or merely the desire to instrumentalize women's rights in service of political ends. As Monica Marks makes clear, "Tunisia's international reputation as a women-friendly backwater surrounded by patriarchal states was the result of considerable image manipulation and regime performance."

The Arab Spring has brought freedom and democracy to Tunisia in a number of ways. Tunisians today "are finally able to contest the legacy of regime feminism and craft a more representative framework for guiding the state's relationship with women's rights." While many secularists have welcomed the country's democratic transformation, others are worried "that democracy might unleash long-percolating conservative trends in Tunisian society, the most dangerous of which they generally consider to be Islamist currents." Yet it is those very currents that have elevated the political status of women. For example, the representation of women has grown in the Constituent Assembly, in which 49 out of 217 members are women.

Surprisingly, despite the culture clash between secularist and religious feminists, both desire upholding the PSC. Indeed, as Ennahda's position has evolved on this issue, the gap between the two groups has narrowed. The vast majority of Tunisians seem "to embrace the code as a proud piece of national legislation that advances women's rights and authentically represents what many indigenize as 'Tunisian Islam'—an Islam characterized by tolerance, moderation and progressive openness to the outside world."

Yet women's rights continue to be a polarizing issue. This polarization intensified after the appearance of Salafist, or radical Islamic fundamentalist, groups who openly reject any political or social formula that does not impose a strict religious orthodoxy on Tunisia. For many left-wing and secularist men and women, Ennahda and Salafism are indistinguishable, no matter how much the former openly rejects the radicalism and violence-prone behavior of the latter. It seems unlikely that the current schism between secular and religiously conservative women will end anytime soon. Regardless of whether or not Islamist political power remains dominant in the near and intermediate future, Tunisian society has become profoundly Islamicized, leaving the more secular segment of Tunisian society feeling embattled and marginalized.

In this regard there has been an ironic historic inversion. While authoritarianism had privileged the more secular and well-to-do women, albeit in a controlled and manipulated fashion, democracy has empowered the more religiously minded females. The only hope in overcoming this cultural chasm is through enlightened constitutional and electoral engineering that give voice to all segments of Tunisian society. Toward this end the National Constituent Assembly, elected to office on October 23, 2011, has the sovereign authority to draft a new constitution, to be followed by elections for a permanent legislative body tentatively scheduled for fall 2013.

The status of women's rights in the other Maghrebi states remains inferior to that of Tunisia despite recent improvements in Morocco where an amended family code or *moudawana* (2004) now allows women to initiate divorce and sets the legal age of marriage at 18 years of age. Yet there still exists a wide gap between the written law and practice, especially as applied to rural women and children. Indeed, despite the law, the instances of child marriage rose from 30,000 in 2009 to 34,000 in 2011, according to Morocco's Ministry of Justice. This has been enabled, in large part, by Article 20 of the moudawana that allows judges to use their "judicial discretion" to allow minors to be married.

While political Islam in Morocco, like in Tunisia, is in a governing position, a more radical Salafist brand of puritanical Islam has emerged there as well. One of its spokesmen, Sheikh Mohamed Ben Abdurrahman al-Maghraoui, issued an underage *fatwa* or Islamic legal decree in 2008 suggesting that marriage was permissible for girls as young as nine years of age. Inasmuch as Morocco continues to be governed autocratically with the current monarch, King Mohammed VI, promoting a modernist interpretation of women's rights, it is unlikely that there will be a serious deterioration of those rights. Given the increased Islamization of society, combined with persistent social cleavages and economic inequalities, a democratic transition in Morocco may well result in a contraction, not expansion, of women's rights. ∎

Islamism and terrorism

Terrorism constitutes a serious threat to the peoples and governments of all five states of the Arab Maghreb Union (UMA). While debates among academics and policymakers continue about the origins, sources and impacts of terrorism in the region, the post-Arab Spring period has clearly witnessed an increase in militant activity due to the emergence of a radicalized jihadist movement encompassing large swaths of the Sahelian-Saharan corridor. The January 16, 2013, attack on the Algerian

WONSOO/CARTOONARTS/NYTS

gas facilities in Al Amenas, in which 39 foreign hostages were killed along with 29 militants, represents the most daring and bloody confrontation with terrorists since the end of the Algerian civil war in 1999. Although it is clear that the overwhelming majority of Muslims in the Maghreb are not terrorists, it is equally clear that the overwhelming majority of terrorists in the region are Muslim. What then is the relationship between Islamism and terrorism in North Africa?

Complicating the relationship between Islamism and terrorism is the overlapping use of violence and rhetoric by both those involved in indisputable acts of brutal killing and Salafist groups who participate openly in the political process. Since the Arab Spring, there has been a proliferation of Salafist groups in North Africa that have requested and received legal authorization to openly participate in politics. In Tunisia alone, for example, at least five Salafist-related groups are openly engaged in propagating their ideas. Some are more concerned with social issues, such as Rahma and Asala; others have close ties to An-Nahda such as the Reform (Islah) Front; still others are more radical in orientation, such as Hizb ut-Tahrir and Ansar Sharia, the latter advocating militant jihadism with deep ties to international jihadism. Morocco, a country that has so far avoided the worst excesses of the post-authoritarian breakdown in the region, has felt it necessary to incorporate Salafism within the political arena as well. In June 2013, for example, a new Salafist group was given legal recognition, thus allowing the Party of Renaissance and Virtue to propagate its ideas in a putatively nonviolent manner.

Although some analysts have sought to distinguish Salafist groups into three separate categories—quietists (those who refrain from politics, concentrating exclusively on preaching a purist version of Islam), activists (those who engage in politics) and jihadists (those who engage in violence to attain their goals), such distinctions are often blurred at the level of action. This was particularly the case when the American Embassy in Tunis was violently attacked on September 14, 2012, by Salafists who destroyed some of the embassy compound while replacing the American flag with that of the black Salafist flag.

Equally difficult in discerning fundamental differences between terrorist groups and Salafists is the common invocation of Islamic rhetoric (Allahu Akhbar or "God is Great") whether engaged in violent killing or mobilizing popular support during politically sanctioned demonstrations. For this article,

terrorism is defined as the systematic use of violence to create a general climate of fear in a population in order to bring about a particular political objective. In the context of the Maghreb, the group most clearly identified as "terrorist" is the Al Qaeda branch in North Africa, Al Qaeda in the Islamic Maghreb (AQIM). AQIM emerged in the aftermath of the violent civil war in Algeria, which left nearly 200,000 people dead over a ten year period (1992–2002). Some of the more militant Salafist groups in all five countries of North Africa may from time to time engage in violent acts, including those in which people are killed. However, they remain, in their essence, political movements seeking to impose a puritanical view of orthodox Islam. This could be through legitimate political means or through street protests and other forms of social mobilization, legally sanctioned or not.

A recent series of political assassinations and terrorist attacks in Tunisia by Salafist groups challenges the validity of many of the analytical distinctions made by academics and policymakers between quietist and militant Salafists and between the latter and hard core AQIM terrorists. For Tunisia, whose

history of nonviolent political behavior goes back to the pre-independence period, to spiral into mindless violence highlights the increased radicalization of the political landscape in the post-Arab Spring Maghreb. Within a six-month period, two left-wing politicians were assassinated by the same Salafist militant, followed by the killing of eight Tunisian soldiers in the eastern mountainous region of Mount Chambi by AQIM-linked terrorist groups. These and less violent but no less disruptive actions by militant groups in Tunisia have undermined the country's democratic transition, if not its very political integrity. Following the former regime's ouster, the country has been in a state of continuous turmoil, torn apart by a security vacuum, chronic economic problems, ongoing strikes and various protest movements as well as the release and return from exile of numerous jihadis.

The flood of weapons after the collapse of the Libyan regime; the instability in Mali; the porousness of the Algerian border; the unresolved conflict in the Western Sahara; the presence of AQIM forces in the Sahelian-Saharan corridor; the steady back-and-forth flow of Tunisian jihadist fighters going to

Chadian soldiers show a flag of AQIM and weapons recovered after violent clashes with Islamist militants in northern Mali in March 2013. The Chadian government claims its troops have killed Mokhtar Belmokhtar, the one-eyed Islamist leader who masterminded an assault on an Algerian gas plant that left 37 foreign hostages dead. (ALI KAYA/AFP/GETTY IMAGES)

GUNS FROM LIBYA

MALI

MICHAEL DE ADDER/ARTIZANS.COM

and coming from battleground zones in Iraq, Afghanistan and Syria—all have accentuated the terrorist dimension of the post-authoritarian political order in North Africa that left every country in the region vulnerable to dissent, disorder and divisions. The continuous outflow of arms from Libya, the military coup and subsequent Islamist takeover in northern Mali and the cross-border attacks on Tunisia all represent a qualitative shift in the balance of power in the region, which was only improved by the French-led intervention in northern Mali in January 2013.

What was once viewed as an "Algerian problem" has now metastasized throughout the region. Each of the five Maghrebi countries, including the Western Sahara, is now a potential theater of terrorist operation. No single country is exempt from AQIM-launched attacks as recent violent confrontations taking place in Libya, Tunisia, Algeria, Mali and Mauritania have confirmed. All this suggests that AQIM will become a greater threat in the future as it spreads further from its roots, rather than fragmenting.

What is particularly disturbing in this phenomenon is the rapid fusion of Salafism with jihadism in which the so-called quietist and preaching dimensions of Salafism are losing ground to their more violent counterpart. The net effect has been one of ambiguity and confusion regarding who does or does not constitute an Islamic threat. Thus, the democratic opening has paradoxically opened up significant space for a broad range of Muslim activists, including more violence-prone Salafist radicals willing to engage in terrorist activities. As Islamism has penetrated virtually every aspect of Maghrebi societies, it has become difficult if not impossible to distinguish those who see Islamism as a legitimate political force from those engaged in terrorism. For the latter, Islam is but a camouflage for more extra-religious objectives, some mundane and materialistic, others more existential.

Provisional or permanent?

A process that began decades ago, often manipulated from above but ultimately embedded from below, Islamism today has come to permeate all five societies of North Africa, making it virtually impossible to identify, articulate, or aggregate a civil political order that separates the secular from the sectarian. This suggests that a complex dialectic between faith and freedom operating in a more open political environment will define the Maghreb's near and intermediate future, a future that surely will involve struggles, some violently radical and murderous, over the meaning of liberty, freedom, democracy and the role of religion in public life. Provided the region's history of dictatorial rule, it should come as no surprise that both secularists and Islamists are struggling in the post-Arab Spring era to establish a more representative, just, accountable and democratic political order through cooperation and compromise, not by ideological puritanism or the imposition of a singular world view.

As of now, state and society are locked in ideological combat on how democracy will or will not determine the region's political future. The current struggles taking place in all of North Africa, from Egypt in the east to Mauritania in the west, reflect the precariousness of the transitional process. At one time, Tunisia suggested the greatest hope but has increasingly descended into chaos and confusion as Salafist extremism disrupts what was hoped to be a relatively peaceful emergence out of authoritarianism into democracy. The terroristic regional environment in which all five countries find themselves is aggravating the internal conflicts and contradictions within Maghrebi societies. Such an environment fuels deeper suspicions among secularists that so-called Islamic moderates are really little different from their Salafist and AQIM counterparts.

Whether they like it or not, however, secularists have to accept that Islamism, both as an expression of social identity and as an instrument for political activism, is here to stay. For their part, Islamists must come to terms with the meaning of democracy, "how and under what conditions [can Muslims] make their religion compatible with desired notions of democracy; how can they legitimize and popularize an inclusive reading of their doctrine [that enshrines] citizen participation, individual rights, pluralism and tolerance."

It is within this deeply divided and highly contested political environment that the U.S. finds itself as it seeks to craft policies that are respectful of national sentiments while advancing American interests.

Policy challenges

North Africa's Arab Spring presents both challenges and opportunities for U.S. foreign policy. The U.S. is currently in a very delicate position in North Africa, for while it has good working relations with each of the five governments, democratically elected and not, the same cannot be said about the region's mass publics, who continue to harbor deep suspicions about American intentions in the Maghreb. Both Islamists and secularists throughout North Africa view the U.S. with equal mistrust, as the experience in post-coup Egypt has demonstrated. Given the multiple challenges it currently faces, Washington should engage in a multilevel strategy that enhances regional security through better military coordination with relevant forces while keeping open all lines of communication with appropriate political actors both in and out of power, whether secular or Islamist. Some specific options may include:

■ Should the U.S. pressure Algeria and Morocco to begin serious negotiations over the Western Sahara conflict? The Saharan issue has poisoned relations between both countries ever since Spanish colonial forces vacated the area in 1975. It also complicates if not fundamentally undermines the ability of regional and international actors to develop an effective antiterrorist strategy that relies on shared intelligence information and coordinated military action against an enemy that operates across national boundaries.

■ However much critics of U.S. foreign policy in the region argue that it is a contrived and manipulated issue used to foster imperialistic interests, the U.S. needs to come to terms with the fact that

The city of Laayoune, Morocco, is reflected in the shattered windows of a bank that was ransacked by Saharawi mobs in November 2010 when the city was racked by violence in response to a protest camp being torn down by Moroccan security forces. (BRYAN DENTON/ NEW YORK TIMES/REDUX)

terrorism in North Africa is real, constant and threatening. AQIM's wide-ranging presence in the Saharan-Sahelian corridor was best demonstrated in the attack at the Al Amenas gas plant in Algeria in January 2013. Given this new reality, should the U.S. expand its "war on terror" to incorporate regional actors more directly and decisively than has been the case in the past? While AQIM has yet to directly target the U.S., it continues to engage in constant armed attacks within and outside Algeria, including in Tunisia, Mali and Libya. The closing of the majority of American embassies in North Africa on August 4, 2013, as precaution against a terrorist attack reflects the intensified nature of terrorist activity in the region. As one terrorism expert has indicated: "the scope of the [embassy] closings is a sign of how diffuse the terrorist threat has become, and how difficult it is to guard against."

■ Related to the above, Washington should be careful not to label all radical Islamist forces as terrorists. This is especially the case with Salafism. As this more fundamentalist interpretation of Islamic activism is expanding in influence and importance throughout the region, however numerically small its followers may be, lumping all Islamists

forces into the "terrorist" category could eventually work against the U.S.

■ Although Washington has been unsuccessful in Egypt in promoting a policy that recognizes the need for the incorporation of all political actors within the political process, both Islamist and secular, should it continue this strategy in North Africa? As it is, the after effect of the Egyptian coup has already negatively impacted Tunisian public opinion, creating a great deal of suspicion about U.S. intentions in the country where both secularists and Islamists accuse Washington of favoring the other side.

■ While terrorism and radical Islam pose serious problems for U.S. interests in the region, Washington should not lose sight of the importance of cultivating civil society in North Africa. All countries in the region, whether in transition or adaptive in their control mechanisms, are increasingly becoming responsive to the demands civil society actors are beginning to make on their elected leaders. As such, the U.S. could engage civil society more directly through active participation in cultural, educational and scientific exchanges. In this regard, the Fulbright Program could be revived and expanded in all five countries of the Maghreb. ■

 Don't forget to vote! www.greatdecisions.org/ballot

discussion questions

1. Given the prevalence of terrorism in the Maghreb, to what extent can the U.S. coordinate its forces with regional leaders so as to ensure cooperation and shared intelligence? Further, what role does the U.S. play in ameliorating relations between Morocco and Algeria over their inability to reach a compromise concerning issues such as the Western Sahara? Do compromises between the Maghreb leaders need to occur before cooperation about more global issues such as terrorism can be addressed?

2. How compatible is Islamism with democracy, particularly in light of considerations such as political parties and elections? What comparisons can be drawn between Islamic movements in the Maghreb and other regions of the Middle East? How similar have the paths toward Islamism and democracy been for the countries of the Maghreb?

3. Tunisia's family code, known as the Code of Personal Status, serves as a deviation from traditional Islamic patriarchy. The Tunisian laws establish equality between men and women and place a stance against polygamy. What role do women play in the current social and political spheres of the other countries of the Maghreb? How has the Arab Spring impacted the role of women in the region?

4. Civil society marks an important bridge between political leaders and the rest of the population. In what ways could civil society in the Maghreb be expanded? What difficulties do advocates of an improved civil society face in the Maghreb? What happens to civil society in stages of radical Islam?

5. The Arab Spring marks an important shift in the way countries of the Maghreb have been perceived in the international community. As such, how has U.S. foreign policy toward countries of the Maghreb developed since the Arab Spring? Is it best to approach these issues in a way that is individually tailored to each country of the Maghreb, or is the U.S. better positioned to incorporate an overarching blanket strategy toward the countries of the Maghreb?

suggested readings

Akhavi, Shahrough, **The Middle East: The Politics of the Sacred and Secular**. London: Zed Books, 2009. 291 pp. $29.95 (paper). The way in which the sacred and secular compete for political prominence in the Middle East.

Bayat, Asef, **Making Islam Democratic: Social Movements and the Post-Islamist Turn**. Stanford, CA: Stanford University Press, 2007. 320 pp. $22.95 (paper). Uses social movement theory to demonstrate how Islam can and must become democratic.

Brown, Nathan J., and Hanzawy, Amr. **Between Religion and Politics**. Washington, DC: Carnegie Endowment for International Peace, 2010. 213 pp. $19.95 (paper). How religion and politics interact in the Middle East and North Africa.

Burgat, François, **Face to Face with Political Islam.** London: Tauris, 2003. 288 pp. $32.00 (paper). Provides a sympathetic view of political Islam as it confronts the authoritarian state in the Middle East and North Africa.

International Crisis Group, "Tunisia: Violence and the Salafi Challenge," **Middle East/North Africa Report** No. 17 (February 2013), 48 pp. Excellent and thorough report on the rise of the Salafi movement and the political aftermath of the assassination of Chokri Belaïd, a prominent left-wing politician in Tunisia.

Kepel, Gilles, **The War for Muslim Minds: Islam and the West.** Cambridge, MA: Harvard University Press, 2004. 336 pp. $22.00 (paper). A fortelling examination of the role of global terrorism and U.S. foreign policy in shaping contemporary Islamist movements.

Laremont, Ricardo, ed., **Revolution, Revolt and Reform in North Africa.** London: Routledge, 2013. 192 pp. $51.95 (paper). Descriptive account of Arab Spring revolutions, with focus on North Africa.

Roy, Olivier, **Holy Ignorance: When Religion and Culture Part Ways**. New York, NY: Columbia University Press, 2010. 259 pp. $27.50 (paper). An exploration of the modern disconnection between faith communities and sociocultural identities as a catalyst for fundamentalism by one of the world's most distinguished political Islam experts.

Wright, Robin, ed., **The Islamists are Coming: Who They Really Are.** Washington, DC: Woodrow Wilson Center Press, 2012. 176 pp. $19.95 (paper). Edited by Robin Wright, this volume provides an analysis of the rise of Islamist parties in a post-Arab Spring world. With chapters from a variety of experts, this compilation covers a number of countries, including Algeria, Egypt, Tunisia, Morocco and Libya.

———, **Rock the Casbah: Rage and Rebellion Across the Islamic World.** New York: Simon & Schuster, 2011. 320 pp. $26.99 (hardcover). Veteran reporter Robin Wright goes to Egypt and Tunisia, home to a region-wide rebellion against long standing autocrats. She describes these events in the words of the very people living through them.

TO LEARN MORE ABOUT THIS TOPIC AND TO ACCESS WEB LINKS TO RESOURCES GO TO www.greatdecisions.org

Energy independence:
Inflated Expectations or New Opportunities?
by Jonathan Chanis

A pipeline runs from the Federal Strategic Petroleum Reserve facility known as Big Hill, September 20, 2000, near Beaumont, TX. It is one of four crude oil storage sites run by the U.S. government. The reserve, created in 1975 after the Arab oil embargo, is intended to provide a stopgap in case of disruptions in oil imports. It has been used only once, during the Gulf War in 1991. (JOE RAEDLE/NEWSMAKERS/GETTY IMAGES)

In many ways, a person's view on petroleum and U.S. foreign policy is a Rorschach test on the role of corporations domestically and the U.S. globally. Traditionally, the more liberal elements of the U.S. political spectrum have argued that the quest for petroleum and a need to maintain the ability to "cut off" petroleum to other states drives the U.S. toward a highly interventionist and belligerent foreign policy. To many, this includes "going to war for oil." This position often goes hand in hand with a negative attitude toward multinational corporations, especially international oil companies (IOCs), and their political actions domestically.

Interestingly, over the last decade or so, some on the opposite side of the political spectrum have adopted a position similar to the progressive critique on oil and foreign intervention. However, the conservative critics are much less concerned with the domestic multinational aspects of the issue, and they are generally supportive of domestic oil and gas exploration and production.

In between these more polarized views are many academics, policy analysts and politicians who see U.S. petroleum policy as just one variable among many affecting U.S. foreign policy. But it is undeniable that the U.S. serves as the de facto guardian of the international trade in petroleum, and that the global petroleum supply chain functions the way it does because the U.S. and many supporting coun-

JONATHAN CHANIS *has worked in investment management, emerging markets finance, and commodities trading for over 25 years. Currently he manages New Tide Asset Management, a proprietary vehicle focused on global and resource investing. He previously worked at Tribeca Global Management and at Caxton Associates where he traded energy and emerging market equities, and commodities and currencies. Mr. Chanis holds a Ph.D. in Political Science from the Graduate School, CUNY, and a B.A. in Economics from Brooklyn College. Over the last four years, he has taught graduate and undergraduate courses on, among other subjects, energy security, international politics, and political economy.*

tries (such as Saudi Arabia and Russia) accept the body of formal and informal rules and norms that regulate international interaction over petroleum. In the jargon of political science, this is called an "international regime."

Since the first oil shock in 1973, America's energy vulnerability and its foreign policy have been linked. As explained below, there has been a recognizable pattern whereby higher petroleum vulnerability constrains foreign policy options, and lower petroleum vulnerability expands foreign policy options. If U.S. dependence on foreign energy continues to decline, as it most likely will, this pattern should repeat itself, thereby increasing the range of foreign policy options available to U.S. policymakers.

Petroleum and foreign policy

The crux of the petroleum-foreign policy issue is the degree to which concern over petroleum distorts American foreign policy by involving the U.S. in regions where it would otherwise have little or no interest. While one can argue about degree, it is impossible to reasonably assert that U.S. concern for petroleum has no impact on U.S. foreign policy and military intervention. If nothing else, a significant share of U.S. defense spending and diplomatic activity is focused on protecting global petroleum trade and many producer countries, especially in the Persian Gulf.

One of the most interesting aspects of U.S. international petroleum policy is that no one really knows how much the military aspects cost. At the very least, there is no publically available U.S. government figure for this cost. The last time the U.S. government attempted to calculate the cost of petroleum defense was in 1992. At that time, the Congressional Research Service estimated total U.S. military spending on oil-related security during the 1980s at approximately $71 billion. This represented approximately 17% of the defense budget.

More recently, a 2009 Rand Corporation study placed the oil defense burden at approximately 15% of defense spending. While 15% might not sound like a large amount, with an annual defense budget in excess of $500 billon, the dollar figure is over $75 billion *per year*. Moreover, other analysts, such as Anita Dancs, put this figure at $166 billion, more than double the Rand estimate.

One of the problems with this type of analysis is that it is very hard to know what missions and forces are used for petroleum defense. Even something seemingly obvious, such as U.S. naval forces patrolling against pirates in the Indian Ocean is ambiguous. (What percent of ships being protected are oil tankers as opposed to container ships, fishing boats, etc.?) Military forces are multipurpose and (to an extent) fun-

gible. And even if the petroleum protection mission were eliminated, not all forces earmarked for this role would be eliminated.

Knowing the actual cost of U.S. international petroleum policy is further complicated by non-Defense Department-related expenditures such as military and economic aid to energy rich states or their neighbors. Annual aid to countries such as Colombia, Iraq, Jordan, Kazakhstan and Nigeria is in the tens of billions of dollars. Would all of this aid flow to these countries (particularly in the amounts they do), if these countries did not have petroleum or some relationship to petroleum?

Even the $25.7 billion the U.S. has spent on constructing, maintaining, and stocking the Strategic Petroleum Reserve (SPR) probably should be included in a total cost estimate. And of course, there is the financial and opportunity costs of the diplomatic corps' focus on problems in places that few Americans would care to visit, and where even fewer (outside the petroleum industry) have any business.

In any event, while the expenses are clearly large, no one really knows the actual costs of U.S. international petroleum policy and the U.S. government has shown no interest in figuring it out.

Petroleum and modern life

But why is petroleum so central to U.S. energy policy? First, petroleum has a unique role in modern societies because its products are ubiquitous. Oil is in virtually everything people consume or with which they interact, whether it is at the gas pump or in plastics and pharmaceuticals.

Second, oil is unique in its importance because of its role in personal mobility and commerce. The U.S. is almost entirely dependent on petroleum for personal transportation, and businesses are almost equally dependent on petroleum to support their supply and distribution systems. In 2012, Americans consumed 18.6 million barrels per day (mmbd) of petroleum products; 47% of this was gasoline and 7.5% was jet fuel.

Third, oil's ownership is concentrated in the hands of a small number

Global Crude Oil Proved Reserves

		Billion Barrels	% World Total
1	Saudi Arabia	267.0	17.5%
2	Venezuela	211.2	13.9%
3	Canada	173.6	11.4%
4	Iran	151.2	9.9%
5	Iraq	143.1	9.4%
6	Kuwait	104.0	6.8%
7	United Arab Emirates	97.8	6.4%
8	Russia	60.0	3.9%
9	Libya	47.1	3.1%
10	Nigeria	37.2	2.4%
11	Kazakhstan	30.0	2.0%
12	Qatar	25.4	1.7%
13	U.S.	23.3	1.5%
14	China	20.4	1.3%
15	Brazil	14.0	0.9%

Source: EIA "Crude Oil Proved Reserves." All figures are for 2012, except the U.S., which is 2011.

of states. Well over 80% of global petroleum reserves are controlled by national oil companies (NOC) and their governments. This gives the petroleum supply chain very strong oligopolistic characteristics, i.e., there are a small number of dominant producers that collude in an attempt to raise prices and deny IOCs access to their reserves.

And finally, oil is unusual because governments are deeply involved in its production and consumption. Besides restricting access to most of the lowest cost production acreage, governments also constrain IOC and NOC activity in numerous other ways. Governments limit intercompany competition and cooperation (e.g., anti-trust regulations for IOCs, and political restrictions on NOC intercompany cooperation with IOCs), and they set environmental standards, health and safety standards, and even petroleum product specifications. Governments pervasively and decisively set the conditions under which the industry operates.

None of the above is meant to assert that the forces of supply and demand are not important in the production and consumption of petroleum. They are, in fact, critically important. It is merely to note that petroleum markets exist under very specific political arrangements, especially in regard to who gets to "make the rules" both domestically, and to an extent, internationally. ∎

Energy security and petroleum

Energy security is about the availability of reliable and affordable fuel and power. In the most general sense, it comprises all sources of energy, including coal, hydroelectric, natural gas, nuclear, petroleum, and other alternatives such as biomass, geothermal, and wind. Energy security refers to the establishment and maintenance of a resilient infrastructure for fuel and power delivery and an ability to manage disruptions to supply. It also means having sufficient fuel to power the economic and commercial life of the country. Petroleum dominates discussions about energy security because the other sources of fuel and power are primarily produced domestically.

In thinking about energy security, it is useful to differentiate between energy used in the transportation sector and energy used in the electric power generation sector. According to the U.S. Energy Information Administration (EIA), almost 95% of all transport in the U.S. is powered by products refined from petroleum. In the U.S. today, unlike in the 1970s, virtually no petroleum is used in the commercial power generation sector. When considering energy security, it is important to avoid conflating petroleum in the transportation sector with energy in the power generation sector. Conflating the two often leads to muddled thinking and unrealistic policy proposals about how quickly alternative sources of energy, such as wind and solar, can replace petroleum. Thinking about this in terms of "energy transitions" minimizes this confusion.

Energy transitions have to do with changes to "prime movers" or the initial source of energy used to do work. For most of human history, the "prime mover" was human and animal muscle-power. Biomass, especially wood, was also an important source of power well into the Industrial Revolution. It was not until approximately 1885 that coal displaced wood as the primary U.S. energy source. And it was not until the early 1950s that petroleum replaced coal. Currently, as can be seen from the chart below, petroleum supplies over one third of all U.S. energy. The U.S. and the world will eventually transition away from petroleum, but this transition will take decades, not years.

The problem with petroleum and the need for transitioning away from it does not stem from the fact that the world is running out of petroleum; the problem is that 70% of the world's petroleum reserves are held by members of the Organization of Petroleum Exporting

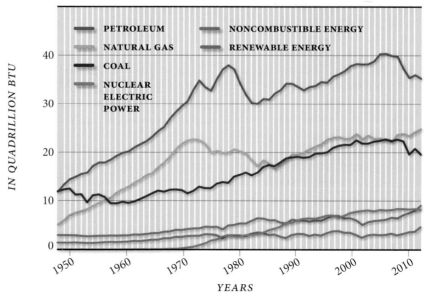

U.S. Evolving Energy Sources: 1949–2011

PETROLEUM
NATURAL GAS
COAL
NUCLEAR ELECTRIC POWER
NONCOMBUSTIBLE ENERGY
RENEWABLE ENERGY

IN QUADRILLION BTU

YEARS

SOURCE: U.S .ENERGY INFORMATION ADMIISTRATION   LUCIDITY INFORMATION DESIGN, LLC

Oil ministers from the Gulf Cooperation Council pose for a group photo during a meeting in Riyadh, September 24, 2013. Saudi Arabia pumped oil at a record rate of more than 10 million barrels per day (mmbd) in August, helping to cushion the market from the virtual shutdown of Libya's exports and reduced output from other countries including Nigeria and Iraq. (FAISAL AL NASSER/REUTERS/LANDOV)

Countries (OPEC) and they collude to keep prices high. They do this in the short run often by attempting to restrict production, and in the long run by underinvesting in petroleum production capability. The economic problem of collusion is exacerbated by the political difficulties caused by several colluding states being openly hostile to the U.S., and others being ambiguously aligned with it. The disproportionate impact that a small number of states can have on global oil supplies means that, under some circumstances, those states can take actions for economic or political reasons that may threaten the U.S. or its allies. Additionally, given the geographic concentration of petroleum resources, political or military disturbances in these areas can disrupt the production of petroleum and its transfer to the U.S., its allies and its trading partners.

In other words, most countries producing and consuming petroleum are highly sensitive to each other. Wars, political disruption, labor strife, and even bad weather often immediately affect countries thousands of miles away. This occurs because the production and consumption of petroleum is a global undertaking involving hundreds of countries, thousands of companies,

millions of workers, and billions of consumers. The petroleum supply chain is a tightly knit, highly interdependent system that has to produce massive amounts of refined product, every day, 365 days per year. When something occurs to reduce the amount produced, all other parts of the system usually adjust to the change. But high sensitivity is not the same as high vulnerability and all countries are not equally vulnerable.

Take, for instance, the events surrounding the October 1973 Arab-Israeli War, which represents the best example of a group of states trying to harm the U.S. by controlling oil exports. In an attempt to force the U.S. to withdraw its support for Israel, Saudi Arabia and its Arab allies in OPEC reduced petroleum production and embargoed petroleum sales to the U.S. and several of its allies. Although the actual production cutback was only 7-8% of global supply, prices rose from approximately $3 to over $12 per barrel within a few months.

Although oil is a very blunt weapon (i.e., it often harms a producer's friends, as well as its adversaries), the first oil shock , between 1973 and 1975, proved to be damaging to the U.S. economy. The jump in oil prices made large parts of the American manufacturing sector

obsolete; it decreased productivity, increased unemployment, and lowered real wages, and given the U.S. Federal Reserve's response of accommodating the oil price rise by increasing the money supply, it arguably set the U.S. off on an inflationary wage and price spiral. There were gasoline shortages, lines at filling stations, and eventually rationing. Outbreaks of violence related to obtaining gasoline were not uncommon. The recession induced by the 1973–75 oil shock was the worst recession since the 1930s, and it was not eclipsed until the great recession of 2007–09.

The second oil shock, or the price increase associated with the Iranian Revolution in 1979 and the outbreak of the Iran-Iraq War in 1981, was less of a deliberate attempt to damage the U.S. The second shock is an excellent illustration of the fact that the U.S. can be negatively affected by events that are not specifically or entirely directed against it.

During the late 1970s, Iran was producing almost 6.0 million barrels a day (mmbd) of petroleum and the U.S. was importing approximately 3% (or 0.5 mmbd) of its oil from Iran. After the revolution, Iranian production quickly declined to approximately 1.5 mmbd. In spite of the fact that the U.S. imported very little Iranian oil, it, like every other importing country, suffered tremendously as global oil prices rose from approximately $12, to over $40 per barrel. This price spike led to the 1980 and 1981 recessions just as the First Shock led to recession in 1974–75.

The grand accommodation and the new regime

In the aftermath of the oil shocks, the U.S. government enacted a number of policies to mitigate future disruptions. Domestically, there were measures to increase the natural gas supply and coal consumption; the Strategic Petroleum Reserve and Department of Energy also were established. Internationally, the major importing countries created the International Energy Agency (IEA), and U.S. presidents from Richard Nixon onward pledged to reduce

America's reliance on petroleum from the Middle East. But a number of developments, especially the nationalization of most IOC petroleum holdings and the rise of national oil companies, profoundly altered how the global petroleum supply chain worked and limited how the U.S. could respond.

In analyzing this, it is important to note that the problem for producers and the industry is not that oil prices have been too high; the real problem was, and remains, that a competitive or free market oil price would be substantially below what it has been, or currently is. Consequently, starting in the 1920s several major oil companies formed a cartel, later dubbed the "Seven Sisters," and colluded to raise prices. This cartel was sanctioned by both the U.S. and British governments.

During this period, nearly all benefits of the distorted price flowed to the oil companies, not the producing countries. But by the end of the 1960s, the OPEC countries began pressuring the IOCs to raise the prices they were paying and, under increasing threat of nationalization, the IOCs began accommodating these demands. Global oil prices rose by more than 50%, from less than $2 per barrel in 1970, to over $3 per barrel in 1973. But the producing states wanted to capture even more of the profits.

The October 1973 War was a perfect pretext to accelerate the nationalization of oil resources and force out foreign companies and their workers from the oil-rich countries such as Kuwait, Qatar, and Saudi Arabia. The 1970s nationalizations profoundly altered the way consuming countries procured oil and the security of their supplies simply by changing who controlled production and investment decisions. With OPEC's rise, collusion to increase oil prices was transferred from the private sector IOCs to producer governments. However, for the U.S., there was a big difference between a cooperative, Western-oriented private cartel, and an antagonistic, foreign-controlled, quasi-oligopoly.

At first, the U.S. was uncertain about how to respond and it considered invading the Persian Gulf to seize the oil fields. The U.S. Congress even held public hearings on the "feasibility" of such action. But eventually Washington decided to peacefully accommodate the new reality. What the U.S. then did, from a position of considerable weakness, was accede to the creation of a new international regime, for the production and distribution of petroleum. The U.S. tried to shape this regime, but it could not stop a number of features from being included that were far from optimal for U.S. consumers. It is this regime that still guides the production and distribution of petroleum today.

One of the most important changes was an acceptance by the U.S. of OPEC's collusive activities. As the Seven Sisters transfer-pricing system broke down, the U.S. Department of Justice (DOJ) diligently enforced anti-trust laws against the IOCs but ignored the NOCs. Even when private legal suits, such as that brought by the International Association of Machinists in 1981 were brought against OPEC, the U.S. government intervened in support of OPEC and its collusive practices. And when the U.S. Congress periodically attempts to pass a resolution calling on the President to apply U.S. anti-trust law to OPEC, the administration opposes it (as happened in 2007).

The legal issues involved in anti-trust suits are complicated and when a U.S. administration wants to support OPEC it can find many justifications including sovereign immunity, foreign sovereign compulsion, prosecutorial discretion, and so on. The point, however, is that if the presidents of Chevron or ExxonMobil did what the presidents of most NOCs do, they would be put in jail. There is a double standard for how IOCs and NOCs can act within the U.S. This issue is not one of jurisdiction. The U.S. DOJ has pursued and has succeeded in many foreign anti-trust cases. The issue is one of policy. Every administration has made the national security decision that anti-trust suits should not be pursued because the U.S. needs the oil and threatening NOC leaders with jail was not going to help the U.S. procure it.

A second key feature of the current regime is that the IOCs are largely blocked from developing the oil and gas reserves of OPEC and most other countries. Every country has the right to decide how its resources are developed, but what is interesting again is the double standard. Many countries that bar or seriously restrict U.S. companies from participating on their territory, including Brazil, China, Mexico, and most of the OPEC countries, generally have greater opportunity to engage in oil and gas projects in the U.S. To varying de-

Los Angeles, CA, October 1972. Gas prices are not listed on the signboard at Gilmore Station due to the energy and gas crisis. (HENRY DILTZ/CORBIS)

grees, this lack of investment reciprocity is a hallmark of U.S. relations with nearly all petroleum producing states. The only significant petroleum producing states with which the U.S. has near reciprocal access are Australia, Britain, Canada and Norway.

A third component of the new regime has been the U.S. commitment to defend the Persian Gulf and the freedom of navigation necessary for global transshipment of oil. The U.S. had been gradually increasing its military presence in the Persian Gulf, but the British withdrawal from east of the Suez in 1971 made the lack of regional security more problematic. After the Iranian

Revolution and the Soviet invasion of Afghanistan in 1979, the U.S. became directly involved. In January 1980, President Jimmy Carter declared that "…an assault by any outside force to gain control of the Persian Gulf region will be regarded as an assault on the vital interests" of the U.S. The Carter Doctrine and subsequent corollaries, declarations, directives, and strategies remain a pillar of U.S. policy. Part of this commitment includes an implied security guarantee to Saudi Arabia.

By acceding to this new international petroleum regime, the U.S. was attempting to create offsetting dependencies with Saudi Arabia and other

Persian Gulf producers. It wanted those countries to be beholden to the U.S. for such things as military security and the creation and maintenance of an international banking system welcoming to their investments. By creating offsetting dependencies, the relationships, or more properly the vulnerabilities, became more symmetrical. If the Saudis need the U.S. as much as the U.S. needs the Saudis, then the U.S. is more secure. In particular, it was thought that mutual dependence would encourage Saudi Arabia and other Gulf producers to balance their interest for higher petroleum prices with the needs of U.S. consumers for lower prices. ∎

Prices and the petroleum investment cycle

It might surprise some, but from the mid-1980s to the very early 2000s, the U.S. government occasionally complained to Saudi Arabia that oil prices were too low. During this period, there were even a few days when oil traded below $10 per barrel and if such ultra-low prices continued, it would have destroyed the U.S. domestic petroleum industry and left the country totally dependent on imports. Given the experience of the 1970s, this would have been unacceptable to any U.S. administration.

Over the last few years, however, prices have been "too high." (See the chart below.) This time, if the U.S. complained, the Saudis, even if they agreed, could do little because they were already producing at full capacity. They physically could not increase production, at least not for several years.

For the U.S., there is an optimum price range that promotes sufficient domestic production (thereby reducing the threat of foreign disruption), while at the same time not harming consumers. For Saudi Arabia and several other producers, there also is an optimal price range that ensures the long-term viability of their massive oil reserves while at the same time meeting short term revenue needs. Problematically, the optimum price for the U.S. often is lower than the optimum price for Saudi Arabia. And even if there were agreement about the optimum price, forecasting future petroleum demand and calibrating investment to meet this demand is extremely difficult.

The petroleum cycle is caused by the enormous amount of money necessary to develop petroleum resources, and by the long lag time between the initial conception of a project and first production. In its simplest form, the petroleum cycle is synonymous with the investment cycle, only lagged by 7-10 years. But investment cycle planning is complicated by two key factors: (1) the

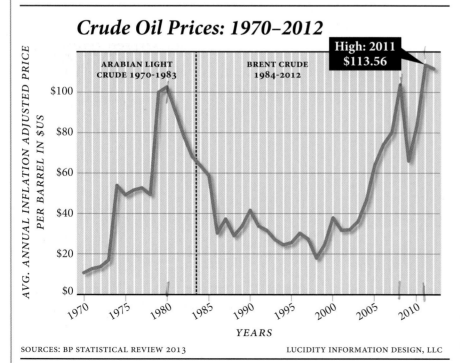

Crude Oil Prices: 1970–2012

ARABIAN LIGHT CRUDE 1970-1983

BRENT CRUDE 1984-2012

High: 2011 $113.56

AVG. ANNUAL INFLATION ADJUSTED PRICE PER BARREL IN $US

$100
$80
$60
$40
$20
$0

1970 1975 1980 1985 1990 1995 2000 2005 2010

YEARS

SOURCES: BP STATISTICAL REVIEW 2013   LUCIDITY INFORMATION DESIGN, LLC

nationalizations of the 1970s destroyed the globally integrated investment process maintained by the Seven Sisters, and (2) demand cycles are much shorter than investment cycles—the two are "asynchronous."

In its most simplified form, the petroleum cycle works like this: high prices induce high investment; high investment creates higher production that leads to low prices; low prices stop investment; stopped investment leads to insufficient supply that in turn creates high prices, which brings back high investment, and so on.

Under the current regime, the world has experienced three distinct investment phases, and one could argue (as below) that the world is on the cusp of the next, very significant down phase. These phases can be viewed from the perspective of prices or actual investment expended, but the price gauge is easier to follow. (Cycle demarcations change slightly depending on which gauge is used.)

The first phase, from 1970 until 1981, was caused by rapidly increasing global demand and inadequate investment in production capacity in the late 1960s and early 1970s. As prices climbed in the 1970s, however, investment in petroleum production grew to massive proportions. New areas, such as the North Sea, Alaska, and deep-water Gulf of Mexico were brought into production. With the addition of all this capacity, conditions were right for the second phase from 1981 until 1998.

As a result of all the new production, oil prices collapsed after 1981 and investment followed shortly thereafter. The third phase, 1998–2012, is particularly interesting because although prices started to rise in 1998, it took several years for investment to increase. Few people, including many oil company managers, believed prices would remain high, so investments were delayed. But by 2004–05, the IOCs and some NOCs were convinced that the increase was durable and they began investing. By 2007 the investment flows were enormous. The result was a massive expansion in production in places like Brazil, West

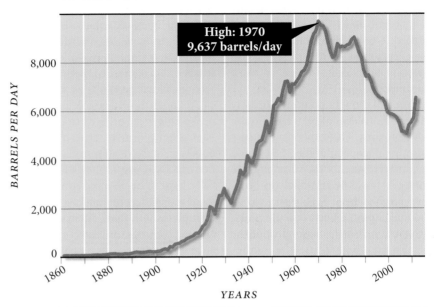

Crude Oil Production: 1860–2012

High: 1970
9,637 barrels/day

BARRELS PER DAY

8,000

6,000

4,000

2,000

0

1860 1880 1900 1920 1940 1960 1980 2000

YEARS

SOURCE: U.S .ENERGY INFORMATION ADMINISTRATION   LUCIDITY INFORMATION DESIGN, LLC

Africa, the ultra-deep Gulf of Mexico, North Dakota in the U.S., and Alberta in Canada.

From 2008 until the spring of 2013, U.S. crude oil production increased approximately 45% to 7.3 mmbd; from 2005 to 2012, U.S. natural gas production increased 30% to approximately 66 billion cubic feet (bcf) per day. This is the "oil and gas revolution" that has

been making headlines and it shows little sign of slowing.

Under the EIA's "best case" forecasts, U.S. crude oil production will rise to 10 mmbd by 2040. When one adds in other supply components, EIA has total U.S. "liquids" production in 2040 at 18.2 mmbd. This would almost make the U.S. self-sufficient in the production of petroleum, depending on

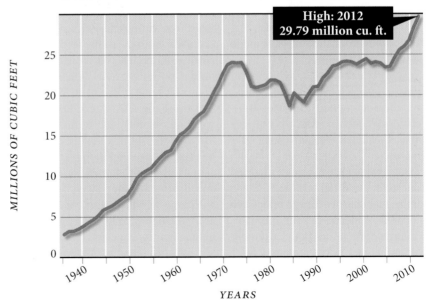

U.S. Natural Gas Gross Withdrawals

High: 2012
29.79 million cu. ft.

MILLIONS OF CUBIC FEET

25

20

15

10

5

0

1940 1950 1960 1970 1980 1990 2000 2010

YEARS

SOURCE: U.S .ENERGY INFORMATION ADMINISTRATION   LUCIDITY INFORMATION DESIGN, LLC

one's demand estimates. In 2007, U.S. net imports amounted to 12.3 mmbd of crude oil and petroleum products; by the first half of 2013, net imports had dropped to 6.9 mmbd. If the EIA "best case comes to pass, imports will fall to approximately 1.5–2.0 mmbd, or 7% of consumption.

Extremely low imports significantly reduce U.S. vulnerability to foreign supply disruptions. There still can be negative price impacts, but the U.S. would be *relatively* better off because physical shortages would be less likely to occur (particularly if the U.S. continues to ban crude oil exports), and economic damage would be less because most of the revenue from higher prices would remain in the U.S. High oil prices would be bad for the U.S., but they would be a lot worse for other oil importers. Also, depending on the specifics of the disruption, there is a good chance prices would go up less in the U.S. than in other areas such as Europe or East Asia.

As importantly, what is happening in the U.S. is indicative of changes taking place in several other locations, especially Canada, Brazil, and West Africa. After 6–8 years of very high investment, global oil production capacity is once again sufficient to exceed demand. And this does not even account for the possibility that Iraq, Mexico and Russia could add significant capacity. The world once again is building up a larger margin of safety that can compensate for localized supply disruptions. (EIA estimates that OPEC surplus production capacity alone soon will reach 4 mmbd.)

Spare production capacity is critical for petroleum security. Traditionally, when surplus capacity reaches high levels, prices decline. And when prices decline, U.S. energy security generally increases.

The above is stated, neither to assert that oil prices will fall back to $25, nor to argue that sharply higher prices are impossible. Indeed, at some point in the intermediate future both extremely lower and higher prices are possible, if not probable. But what the petroleum investment cycle indicates is that if there is a continuation of the current elevated prices, then the price decline of the next down phase of the investment cycle should be deeper and last longer than first anticipated. A Chinese induced "super-cycle" may set a floor under prices, but that just makes it easier for the U.S. to have an optimum price allowing it to balance high domestic production with a more moderate gasoline price.

Although the full petroleum independence case may be hard to obtain, the increasingly positive impact of increased domestic (and global) petroleum production on U.S. energy security is meaningfully large. The benefits come not just from reduced vulnerability to foreign disruptions, but from other sources including the positive impact on the balance of payments, increased domestic employment, and, importantly, a lower level of economic disruption should global petroleum prices rapidly rise.

The petroleum cycle and U.S. foreign policy

Each phase of the petroleum cycles has been accompanied by very different policy challenges for the U.S. In the high price phase, the U.S. had to deal with such things as the negative macroeconomic impact of higher energy prices, resource nationalism in oil producing countries, and foreign adversaries emboldened by flush treasuries. In the lower price phase, the primary challenge for the U.S. was to manage the instability in exporting countries since lower oil prices tend to destabilize those countries. Perhaps the best historical example of the importance of petroleum cycles and their impact on foreign policy is Soviet-American relations at the end of the Cold War.

During the 1970s, when oil and gas were significantly increasing in price, the Soviet Union was able to finance an expansive foreign policy. It also was able to augment its traditional military and diplomatic activities in Europe with a new inducement for European accommodation to its policy goals. This inducement was access to ever-larger amounts of oil and natural gas.

In addition to the enhancement of Soviet power in Europe, the upturn in the petroleum cycle and the increased revenue helped the Soviet Union main-tain a series of client states in Africa, Latin America, and the Middle East. While one can debate the precise role higher commodity revenue played in supporting these clients, the U.S. was sufficiently alarmed about the success of Soviet policy in the Middle East that President Carter issued his previously mentioned doctrine.

Greater oil and gas revenue also enabled the Soviet Union to compensate for and cover up the fatal defects of its economic system. But by 1986, when global oil prices had fallen more than 75%, the Soviet Union was virtually bankrupt. Not only did it not have the financial resources to continue its previous policies, it had to start accommodating the U.S. so that it could gain greater access to Western loans and (it hoped) investment.

While the commodity collapse of the 1980s was not the only reason for the downfall of the Soviet Union, it certainly was one of the more important reasons. The Soviet-American bilateral relationship is an excellent illustration that petroleum cycles are important, not just because of whom it strengthens, but because of whom it weakens.

Elements of power and oil

U.S.-Soviet relations presented one of the most extreme examples of the petroleum cycle's impact on foreign policy; but one can also make direct parallels to today's world. Generally, the petroleum cycle creates very broad groups of international winners and losers. When oil prices fall, the losers are obviously those states with high oil exports and a large dependence on the revenue that these exports generate. Saudi Arabia and the rest of OPEC clearly will face an even more challenging international environment when and if the cycle turns down. But even non-OPEC states, such as Brazil and Canada, would be seriously affected by a decline in the price of petroleum. Conversely, the winners are the major petroleum importing countries, especially China, Japan, India, Korea, Germany and France. And given the U.S.' transition from a major importer to a minor importer, it too should be a winner.

While broad generalizations about the significance of changes in the petroleum cycle are possible, they are less useful for making policy because petroleum prices and dependencies do not necessarily impact every country equally. Even if two countries have the same degree of dependence on oil export revenue, or consume similar amounts of imported oil, there are many other variables that have to be considered if one is to understand the impact of petroleum on that country's foreign policy. This occurs because the "power positions" of countries are composed of a variety of resources, and oil is only one such element.

In order to become more policy relevant, one needs to be specific about each country's situation, and in order to do this, one can apply an "elements of power" analysis. Hans Morgenthau, in his classic study, *Politics Among Nations,* differentiated between the "permanent" and the "nonpermanent" elements of power. He grouped them roughly as follows:

Permanent Factors

- Climate
- Demography
- Geography/Topography
- Hydrology
- Natural Resource Endowment (including petroleum)

Nonpermanent Factors

- Political System
  Legitimacy, leadership, diplomacy
- Military
  Quality and quantity of armed forces (including leadership)
- Social & Economic
  How the population is organized and mobilized
- Industrial Capacity
  Technology/Informational Usage
- Psychological National Character & Morale ("degree of determination")

Many of the above variables are hard to quantify and some even are impossible to quantify. Consequently, many analysts of international affairs do not like this approach because it can be so subjective. Nonetheless, elements of power analysis can be useful, par-

(JOHN TREVER/POLITICALCARTOONS.COM)

ticularly when it comes to the "permanent factors" of power, and especially natural resources.

Traditionally, military power had been the primary gauge of international strength. But since the end of the World War II, military force has been less useful. If military power has become less indicative of power potential, then how does petroleum fit in? And how do shifts (over time) in who has petroleum and who does not, fit in?

As noted, petroleum is essential for modern life. Clearly, its impact on a country's power potential is meaningful and which countries have it and which do not matters. Possession of petroleum, in some cases, can be the basis for creating asymmetric relations of vulnerability. Writing in 1978, Morgenthau remarked: "The emergence of oil as an indispensable raw material has brought about a shift in the relative power of the politically leading nations." Without petroleum, Saudi Arabia, for example, would be a much less important state, and it would be much more vulnerable to actions by other states. By contrast, Europe's increasing inability (or refusal) to produce petroleum from its territory is increasing its vulnerability by compelling it to create more countervailing relationships, i.e.,

balance the asymmetries. And every time a country is compelled to create one of these countervailing relationships it gives up some of its freedom to maneuver.

Policy questions

Hans Morgenthau thought that the most important factor for a nation to possess was superior diplomacy, but he also recognized that if diplomacy is weak, that at least the more permanent factors of power, such as bountiful natural resources, could help compensate for this weakness. One can debate the strength or weakness of current American diplomacy, but there is little doubt that the U.S. is reassuming a powerful position in the world of petroleum.

To many observers, increased U.S. oil and gas production may allow the country to reduce its global presence, particularly in the Middle East. The disentangling of the U.S. from such overseas commitments would reduce defense costs and shift the burden of intervention to other states. Whether one agrees with this view largely depends on how one assesses the significance of increased U.S. oil and gas production and of how far the U.S. can go in isolating itself from energy disruptions and other events around the world. ■

 Don't forget to vote! www.greatdecisions.org/ballot

discussion questions

1. Is the U.S. really less vulnerable to a disruption of its petroleum supply? What does vulnerability mean? Is the "balance of vulnerability" again shifting in a manner such that OPEC has less power because the U.S. needs them less? What would an "elements of power" analysis say about the United States today?

2. If lower petroleum vulnerability is real, should the U.S. reduce its global activities, especially in the Persian Gulf and Middle East? Should not other countries with more serious petroleum problems like China, India, France and Germany be more actively engaged in the Middle East? Is it good for the U.S. if these countries become more engaged globally?

3. Should the U.S. pursue policies that encourage the greater use of competitive markets for the allocation of petroleum? In particular, should it use domestic anti-trust laws to attempt to reduce the amount of collusion among OPEC states? Is this realistic? Is it dangerous?

4. Should the United States require reciprocity in terms of investment access when dealing with foreign investment in the U.S. oil and gas industry? Would an effort akin to the World Trade Organization be useful?

suggested readings

Bryce, Robert. **Power Hungry: The Myths of "Green" Energy and the Real Fuels of the Future.** New York, NY: PublicAffairs, 2010. 448 pp. $18.99 (paper). A provocative but extremely well researched argument for the U.S.'s continuing use of fossil fuels.

Collier, Paul. **The Plundered Planet: Why We Must—and How We Can—Manage Nature for Global Prosperity**. New York: Oxford University Press, 2010. 288 pp. $16.95 (paper). Award-winning author Paul Collier explores the potentially devastating effects of mismanaged natural resource exploitation for the world's poorest populations and proposes realistic and sustainable solutions to these difficult problems.

Crane, Keith, Goldthau, Andreas, Toman, Michael, Light, Thomas, Johnson, Stuart E., Nader, Alireza, Rabasa, Angel, and Dogo, Harun. "Imported Oil and U.S. National Security," RAND Corporation, 2009. Available free online at <http://www.rand.org/content/dam/rand/pubs/monographs/2009/RAND_MG838.pdf>. Chapter 5 reviews the issues and methodology for estimating the petroleum-related defense burden.

Dancs, Anita, "The Military Cost of Securing Energy," National Priorities Project, 2008. Available free online at <http://vcnv.org/files/NPP_energy_defense_spending_full_report.pdf> Also reviews the issues and methodology for estimating the petroleum related defense burden, but comes up with starkly different numbers.

Gause, Gregory F. **Saudi Arabia in the New Middle East**. New York: Council on Foreign Relations, 2011. 60pp. Available free online: "< http://www.cfr.org/saudi-arabia/saudi-arabia-new-middle-east/p26663>. A concise, yet wide ranging review of Saudi Arabia and the issues complicating its polices.

Hofmeister, John. **Why We Hate the Oil Companies: Straight Talk from an Energy Insider.** New York, Palgrave Macmillan, 2010. 272 pp. $16.00 (paper). An honest account of current petroleum industry problems. The former Shell Oil Company president's "Forget the Free Market" chapter is particularly useful.

Inkpen, Andrew and Moffett, Michael H. **The Global Oil & Gas Industry: Management, Strategy and Finance**. Tulsa, OK: PennWell Corporation, 2011. 455 pp. $89.00 (hardcover). A nontechnical book for readers with technical backgrounds that covers a wide-range of topics critical to understanding the business of oil and gas.

Levi, Michael. **The Power Surge: Energy, Opportunity, and the Battle for America's Future**. New York: Oxford University Press, 2013. 272 pp. $27.95 (hardcover). Michael Levi looks at America's two simultaneous energy revolutions. After decades of decline, the oil and gas industry is once again expanding, all while eco-startups are actively exploring alternative sources of energy. Levi explains what this will mean for America's economy and energy security.

Smil, Vaclav. **Energy Myths and Realities: Bringing Science to the Energy Policy Debate**. Washington DC, AEI Press, 2010. 213 pp. $34.95 (hardcover). Combines economic analysis, environmental science, and a deep knowledge of history to produce a series of chapters discussing many of the most critical and controversial energy issues.

Yergin, Daniel. **The Prize: The Epic Quest for Oil, Money & Power**. New York: Free Press, 2008. 928 pp. $22.00 (paper) Originally published in 1991, **The Prize** is the 1992 Pulitzer Prize winner for nonfiction, and a comprehensive history of one of the world's most important commodities: oil.

——— **The Quest: Energy, Security, and the Remaking of the Modern World**. New York: Penguin Group, 2012. 832 pp. $20.00 (paper). Yergin's sequel to his Pulitzer Prize-winning book The Prize intelligently and entertainingly demonstrates energy's critical role in global politics and economics. Yergin asks difficult questions and tells the stories of individuals and technologies that are shaping our future.

TO LEARN MORE ABOUT THIS TOPIC AND TO ACCESS WEB LINKS TO RESOURCES GO TO www.greatdecisions.org

Food and climate
by William Sweet

An Egyptian farmer holds a handful of soil to show the dryness of the land due to drought in a farm formerly irrigated by the river Nile, in Al-Dakahlya, about 75 miles from Cairo, in June 2013. (MOHAMED ABD EL GHANY/REUTERS/CORBIS)

When there are abrupt changes in the weather, the first thing everyone traditionally worries about is how agriculture, food supplies and food prices will be affected. Obviously we can't live without food. Yet, with the overwhelming preponderance of people in the advanced industrial societies living in cities, the centrality of weather and food is easily lost sight of. Perhaps this partly explains why the subject of climate change and food security has been slow to climb to the top of the global policy agenda.

Last year, the subject suddenly received much more attention. In June 2013, the World Bank issued the second installment of a report on climate change, "Turn Down the Heat," looking at relatively near-term food impacts likely to result in a world that is two or four degrees Celsius warmer, the lower- and higher-end consensus projections for world warming in this century. The bank's initial report, published at the end of 2012, had predicted that were the world four degrees warmer by the end of the century, there would be devastating effects on water and food, prompting tens of millions of refugees to flee degraded environments.

The newer report, done at the behest of World Bank President Jim Yong Kim, addressed nearer-term implications. Some of them are disconcerting, to say the least. For example, with warming of 1.5°C in sub-Saharan Africa, about 40% of the areas currently planted with maize would no longer be suitable for corn production; there also would be "significant negative impacts on sorghum suitability in the western Sahel and southern Africa."

In Southeast Asia, increasingly frequent seawater flooding, salt intrusion and coastal erosion will occur as sea levels rise more than average near the equator. Aquaculture, agriculture and marine capture fisheries will be "particularly at risk" in the Mekong, Irrawaddy and Chao Phraya deltas. Southeast Asia will face heat extremes that are virtually unknown today in 60%–70% of the region.

WILLIAM SWEET *is the author of* Kicking the Carbon Habit: The Case for Renewable and Nuclear Energy *(Columbia University Press, 2006). He is developing a book about climate diplomacy.*

In South Asia, the area where the largest number of malnourished or outright hungry individuals live and where total population is expected to grow in the next four decades from 1.6 billion to 2.2 billion, the consequences of global warming will be particularly dire for the water cycle. Dry areas and dry seasons will be become drier; wet areas and seasons get wetter. Monsoon intensity is likely to increase, especially at the more pessimistic projections of warming. Even in the more optimistic projections, Himalayan glaciers will retreat and the Ganges, Indus and Brahmaputra river systems will suffer increased flooding and reduced dry season flows.

Some aspects of that assessment—such as the complex effects of glacier retreat—may be controversial. Nevertheless, the assertion that wet places will get wetter and dry places drier has been a fundamental conclusion of climate models going back to their earliest days, and has withstood critical scrutiny again and again.

Impacts and causes

World Bank President Kim may have been one of the most influential voices discussing climate and food security, but his was by no means the only one. On June 17, 2013, UN Secretary General Ban Ki-moon took the occasion of the World Day to Combat Desertification to remind people of droughts that drastically affected food security in the Horn of Africa and Namibia, not to mention a drought in the U.S. that affected four fifths of the country's agricultural land. Luc Gnacadja, executive secretary of the UN Convention to Combat Desertification, said that over 1.6 billion people have died because of droughts since 1979.

In a rich country like the U.S., people do not die of starvation when there is a serious drought, and farmers are protected by government-supported crop insurance programs. Still, an event like last year's is worrisome enough. Two weeks before World Desertification Day, U.S. Secretary of Agriculture Tom Vilsack announced that the U.S. Department of Agriculture (USDA) would establish seven Regional Climate Hubs to work with farmers and foresters on hazard and adaptation planning. Vilsack noted that the USDA had already produced service-oriented climate adaptation plans and two major assessments of climate impacts, one for agriculture and one for forestry.

The action plan described by Vilsack on June 5 was not confined to climate change consequences but also addressed agriculture's contributions to global warming. A "carbon management and evaluation tool" will help farmers calculate how much efforts at conservation can reduce their greenhouse gas emissions. Technical experts on soil management will benefit from the online release of data collected by the USDA since 2010 on the amounts and distribution of carbon stocks in U.S. soils under a variety of land covers and management techniques.

These programs are reminders that world agriculture is not merely a victim of climate change but also a major contributor to it. One recent authoritative assessment indicates global food systems may account for as much as one third of total annual greenhouse gas emissions.

Extreme events

Without a doubt, the attention being given food and climate originated in the series of extreme weather events in recent years that produced sharp spikes in world food prices. The most notable such events in 2007–08 resulted from droughts in Australia, Eastern Europe and Ukraine, as well as flooding in the U.S. Midwest. Sometimes a relatively confined weather event in a country not normally considered one of the great grain exporters could have a remarkably outsized effect: In 2010, desiccating winds and fires near Moscow prompted Russia to ban wheat exports, sending world wheat prices to a two-year high.

To what extent can such events be blamed on climate change? By 2010, scientists from all over the world were convening for workshops to discuss statistical methods of assessing extreme weather events. Last year, the Intergovernmental Panel on Climate Change (IPCC), the organization of climate scientists that delivers regular status reports, produced one such report specifically on implications of extreme climate events. A creature of the UN Environment Program and the World Meteorological Organization, the IPCC recruits thousands of volunteer scientists to report regularly on climate change.

In September 2012, the *Bulletin* of the American Meteorological Society produced a package of articles assessing extreme climate events of 2012. Eighteen teams from around the world contributed, with the U.S. National Oceanic and Atmospheric Administration (NOAA) playing a major role. They focused on 12 events and identified climate change as a significant factor in about half of them. Among the events they considered in particular detail were the U.S. heat wave, Hurricane Sandy and the heavy rainfall that afflicted both northern Europe and eastern Australia. They found, for example, that even though a storm like Sandy was and will remain extremely improbable by any analysis, lower Manhattan can expect to be flooded every couple of years by the end of the century if sea level rise is at the upper end of scientific projections. As for the U.S. heat wave, they determined that while it could be largely explained by normal climate variability, temperatures like those experienced in 2012 will become four times as probable in the coming decades.

James Hansen, the pioneering climate modeler and one of the first atmospheric scientists to draw public attention to human-induced climate change, assessed some of the earlier extreme climate events. In an article authored by Hansen and his colleagues, they said, "There is no need to equivocate about the summer heat waves in Texas in 2011 and Moscow in 2010" because those events were so far outside the range of normal probability. Those two events, in addition to the French heat wave of 2003 that cost hundreds of lives, "almost certainly would not have occurred in the absence of global warming."

Precedents

History shows that agricultural shortages caused by chance weather and climate events can have drastic political effects. One such event, a grain harvest failure, food shortage and price spike on the eve of the French Revolution—"a serious accident of the kind that happened periodically," as one scholar has put it—was a major driver of uprisings both in the countryside and in Paris. The famine was widely blamed at the grassroots level on a suspected "aristocratic conspiracy" against the revolution; it generated the "Great Fear" that swept the country, contributing ultimately to the Terror and then (in the form of the "levée en masse" or mass mobilization) to Napoleon's military campaigns against all the countries trying to contain and roll back the revolution.

Flash forward to the present. Last year, *New York Times* columnist Thomas Friedman drew attention to the role high world food prices played in setting the stage for the Arab Spring. Friedman described the results of a report, "The Arab Spring and Climate Change," that was jointly produced by the Center for American Progress, the Stimson Center and the Center for Climate and Security. One essay, by Oxford University

geographer Troy Sternberg, said that in 2010–11, just as the Arab Spring uprisings were breaking out, "a once-in-a-century winter drought in China," together with droughts and floods in other major grain producing countries, "contributed to global wheat shortages and skyrocketing bread prices in Egypt." Since most grain produced in the world is not traded, any significant production shortfall in a significant exporting country immediately translates into much higher prices.

Thus, the effects of the 2010–11 shortfalls were most severe for countries dependent on grain imports, and as it so happens the nine top importers of grain per capita are all in the Middle East. No other country relies more on imported grain than Egypt. According to the UN Food and Agriculture Organization, "bread provides one third of caloric intake in Egypt, a country where 38% of [average household] income is spent on food." The doubling in global food prices from June 2010 to February 2011 had a drastic effect on an Egyp-

tian family's ability to obtain the food it needed. Egypt in 2010–11, France in 1775–76: The parallels are uncanny. In the 18th century, as the great historian of the French Revolution Georges Lefebvre spelled out, the average working man or peasant in France needed two or three pounds of bread per day; it was overwhelmingly the mainstay of the common person's diet. For such a person to get by, wrote LeFebvre, "it was estimated that bread should cost no more than two sous a pound. [But] in the first half of July [1789] the price was twice this figure. In the provinces it was much higher, reaching 8 sous or more."

In hindsight, it was a short step from those conditions to the morning of October 5, 1789, when the working women of Paris, led by a man carrying a mounted bayonet with a loaf of bread stuck on it, brought the king, queen and dauphin back to Paris from Versailles. As they marched, relates LeFebvre, they chanted that they were bringing back the "baker, the baker's wife and the baker's boy." ∎

Food security

In the days of the ancien régime, from time immemorial the monarchy had tightly regulated domestic grain markets and maintained reserves to get the country through periods of famine or shortfall because grains and bread were so essential to the daily survival of the French people. Though transporting grain from one part of the country to another in the event of crisis could be difficult, the general expectation was that the monarchy would make sure everyone was fed. In the 18th century, however, progressive thinkers of the French Enlightenment took note of advances in agricultural technology and technique in England, where freer market conditions prevailed. A school of French economists known as the Physiocrats advocated opening French grain markets to world market forces, which gradually got the attention of the monarchy. On the eve of the revolution and as it unfolded in its first year, the monarchy vacillated between the two

approaches. The French people seemed to blame whichever faction was in the ascendancy at any given time for shortfalls, whether it was the pro-regulatory or market-friendly group.

Here too there are parallels to the contemporary world. In the last decades, economic development agencies and specialists have been sharply split between those who advocate freeing up global markets in grains, rice and other staples, and those critical of such policies. Everyone has his own bogeymen.

Among those who advocate free market systems, and whose influence dominates major international organizations like the World Bank and International Monetary Fund, typical objects of scorn include urban elites who insist on subsidized or controlled food prices, which discourage agricultural production; export restrictions like the ones Russia imposed after the 2010 fires because they amplify price spikes and prevent markets from responding ad-

equately to food emergencies; and farm subsidies in rich countries, which undercut efforts to encourage production in less well-off countries.

Critics of that "Washington consensus" are deeply suspicious of the multinational companies that benefit from greater free trade in agricultural inputs and outputs, the brokers and speculators who skim off big premiums from the trade, and the technologies that advanced countries encourage poor countries to adopt without adequate attention to unintended consequences in unfamiliar situations.

If there were to be a global-scale agricultural shortfall, whether the result of extreme climate events or not, one or both of those two ideological factions would certainly be blamed, just as regulators and deregulators were blamed equally and at the same time during the French Revolution. It would be easy for a satirist in the tradition of Swift or Voltaire to make fun of the battles. But at the heart of the argument is a serious difference of opinion over the meaning of the term "food security."

When it comes to defining, adherents to the Washington consensus tend to put the emphasis squarely on quantitative production. Their main concerns are whether social, economic and political conditions favor the rapid introduction of advanced technologies and procedures in order to feed a growing world population. Critics of the aforementioned approach put more emphasis on the distribution of food and access to staples; they tend to look at the issue of local social, economic and political conditions in a rather different way.

Washington consensus critics often take their cues from the Nobel Prize-winning economist Amartya Sen, who argued that famine never is just the result of a quantitative shortfall and is always the consequence of something going awry in the distribution system. Sen argued that in modern times famines have not occurred in democracies because democratic institutions, like a free press, virtually guarantee that food will get to the people who urgently need it.

As the world is not a democracy, the distributionist argument may be of limited relevance when it comes to predicting a global-scale catastrophic famine from extreme climate events. But it is plainly of great relevance to questions of what can be done to prepare for and adapt to incremental, year-to-year climate change, the subject that has dominated discussions of global warming and food security so far.

Dangers and relief

In 2009, the UN Food and Agriculture Organization (FAO) characterized climate change and food security in terms that ought to satisfy both the productionist and distributionist camps: "Climate change negatively affects the basic elements of food production, such as soil, water and biodiversity. More broadly it affects all four dimensions of food security: food availability, food accessibility, the stability of the food supply and the ability of consumers to use food, including food safety and nutritional value."

The language comes across as stilted, to be sure, and the general tone may seem facile. The same could be said about the long programmatic sections of the report that follow: "Countries need a sound understanding of the current and future vulnerabilities […] FAO seeks to develop innovative, user-friendly tools and methods to support decisionmakers […]"

The World Food Program's (WFP) assessment in December 2010 has a more specific emphasis. Based on a survey of 43 WFP country offices conducted the previous year, the report considers WFP's experience with climate change to date and makes recommendations. More than half of the country offices' responses indicated that a changing climate was most threatening poor sectors of the population already vulnerable to hunger and malnutrition. Three quarters of the countries where WFP worked had projects with elements related to climate change and/or disaster-risk reduction. The report cautioned against "rebranding" all the organization's development activities in terms of climate change, but it said it would be "irresponsible of WFP not to consider climate change as a central challenge to be internalized into its policy, planning and operations dimensions."

Systemic threats

How will agricultural systems be affected by climate change? Who will be hit the hardest? There is no doubt that water access will be the number one issue. An FAO evaluation in 2011, "Climate Change, Water and Food Security," noted that recent scientific studies predicted "a substantial increase in irrigated areas in response to global temperature rise, higher rates of crop water use, and declining and more variable rainfalls." In other words, as world temperatures rise, agricultural water needs will rise even as the availability of water becomes more unreliable.

The FAO's evaluation cited an analysis by the International Institute for Applied Systems Analysis in Austria, which projected "a 45% increase in irrigated land in southern Asia, Latin America and Africa to meet future food demands." It stated,

This translated into a 66% increase in water requirement over present use when climate change was taken into consideration….The broad conclusion is that the additional water required because of climate change will be nearly as great as the net increase in demand from present day to 2080 to meet additional food and other needs.

That is, the increase in water needs from now to 2080 attributable to climate change will be roughly equivalent to the increases associated with growing population and improving diets.

Of course, much depends on just how big the temperature rise is in the next 75 years and on where one happens to live. If for example the rise is in the range of 1–3°C, crop yields will actually improve in temperate zones and only deteriorate if the rise exceeds 3 degrees. In the tropics, on the other hand, yields will decrease as the temperature rises by 1–2 degrees, a scenario that is a virtual certainty and, by general scientific consensus, the best foreseeable case.

The FAO notes that in many countries of the world, water withdrawals for irrigation are exceeding natural replenishment of aquifers, and that in many major river basins—the Indus, Nile, Jordan, Syr Darya, Amu Darya, Yellow River and Mekong—water is already fully allocated or almost fully allocated. But not all the FAO's news is terrible. The report notes that it is in some ways more optimistic about the future than studies like the Stern climate review, the influential 2006 report produced by former World Bank chief economist Nicholas Stern, or some studies from the IPCC. (An important IPCC report on climate and food is due out in March 2014.)

"Since the 1970s," the FAO states, "the extensive development of irrigation supplies and flood control has smoothed out the impacts of climate variability and, with the benefit of Green Revolution farming techniques, increased productivity to the point that commodity prices fell year on year in real terms until the early 2000s."

There is a sense both here and in other literature that with intensified agricultural extension work ("feet in the fields"), the development of new crop strains that are resistant to higher temperatures and tolerant of lesser or greater amounts of water, and rigorous testing of the new varieties as well as new methods in real-world agricultural situations, the impacts of climate variability may be largely finessed once again.

Regional impacts

The overwhelming focus of developing new technologies and procedures has been on South Asia and sub-Saharan Africa, on the deltaic rice and aquaculture of Southeast Asia and the rain-fed agriculture of sub-Saharan Africa. This does not mean that the advanced industrial countries are immune to agricultural threats. Because of the spread of the tropics northwards in the Northern Hemisphere, received agricultural practices and whole ways of life in the U.S. southwest and the Mediterranean are coming under a lot of stress. Australia's chronic catastrophic wildfires are evidence of the same trend in the Southern Hemisphere.

Generally, what may sound at first like a cliché—that it will be the world's poorest and most vulnerable who will be most affected by climate change—seems the simple truth of the matter. Thus, organizations like the International Food Policy Research Institute (IFPRI), the FAO, WFP and the Asian Development Bank have conducted and published numerous country and topical studies for South Asia and sub-Saharan Africa, the areas of the world where malnutrition and outright hunger are already rampant, and which have been the focus too of the UN's Millennium Development Goals campaign. Here the goal of halving malnutrition by 2015 seems within reach, but the ultimate aim of eliminating it altogether may be threatened by adverse climate trends.

IFPRI has done detailed climate assessments for Malawi, Niger, Nigeria, Rwanda, Swaziland, Senegal, South Africa, Tanzania, Togo, Uganda, Zambia, and Zimbabwe, among other sub-

A maize farmer in Kenya surveys damage to his crop following unseasonably heavy rains in September 2011. (DAVID BATHGATE/CORBIS)

Saharan African states. In a general assessment of the continent, IFPRI concluded that warming would be greater than the global average rise and that rainfall would decrease in some areas.

Overall, declines in crop yields are expected to be smaller in Africa than in Asia because yields are so relatively low to begin with and fertilizer application is so limited. By the same token, African vulnerability to climate change is higher. There is widespread dependence on rain-fed agriculture in northwestern and northeastern Africa because so many farmers are operating at close to subsidence levels and because so many people generally are very poor.

Ethiopia, in particular, has received special attention as a sensitive case. With four fifths of its population working in agriculture, its economy is especially affected by unusually erratic and extreme rainfall patterns, which will become worse with global warming. The country suffers both frequent droughts and flooding, which besides drowning crops can knock out roads and other infrastructure needed by farmers. Part of the answer, IFPRI suggests, is "rapid development of Ethiopia's hydro-potential, upgrading its road standards, and gradual diversification of the economy away from the more climate-vulnerable sectors."

A notable development associated with climate change in southern Africa is the rapid displacement of savanna by dense wooded vegetation. The thorny plants taking over grasslands represent a threat not only to native species like cheetahs but also to cattle and other livestock raised for food.

In Asia and South Asia broadly, water flow is an issue in the great river valleys where rice, wheat and soybeans are cultivated. Aquaculture is at risk in some of the region's huge deltas, where saline intrusion and storm damage are chronic issues. In Indonesia, for example, a temperature rise of 1°C by 2030 is expected to have a negative impact on the economy generally, especially on soybean and rice production. In China's Yellow River valley, which has one of the highest rates of water withdrawal of any major river in the world and has suffered from drought in the central Asian highlands for many years, climate change is expected to produce huge water shortages in the next decade. A model developed by IFPRI shows that "large food-producing regions, such as the Yellow River Basin, can strongly impact international food prices."

South Asia, due to its chronic poverty and malnutrition, is generally at high risk, with Bangladesh being the extreme case. Situated at the head of the world's largest delta, where the Ganges, Brama-

A new rice variety that can grow in salt water is being developed at the International Rice Research Institute (IRRI) in the Philippines, February 2011. (CHERYL RAVELO/ REUTERS/CORBIS)

putrea and Meghna converge in the Bay of Bengal, the country is notoriously vulnerable to cyclones; in the 1970s, Cyclone Bhola took a half million lives.

Thus, rising oceans represent a huge issue for the country, and not only because of saline intrusion affecting agriculture; as many as 40 million people could be driven from their homes and end up refugees. The Bangladeshi agricultural sector consists to a great extent of tiny holdings, which are farmed extremely intensively, with annual double cropping that is tightly geared to the cycles of dry and rainy seasons (the kharif, pre-kharif and rabi). The FAO projects that warming will increase the probability of dry years, with water flows decreasing in the Ganges, Brahmaputra and Meghna by 27%, 21% and 15%, respectively, by 2050. "In the drought-prone areas [of the West] where there are mostly subsistence farmers, the average farm size is less than 0.4 hectare. Reduced yield levels due to temperature increase and frequent dry spells may lead to decline in household coping strategies."

Of course not all the effects of climate change will be so negative. In Asia, as in Africa, there are cases where the anticipated impacts are ambiguous or even positive. A report from the Asian Development Bank suggests that in Vietnam's Mekong Delta, where a huge fraction of the world's marketed shrimp originate, increased freshwater flow may actually reduce dry-season salinity.

Though storm surges associated with monsoons could be larger, computer projections show only modestly higher water levels during surges.

'No regrets'

What is to be done? As the world contemplates all the ways food security will be affected by climate change, the natural and common-sense approach is to devise mitigating measures independently of how much the world warms in the next decades. This has been the first impulse generally since the 1980s when it became widely apparent that climate change could turn out to be a serious problem. It is a policy approach that usually goes by the name of "no regrets" or "low regrets." In essence, even if climate change should turn out to be not such a serious problem after all, the mitigating measures taken will have been worthwhile in their own right.

Much of what falls under that heading is straightforward and, by and large, not new under the sun: Crop diversification, so as to avoid excessive dependence on any one crop that could be vulnerable to drought or flood; co-development of forest and pasture, so that livestock are shaded and grasslands retain water; zero- or low-tillage farming, to reduce the escape of carbon dioxide from soils into the atmosphere; continued development of new crop strains that will be more resistant to heat, dryness or inundation; soil conservation and rehabilitation, by means of terracing, strip cropping, planting of tree shelterbelts and growing grass atop land vulnerable to erosion.

Somewhat more controversial or contested are objectives connected with "food sovereignty," a notion developed within the framework of the distributionist approach to food security, largely in reaction to the perceived excesses of globalization. Go into a grocery store in Peru today and you may find only imported grains, not quinoa, on the shelves because quinoa has become a fashionable food among the well-off, and the local indigenous people can no longer afford what is now a luxury. You may have the same kind of experience if you go looking for virgin olive oil in a Palermo supermarket. The basic impulse in the food sovereignty movement is to protect native ways of life, including native diets. One strand, which goes by the name Via Campesina, defines itself as a peasant movement opposing what one might call today's globalized enclosures movement—the trend toward ubiquitous commercial agriculture, with large foreign investors buying up land, often for scaled-up monoculture.

Easily the most controversial issues dividing productionists and distributionists have to do with agricultural trade and markets. As in the 18th century, today's productionists tend to see marketization and trade as the right way to boost production and drive technological improvement. Meanwhile, distributionists worry about the negative cultural and dietary effects of commercialization and emphasize the desirability of achieving greater food security by means of aggressive domestic reform.

An exemplary case is the quite successful food and nutrition program Brazil inaugurated in 2003. It involved direct support to small farmers, stabilization of food prices, a minimum wage that doubled in the 1990s and again in the first decade of this century, and public procurement of food for distribution to the needy, one third of it coming from family farms. An especially valuable component, in the assessment of Walter Baethgen, leader of the Latin America and the Caribbean program at Columbia University's International Research Institute for Climate and Society, has been insurance. The segura safra, or "safe crop," guarantees the small farmer, who ordinarily is fearful of investing in new technology or expensive inputs, an income during weather disasters such as a drought so that he or she will not be wiped out in a weather disaster. Larger commercial farmers get insured only if they pass muster in terms of certain designated management standards.   ∎

Food disaster scenarios

It is clear that global institutions have begun to assess what the incremental effects of climate change on local and regional agricultural systems will be, and to help prepare for both a gradual worsening of conditions and local disasters. But what if in a single growing season or two consecutive seasons there were to occur something like a Hurricane Sandy, a drought in the U.S. plains states, dessicating winds in Russia, and devastating flooding in one of the great rice-growing areas in, say, Indonesia, Vietnam or China?

This may seem like an obvious question, but it is one that development aid specialists and policymakers are only just now starting to think about. Thus, a major report issued in March by the IPCC, "Managing the Risks of Extreme Events and Disasters to Advance Climate Change Adaptation," largely confines itself to consideration of the usual incremental changes and advocates the customary low-regrets policies. It does not mention, let alone discuss, a scenario in which an abrupt change in the climate produced a global-scale food emergency.

By the end of this century, according to the IPCC, what is now the hottest day may occur every two years twenty years from now. Once in 20 heavy rainfall might happen twice as often, and there will be drier weather in southern Africa, northeast Brazil, central Europe, central North America and in the Mediterranean. "Actions that range from incremental steps to transformational changes are essential"; but the best for now would be "actions that offer development benefits in the relatively near term, as well reductions in vulnerability over the long term."

Abrupt, drastic changes in climate are well documented, as has been discovered from recovered ice borings in Greenland and Antarctica. So why did the IPPC group responsible for the climate risks report not address sudden, large-scale extremes? According to one eminent scientist who played a leading role in formulating the report, the group's main objective was to get the climate change and climate adaptation communities together, figure out how individuals and communities will be affected, and come up with some constructive reactions. As for the larger question, "you're at the emergence of a new field," he said, and at present "the [scientific] literature is not deep on the large-scale [climate] interactions." The report was just "a first step."

When the same questions were put to a top specialist at a major international lending agency, his immediate reaction was to say, "Funny you should ask." He left the distinct impression that he had just been told to start worrying about the question.

'Nonlinearities'

One can only speculate why so little has been said in pubic on the subject of catastrophic climate change and the global food emergency. The most obvious reason, hinted at above, is that almost by definition, the unpredictable is hard to study scientifically. "We don't know anything about the nonlinearities in the system, and so surprising events are to be expected," said Jerry M. Mellilo, a senior scientist at the Woods Hole oceanagraphic laboratory, speaking at an event last September inaugurating Columbia University's new Agriculture and Food Security Center. Mellilo referred to all the variables in the climate system that are complex functions of each other.

Another reason for inattention to the dangers of a global food crisis —and one that has dogged the climate debate from the beginning—has to do with an understandable reluctance to worry about remote possibilities when there are so many urgent human tragedies that require immediate attention. Why worry about a future world food shortage when half the children under five years of age in today's South Asia suffer from stunted growth because of malnutrition?

The single most important reason is that many people believe it is simply implausible that the world could suddenly run out of staple crops. In fact, the world's food supplies are more diverse than one might suppose, and under normal circumstances, most of the great food-consuming nations are largely self-sufficient. When one thinks of world food one is likely to think first of the Eurasian steppe, the U.S. great plains, and the great river valleys of China, South Asia and the Middle East.

A porter moves a bag of flour onto a truck at a wholesale market in Beijing in July 2013. China's wheat crop suffered severely from frost in the growing period and from rain during the harvest. The resulting import demand could cause China to overtake Egypt as the world's top buyer. (JASON LEE/REUTERS/CORBIS)

But there is much more to it than just that.

When it comes to the three great staples—wheat, rice and corn (maize)—there are large numbers of significant producers. While the biggest producers are big indeed, they are far from the only game in town. China tops the list for both wheat and rice, but the next nine producing countries combined produce three times as much wheat and twice as much rice as China does. In maize, the U.S. position is more truly dominant: It produces about as much as the next nine combined.

To look at those numbers in just a little more detail, India is the next-greatest producer of both wheat and rice after China. Russia and the U.S. usually produce about the same amount of wheat yearly, with France next; Austria, Canada, Germany, Kazakhstan and Pakistan are roughly equivalent. In rice, Bangladesh, Burma, Thailand and Vietnam are all major producers, and the latter three are top exporters.

In terms of self-sufficiency, rice is arguably the world's most important single staple: In the countries where it dominates diets, most people eat it all the time and little else by comparison. So it is perhaps no surprise that such countries see to it that they have more than enough. In normal years, production of rice far exceeds consumption in China, India, Indonesia, Bangladesh and Vietnam.

Agricultural self-sufficiency is well known to have been one of the principal objectives of the Communist Revolution in China.

Thus, as the agricultural economist Rajeev Patel conceded in an April 2008 blogpost, East Asian rice was scarcely affected by the global food crisis at that time:

In China, the prices are barely up at all, and they're lower than last year….This compared to a 200% increase in the Philippines over the same period. South Korea is opening its grain reserves to keep prices down. Japan isn't suffering at all… What distinguishes all three of these countries from others in Asia? First, they have their own domestic production. Second, they augment do-mestic production with domestic grain reserves. Third, they're only able to do this because they're aggressive and powerful negotiators in international trade agreements.

But one should not suppose that the big staples growers are always producing more than they need, that food stocks are being accumulated and maintained, and that in the event of a severe shortfall in one region, countries in other regions would come to the rescue.

World food stocks

A disconcerting development in recent years has been the erosion of global food reserves. Charts illustrating total global production and consumption of the major staples show that after many decades of production being comfortably higher than consumption, the two curves now track each other very closely.

Lester R. Brown, the president and founder of the Earth Policy Institute in Washington, D.C. (and the former founding president of Worldwatch), has been following the trend closely. A generation ago, says Brown, the FAO recommended we have 70 days of "carryover stocks"—the amount of stockpiled food still available when the next harvests begin. The world used to have around 100 days of carryover; the latest number is 68. Brown thinks it should be about 110. "We are only one harvest away from chaos in world food markets," says a slide accompanying the release of his recent book, *Full Planet, Empty Plates*.

Yet "the idea of an international grain stock has never really got much traction," Brown observes, and "there never has been a sincere effort by the international community to develop a grain reserve." As an agriculture official in President Lyndon Johnson's administration, Brown had direct experience with the logistical problems that arise in transporting food to where it is urgently needed, such as during a failure of the Indian monsoon in 1965.

During World War II, to take an even more telling Indian example, there was an acute famine in Bengal, in which millions died of starvation. Amartya Sen personally experienced it, and it is an event sometimes adduced to support his claim that famine arises from distribution-system breakdowns. It is important, though, to be clear what kind of distribution problem it was. In a recent book, science writer Madhusree Mukerjee has shown in detail that the decisive factor was a top-level decision in the British government that it was more important to war morale to keep feeding the English at the levels they expected than it was to prevent starvation and death in Bengal.

The moral of the story is clear: In the event of a global food shortfall, those with the greatest resources will see to their own interests first, regardless of where the most dire problems are. Staples will get to where they are most urgently needed only if there is some agreed-upon procedure or mechanism that guarantees it.

Policy options

The first and most obvious thing the U.S. can do to address climate change and food security is reduce its own greenhouse gas emissions. To that end, President Barack Obama has used his executive authority to the fullest. As spelled out in his 2013 Climate Action Plan and Georgetown University speech, he has strongly discouraged electricity generation by existing dirty coal-fired plants, sharply increased fuel efficiency standards for cars and trucks, and encouraged zero-carbon and low-carbon energy, from wind and solar to nuclear.

He has also largely embraced the revolution in unconventional natural gas (fracking), which has been the main factor responsible for the decline in U.S. emissions since 2007.

Arguably, however, the U.S. needs to put itself behind a global program of agreed-upon greenhouse gas reductions as it looks ahead to the next major climate conference, which will be in Paris in December 2015. At the last such conference, in Copenhagen in December 2009, the president and his secretary of state helped derail the Kyoto program of mandatory cuts as Kyoto became a "dirty word" in U.S. politics, as the EU commissioner for the environment, Stavros Dimas, put it.

But they joined with others in endorsing the underlying Kyoto principle of cuts based on "common but differentiated responsibilities." Whether the president and his new secretary of state will be able to deliver on that pledge at the end of 2014 will depend in no small part on the outcome of the November 2014 midterm elections.

Another outcome of the December 2009 Copenhagen meeting was a pledge on the part of developed countries to provide poor countries with billions of dollars to address climate change.

Not surprisingly, that promise has so far remained largely unfulfilled. But with the risks of incremental climate change climbing higher in global consciousness, the time is ripe for such funds to be made available to help fortify agriculture and prepare for emergencies. Coming up with the money would of course immeasurably improve prospects for getting less-developed countries behind whatever program emerges in Paris.

To a great extent, dilemmas in world food security arise from fundamental trends about which little can be done at a high political level: population growth; the rising share of grain-intensive meat in diets, and—not least—the inevitability of global warming itself, however great the efforts. But some aspects of the situation are policy-sensitive, notably the immensely controversial subject of genetically modified foods (GMO), and synthetic foods.

Regarding GMO, in this writer's view, they have a vital role to play in the development of hardier, higher-yield and more nutritious crops. As the editors of *Scientific American* put it in a recent special issue about food, "We have been tinkering with our food's DNA since the dawn of agriculture."

GMO is a technology that already has delivered enormous benefits to people in developing countries, and promises more. "Recently published data from a seven-year study of Indian farmers show that those growing a genetically modified crop increased their yield per acre by 24% and boosted profits by 50%. These people were able to buy more food—and food of greater nutritional value—for their families."

President Barack Obama wipes perspiration from his face as he speaks on climate change at Georgetown University in Washington, DC, June 25, 2013. (CHARLES DHARAPAK/AP/CORBIS)

One thing GMO cannot help with much is preparation for a global-scale agricultural emergency. GMO can help make global production of food much larger, but at whatever level food is being produced and consumed, there will remain the glaring issue of what to do if suddenly there is not nearly enough to go around at the level people have become accustomed to. Here, synthetic foods may have a role to play.

The whole subject of artificial food is a more serious one than one might have supposed when reports appeared last year that scientists had come up with a ludicrously expensive synthetic hamburger. As described in a recent special issue of *IEEE Spectrum* about what a skeptic might call "fake food," many publicly and privately supported R&D organizations are pursuing ambitious work. Especially where creation of international food reserves are concerned, artificial food could make a contribution. One reason why reserves are so low is because grains and rice are difficult and expensive to store for long periods of time.

Question of reserves

With regard to the establishment of some kind of reserves system both to stabilize food prices and to release in the event of major supply crisis, the U.S. has played a singular role in the

past and may do so again in the future. Partly because of New Deal agricultural support policies throughout the period following World War II, the U.S. consistently produced much more grain than consumed, and there was always land available for growing more if needed. In Europe, where government policies favored maintenance of strong agricultural economies and preservation of the small and medium farmer, there also was excess capacity.

In the past few decades, farm subsidy programs came under sharp attack both from the free trade and Third World agriculture advocates and drew attention to the ways such programs put the poor country farmer at a disadvantage. The trend in the U.S. has been to phase out traditional farm subsidies—only to bring back subsidies in the form of biofuels programs.

A constructive approach would be for the world's biggest producers and exporters of staple crops to reach a formal or informal understanding about the maintenance of reserves and how they would be released and distributed in a world food emergency. The U.S. and countries in Latin America both have central roles to play here. Argentina is a major exporter of grains, and Brazil of soybean; smaller countries like Paraguay, Uruguay and even Bolivia are significant, too. ∎

✔ **Don't forget to vote! www.greatdecisions.org/ballot**

discussion questions

1. Natural disasters such as droughts, fires and extreme weather changes often lead to changes in the global economy such as increased food prices. What specific political steps can be taken to minimize the dangers associated with food scarcity and increased food prices?

2. How can organizations that deal with climate change help place climate considerations at the forefront of foreign policy agendas, not only in the U.S., but elsewhere? Are some countries more inclined to focus their agendas on food and climate issues? If so, why?

3. Factors such as population growth place a strain on global food security. How effective is it to rely on strategies such as genetically modified foods? What role do genetically modified foods play on a political level? Is a reliance on genetically modified foods a sensible option for dealing with crises and food emergencies?

4. In the 2009 Copenhagen conference developed countries pledged to provide poorer countries with resources to combat climate change. To what extent should the U.S. make this aid a priority? What is the most effective way to deliver climate change aid?

5. Increased urbanization and a population of an estimated 8.1 billion by 2030 are some aspects that governments need to deal with. In what ways do these factors relate to climate change, and what consequent strains would be placed on governments?

suggested readings

"The Age of Plenty: Technology Will Let Us Feed 10 Billion People," **IEEE Spectrum Magazine**, 2013. A special issue of the *IEEE Spectrum* magazine. Especially relevant are the articles about the "industrial revolution in genetics" and "fake meat."

Diamond, Jared. **Collapse: How Societies Choose to Fail or Succeed.** New York: Penguin Group, 2005. 608 pp. $18.00 (paper). Jared Diamond's follow-up to his Pulitzer-Prize winning book *Guns, Germs and Steel* explores how climate change and population explosion have caused the collapse of societies in the past and what it means for civilization today.

Klare, Michael. **The Race for What's Left: The Global Scramble for the World's Last Resources**. Picador, 2012. 320 pp. $17.00 (paper). Michael Klare argues that the greatest task of this coming century ought to be radically altering our consumption patterns.

Lomborg, Bjorn. **Cool It! The Skeptical Environmentalist's Guide to Global Warming**. New York: Alfred A. Knopf, 2007. 304 pp. $14.95 (paper). GREAT DECISIONS IN FOREIGN POLICY 2014 guest Bjorn Lomborg argues that the focus ought to be on more cost-effective strategies like investing in green energy research and development rather than attempting today's ineffective and expensive solutions.

"Managing the Risks of Extreme Events and Disasters to Advance Climate Change Adaptation," **Intergovernmental Panel on Climate Change (IPCC)**, March 2013. 582 pp. (PDF). This is an indispensable first authoritative assessment of the subject. Like all such IPCC assessments, it is extremely cautious and conservative, sticking closely to what can be scientifically predicted with high confidence.

Mukerjee, Madhusree, **Churchill's Secret War: The British Empire and the Ravaging of India During World War II**. New York: Basic Books, 2010. 368 pp. $16.99 (paper). An important case study of what happened in one major international food supply emergency.

Pooley, Eric. **The Climate War: True Believers, Power Brokers, and the Fight to Save the Earth**. New York, NY: Hyperion, 2010. 496 pp. $27.99 (hardcover). An insider's guide to the scientists, activists and politicians in the U.S. who are shaping the climate change dialogue.

Turral, Hugh, Burke, Jacob, and Faurés, Jean-Marc. **Climate Change, Water and Food Security.** Rome: Food and Agriculture Organization (FAO), 2011. 174 pp. Free (PDF). Perhaps the most alarming of the authoritative studies on climate change and food security.

TO LEARN MORE ABOUT THIS TOPIC AND TO ACCESS WEB LINKS TO RESOURCES GO TO www.greatdecisions.org

China's foreign policy
by David M. Lampton

Chinese President Xi Jinping (center front), who is also the chairman of the Central Military Commission and general secretary of the Communist Party of China Central Committee, reviews an honor guard on the aircraft carrier, the Liaoning, *in northeast China's Liaoning Province, Aug. 28, 2013.* (LI GANG/XINHUA/EYEVINE/REDUX)

This is a "good news-bad news" story. The People's Republic of China (PRC) is becoming a more normal country in foreign policy terms.

Integrating into the world, the Middle Kingdom is often constrained by global norms and the practices of international organizations, the forces of economic and ecological interdependence, and the need to address threatening transnational challenges that only can be effectively tackled through cooperation. Like other countries, China jealously guards its sovereignty, its leaders find legitimacy in nationalism, and Beijing's foreign policy elite sometimes responds to immoderate domestic public opinion. The PRC foreign policy elite, as elsewhere, must juggle the contending foreign policy ambitions of divergent turf-conscious bureaucracies at home and fight off domestic contenders who may wish to replace them. And finally, Chinese leaders are captive of global technological developments they cannot control but to which they must respond. In these respects China is a normal state; however, being "normal" is a mixed blessing. Being a normal state means that policies often are incon-

sistent with one another and that conflict is built into the making of foreign policy at home and its execution abroad.

What is one to make of Chinese foreign policy in the era of Xi Jinping, China's first-among-equals leader installed at the 18th Party Congress of November 2012? Compared to his predecessor, President and General Secretary Hu Jintao, Xi seems to have wrapped his arms around power promptly, as dramatically indicated by the policy changes he initiated in November 2013 at the party's central committee meeting, the Third Plenum. Among those changes was the creation of a National Security Council that promises to

DAVID M. LAMPTON, *at the Johns Hopkins University School of Advanced International Studies (SAIS), is Hyman Professor, Director of China Studies, and Director of SAIS—China. Dr. Lampton formerly was president of the National Committee on U.S.-China Relations and is author of the new book entitled* Following the Leader: Ruling China, from Deng Xiaoping to Xi Jinping *(University of California Press, 2014). The author wishes to thank SAIS Ph.D. student Amanda Kerrigan for her comments on drafts of this piece and her research assistance.*

7

be powerful, though its full scope and mandate were initially murky. Nonetheless, Xi is saddled with many of the same foreign policy challenges and inconsistencies apparent in Hu Jintao's latter years. What are they? What accounts for them?

Inconsistency in Chinese foreign policy can be seen along several dimensions. On the one hand, President and General Secretary Xi Jinping talks about "a new type of major-power relationship" with the U.S., a relationship built on "mutual respect and win-win cooperation" rather than the very zero-sum thinking that leads to conflict or even war. Yet the very zero-sum thinking Xi decries has made its appearance in a very big way. Xi finds his country locked into a friction-laden relationship with Japan and the Philippines over rocks and atolls in the South and East China seas. The U.S. has complex security commitments to these allies and conceivably could be dragged into conflict. Beijing also decries North Korean nuclear and missile tests but often recoils from strong-arming its small wayward neighbor to cease activities inimical to core PRC interests. While Chinese leaders recognize that the Soviet Union fell in part because it got into a terminally expensive arms race with the U.S., Beijing is still participating in the early stages of an action-reaction cycle with Washington featuring nuclear force modernization, anti-satellite weapons, stealth aircraft, cyber capabilities, maritime power projection and moving robustly into space.

This, in turn, energizes China's neighbors to seek security by strengthening their own militaries and by finding room under the American security umbrella. Both options run counter to the overriding PRC interest of securing a peaceful external environment to provide breathing space for the primary and long-term task of domestic economic, social, and perhaps eventually political modernization. Given these divergent tendencies, how can we understand the drivers of Beijing's foreign policy in the second decade of the 21st century and beyond?

Beijing's behavior springs from its ever-changing domestic society and politics, an increasing economic, military and diplomatic muscle, and a changed international environment. Further, citizens of the PRC are acting in the world, but the party-state elite does not and cannot govern all their activity.

China's leadership projects an image of lockstep uniformity—diversity is one person on the seven-person Politburo Standing Committee wearing a blue tie while the six others sport red ties with their dark suits. Nonetheless, Chinese foreign policy is made against the backdrop of deep intellectual, organizational, regional, economic, societal and leadership divisions. The outside world faces a deeply conflicted China, one that is uncertain how to measure its power, weigh interests, and control its citizens and economic entities, as well as deal with neighbors, powers at greater distance, and failed states. It might be easier to deal with a PRC less internally divided, a China that spoke with fewer voices.

Only since the beginning of the 21st century has Beijing achieved anything approaching global reach. The PRC increasingly has energy and commercial stakes in far-flung areas of the world where it scarcely had been present 20 years ago, putting its citizens and its investments in some of the riskiest, most troubled places on earth. In 2010 it was estimated that 847,000 PRC citizens worked abroad. Private Chinese gold miners in Ghana in 2013, bankrolled by families, villages and companies from Guangxi, Zhejiang and hard-scrabble provinces throughout mainland China,

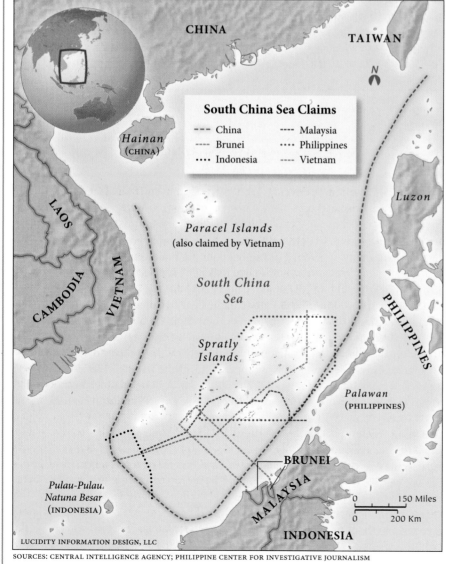

South China Sea Claims

- - - China
- - - Brunei
···· Indonesia
---- Malaysia
···· Philippines
---- Vietnam

CHINA

TAIWAN

Hainan (CHINA)

Luzon

LAOS

CAMBODIA

VIETNAM

Paracel Islands (also claimed by Vietnam)

South China Sea

Spratly Islands

PHILIPPINES

Palawan (PHILIPPINES)

BRUNEI

MALAYSIA

Pulau-Pulau Natuna Besar (INDONESIA)

INDONESIA

0   150 Miles
0   200 Km

LUCIDITY INFORMATION DESIGN, LLC

SOURCES: CENTRAL INTELLIGENCE AGENCY; PHILIPPINE CENTER FOR INVESTIGATIVE JOURNALISM

for example, can create international problems. Chinese miners' rapacious efforts to make money affect Ghanaian workers and environment, thereby negatively impacting China's relations with Ghana, not to mention the PRC's global image. Additionally, significant numbers of Chinese citizens have been killed, kidnapped and/or tortured in such far-flung locations as Pakistan, Ethiopia, Sudan, Libya, the Niger River Delta, Egypt, Zambia and Afghanistan. China is torn between its instincts to promote employment for citizens abroad, protect its people and interests overseas when threatened, and its fear of entanglement in conflicts it may not understand and can ill afford. Beijing also is guided by an American lesson: It is easier to get into trouble abroad than get out of it.

In short, Chinese foreign policy can be understood by the same generic considerations and ambivalences affecting other big powers. While this observation has its reassuring aspects, it means

New members of the Standing Committee of the Politburo, Xi Jinping, Zhang Gaoli, Liu Yunshan, Zhang Dejiang, Li Keqiang, Yu Zhengsheng and Wang Qishan, are introduced in Beijing, November 15, 2012. With the exception of Wang Qishan, each member wears a red tie. (ADRIAN BRADSHAW/EPA/CORBIS)

that managing the U.S.-China relationship is becoming ever more complicated as Beijing and Washington increasingly rub up against each other in air, space and cyberspace, on the high seas, and on land at the world's four

corners. All this notwithstanding, intelligent policy toward the PRC, and vice versa, can help shape a more hopeful and productive future. The U.S.-China relationship can be managed, but it will be far from easy. ■

China's foreign policy and the U.S. response

The years 2009–10 were troublesome for Beijing's foreign policy. Many neighbors and more-distant powers raised the question of whether or not growing Chinese power was fully consistent with their own interests, not least security. Anxieties had been evident in the preceding few years, but markedly increased in 2009–10.

The skill with which Chinese foreign policy had been executed from 1979, when full diplomatic relations were established between China and the U.S., to 2009 had been notable, in part because China self-evidently had domestic and foreign policy leadership focused on internal economic development, and because Beijing had progressively joined international institutions, including the World Trade Organization (WTO) in late 2001. China made mutually beneficial economic progress while still being relatively weak—a re-

assuring conjunction of developments to ever-suspicious neighbors along China's 14 land borders and other maritime nations in the region. During this three-decade-long period Beijing managed to dramatically increase the nation's comprehensive national power (the sum total of military, economic and diplomatic strength) without dramatically increasing the threat perceptions of either its neighbors or distant powers. China's reformist leader Deng Xiaoping, along with his successor President Jiang Zemin, Premier Zhu Rongji, and their foreign policy adviser Vice Premier and Foreign Minister Qian Qichen, deserve credit as skilled leaders.

Often a rising power triggers anxiety throughout the international system as its strength grows. Beijing largely avoided this pitfall in the first 30 years of reform by: settling most of its land boundary disputes on terms advantageous to each

rival claimant (India being a significant exception, as were some maritime disputes); assuming sovereignty over Hong Kong from the United Kingdom in a basically reassuring way on July 1, 1997; moderating Taiwan policy by progressively moving from talk of "liberation," to "peaceful reunification," to "One Country, Two Systems," to "no independence"; helping to economically stabilize its neighbors in the dark days of both the Asian Financial Crisis (1997–98) and the global financial crisis a decade later; and by becoming the principal export market and trade partner for nearly all its neighbors. By wide margins public opinion in 2013 in Pakistan, Malaysia and Indonesia, for instance, saw China's impact on their economy far more favorably than they viewed U.S. impact.

To be sure, prior to 2009 there were scattered anxieties about aspects of the PRC's growing strength as evidenced

Chinese teenagers walk past the Nanjing Road shopping mall in Shanghai. China has emerged as a critical nation in leading the world out of the worst economic recession of modern times. (Q. SAKAMAKI/REDUX)

by concerns about attempted Chinese acquisition of American firms, such as UNOCAL in 2005; a persistent and sizable imbalance in economic relations between the PRC and the U.S.; Beijing's test of anti-satellite capability in 2007; and, the steady increase in the numbers of short- and medium-range missiles in proximity to Taiwan for a considerable time in the 1990s and beyond. Nonetheless, by and large the growth of Chinese power was viewed with relative equanimity by those near and far for the first 30 years of reform.

In 2009 and 2010, at least three developments contributed to a watershed period in Chinese foreign policy:

■ *Chinese Strength during Economic Crisis:* Following the demise of Lehman Brothers in fall 2008, the prolonged economic stagnation in Japan, the EU, and to a lesser extent the U.S., the major western powers became progressively more concerned that their overall dominance was eroding as the Chinese juggernaut plowed ahead. In November 2008, the U.S. National Intelligence Council declared that: "Owing to the relative decline of its economic, and to a lesser extent, military power, the US will no longer have the same flexibility in choosing among as many policy options." China's comparatively blazing GDP growth—which only dipped to a low of 6.2% in one quarter of 2009, compared to negative growth in the EU, Japan and the U.S. for that entire year—served to raise the specter of a dynamic

economic, diplomatic and military PRC behemoth as Western power eroded and talk of the "decline of the West" became more popular.

■ *An Increasingly Confident China.* A staggering contrast in performance between China and the West produced a more confident PRC leadership and populace, one that felt it no longer needed to be excessively cautious about promoting its interests. In 2009, according to a poll by the Pew Global Attitudes Project, 17% of Americans thought their "national economy was in good shape," while 88% of Chinese had this sentiment about theirs. This optimism may be related to China's demographics. Sixty-five percent of the Chinese population is under the age of 35, born in the reform era, a relatively prosperous and optimistic period. This younger population is less encumbered by the fears and sense of limitation that often constrained their elders. Furthermore, this younger cohort more generally feels a sense of entitlement, both personal and national.

■ *Missteps in Handling Foreign Policy Flare-ups.* Finally, in 2010 Beijing maladroitly handled a series of incidents involving the Association of Southeast Asian Nations (ASEAN) and South China Sea claims; North Korea's apparent use of lethal force against a South Korean naval vessel in March and Pyongyang's flagrant, deadly attack on a South Korean island in November (both of which Beijing seemed

somewhat indifferent to); and a highly charged September East China Sea incident involving a Japanese coast guard vessel being rammed by a PRC boat commanded by a belligerent captain. Each of these incidents and their aftermath was handled by Beijing in a manner that sharply increased the concerns of many neighbors (South Korea, Japan, the Philippines, Singapore, Indonesia, Vietnam, India, Australia and even Malaysia), not to mention the U.S.

Consequently, many of China's more anxious neighbors approached a more receptive Washington seeking security reassurance. Combined with the domestic political rewards of looking tough on China going into a general election year in the U.S., and a widespread (albeit a somewhat exaggerated) sense in Washington that it had paid insufficient attention to Asia during the Bush administration, President Barack Obama initiated his administration's Asia "pivot" (later redubbed "rebalancing") in fall 2011. The pivot relied on several core concepts. As the U.S. disengaged from conflicts in the Middle East and Central Asia, some military, diplomatic and economic resources would become available to augment the U.S. position from Northeast Asia through South Asia. In addition, this region was demonstrably of growing economic, security, diplomatic and intellectual importance, and the U.S. needed to create a stable balance of power in the region. However reasonable and essential to stability, the problems in creating a balance of power are twofold. First, no matter how the pivot was phrased or packaged, the message to Beijing seemed clear—more U.S. power in the region and tighter relations with its traditional allies were principally aimed at offsetting growing PRC strength. Second, Washington's rollout of the plan had a notable military component, even though this overemphasis was adjusted over time to underscore economic and diplomatic engagement. This was done, in part, to correct the initial distortion and in part to deal with budget stringencies and other strategic requirements, which limited what was feasible. ■

The drivers of Chinese foreign policy today

What are the principal drivers of Chinese foreign policy? Addressing this question can lead to better understanding of why China seemingly lost its foreign policy way in 2009–10, what is shaping China's response to America's "rebalancing" policy today, and what to expect in terms of China's future foreign policy.

■ **DRIVER ONE:** *Domestic considerations.* The domestic struggle for power, resources, status and privilege is the soil in which foreign policy grows. Leaders must survive domestic political combat to be around to shape foreign policy. Foreign policy is often a "big stick" one domestic party uses to beat another. Moreover, China has its particular characteristics, not least its national narrative of being humiliated and bullied by other powers in the 19th and 20th centuries, particularly by Japan. The legitimacy of the Chinese Communist Party (CCP) rests considerably on its claim to be the agent of national revival and restored dignity—China "stood up" when the CCP seized power in 1949, as Mao Zedong put it. Today, President Xi Jinping talks about "The China Dream": national revival.

In the intervening years since Deng Xiaoping initiated reform in the late 1970s, there have been important political and social changes affecting Beijing's foreign policy. Though political and procedural rights reform in China has been quite limited, change in the PRC political system has been important. Beyond a more regularized and transparent leadership succession process, a more competitive recruitment process for the bureaucracy, greater diversity and higher education among Communist Party members, and diminished ambitions for social control by the state, fundamental changes have occurred. As PRC leaders have become weaker with respect to each other and with respect to society, society and the bureaucracy have become more com-

Chinese migrant workers labor at the construction site of a real estate project in Zaozhuang, Shandong province, July 2013. (LI ZHONGXIAN/IMAGINECHINA/CORBIS)

plex, fragmented and pluralized, hence, it is harder to produce consensus. Individuals and groups lower in society and government have gained more money, human talent and information with which to pursue their own agendas and with which to resist unwanted central policy initiatives. Although the outside world typically operates under the inaccurate assumption that there is a "China, Inc." pursuing a shared vision in lockstep fashion, the world faces a PRC where leaders exert themselves to ride herd on an evermore fractious society.

Bureaucratic and regional division: Whether or not one should credit the Chinese with inventing bureaucracy, they have had a very large and complex one for a long time. Its Communist party is the size of Egypt's population; its state administrative (cadre) force approximately the size of Syria; and its military numbers 2.3 million, about three times the population of the city and county of San Francisco. China's provinces are bigger than most Europe-

an countries. A Chinese governor would be a national leader in most other places, considering the size of population and land area. Scale matters in China!

With such large organizations and no federal system with a binding constitution, rule of law or an independent judiciary—all combining to grant well-defined powers to subordinate levels, private entities, and social organizations—it is difficult to assure timely formulation of policy, effective implementation, or even for Beijing to know what subordinates are doing. Subordinates conceal and distort information, and too many problems frequently overwhelm the elite. Orders up and down the hierarchy are bent by whoever implements them along the way. Truth be told, the wonder is not that China has problems; it is that it performs as well as it has.

This scale and diversity are reflected in China's foreign policy. The military persistently takes more muscular positions on sovereignty and territorial issues than Beijing's economic, trade and diplomatic establishments. The foreign ministry is constantly at loggerheads with the public and state security bureaucracies over visa requirements and border control. Ministries, commissions, localities and state corporations dominating a particular industry (e.g., autos, financial services and electronics) seek to limit competition from foreigners and other domestic firms, while provinces seeking new investment from abroad in these industries may be far more welcoming. The education and health bureaucracies, the military and the state security apparatus all want more money. Provinces encourage citizens to go abroad in search of jobs and fortune, but the foreign ministry has to clean up the diplomatic and security

inces closest to the Democratic People's Republic of Korea (the DPRK or North Korea), there is little tolerance for North Korean instability. These provinces also have many immigrants from the DPRK who do not want to see their relatives across the Chinese border suffer even more. But they also fear an influx of more refugees and losing their business with the north. For example, businesspersons from the Chinese city of Dandong along the Yalu River in Liaoning Province, in clear view of North Korea, have ventures there. Dandong's city fathers envision their city as a regional economic hub that could eventually include the DPRK. Predictably, such Chinese areas resist putting fierce pres-

group of pundits and opinion leaders. These voices and channels are particularly influential on hot-button issues such as relations with Japan, the U.S., sovereignty (e.g., Taiwan, Tibet, Xinjiang, and the South China and East China seas), and specific occurrences that call into question "national dignity" and security, such as the 1999 lethal and mistaken U.S./NATO bombing of the Chinese Embassy in Yugoslavia.

A considerable amount of information on mass popular sentiments in the PRC can be found in a spring 2013 Pew Global Attitudes Project poll. "Unfavorable" ratings of the U.S. by 53% of the Chinese surveyed are higher than the unfavorable ratings of the U.S. expressed by any other Asian country, except Pakistan. PRC citizens under 30 years of age were almost twice as favorable toward the U.S. as Chinese aged 50 and older. There has been a 34% decline in Chinese popular "approval" of Obama's international policies between 2009 and 2013, presumably reflecting the combined effects of the global economic downturn seemingly catalyzed by the U.S. and the "pivot" several years later. However, these polling numbers were taken prior to two positive developments in mid-2013: a U.S.-China summit in southern California in June and a subsequent set of high-level bilateral dialogues in Washington, DC, in July.

Since the global financial crisis began, world public opinion has increasingly viewed China as a potent geopolitical and economic force in the world. As a result, China feels it is regaining its rightful place in the world. Among the many effects of this is a decrease in PRC patience with what is popularly seen as the inequities of some past international arrangements, whether it be U.S. weapons sales to Taiwan, close-in U.S. naval and air surveillance along the Chinese coast, or Japanese refusal to discuss what Beijing considers to be a dispute over islands in the East China Sea (the Diaoyu/Senkaku) after Japan's then-prime minister Yoshihiko Noda unilaterally changed the situation in fall 2012 by purchasing some of the islands.

In some regions of the world, name-

Chinese protesters shout anti-Japanese slogans in front of the Japanese Consulate in Shanghai, China, on September 14, 2012, after new developments in the Diaoyu/Senkaku islands dispute. (EUGENE HOSHIKO/AP/CORBIS)

problems that fortune hunters create. The creation of China's coast guard by merging previously separate maritime surveillance units, fisheries authorities and customs' anti-smuggling units reflects the fact that previously there were so many PRC maritime organizations operating offshore that it nearly was impossible to supervise what was happening. Indeed, it is precisely this bureaucratic Balkanization and warfare that the newly created National Security Council is designed to address.

Local governments also have divergent needs, desires and interests. In the case of China's three northeastern prov-

sure on Pyongyang. PRC veterans of the Korean War, who fought on the side of the DPRK against the U.S. and South Korea, join these Chinese provinces in their reluctance to strong-arm North Korea. Other Chinese groups see no reason to cooperate with sanctions on North Korea until America quits selling weapons to Taiwan.

Public opinion, the media, and nationalism: Public opinion has become an important consideration shaping Chinese foreign policy. PRC mass domestic opinion is conveyed through the increasingly market-driven Chinese media, the Internet and an emerging

ly Africa and Latin America, China has, for the most part, high favorability ratings. However, in the U.S. and Japan in particular, the PRC's "favorability" rating is much lower, feeding a sense among Chinese citizens of a baseline hostility in the negatively inclined countries. That Xi Jinping made his first forays abroad as president to Africa and Latin America should come as no surprise. Xi did come to the U.S. after, but a visit to Japan any time soon would take political courage. It also is unsurprising that Xi has consolidated his power within the CCP, People's Liberation Army (PLA) and citizenry by taking a tough line against Japan.

The Pew poll reports that 41% of respondents in the 39 surveyed countries considered the U.S. to be the "world's leading economic power" while 34% saw China in this light, rising 14% since 2008. Similarly, "In 23 of 39 nations, majorities or pluralities say China either already has replaced or eventually will replace the U.S. as the top superpower," and youth all over the world have a considerably more favorable view of China than older people. Finally, there has been a 24% drop in the Japanese public's "favorability" rating of China since 2008, which plunged to 5% in 2013. This drop may reflect increased tension with Beijing in the East China Sea, the more assertive leadership of Japanese Prime Minister Shinzo Abe since the end of 2012, China's increased power, and President Xi's determination to be seen as a fierce defender of PRC interests.

In short, it is becoming increasingly difficult for Beijing to pursue policies on hot button issues that run counter to domestic opinion on key issues. Chinese leaders prefer to travel to areas in which they feel welcome and get better press, and where they see themselves making more headway. PRC leaders and the Chinese public alike see no particular reason to put up with perceived indignities of the past. Outsiders may construe this as "nationalism," but one person's nationalism is another's patriotism. Whatever the name, it can lead to a more assertive posture in foreign policy. Countries from North America and Europe, to the Middle East, much

of the Asia-Pacific, and parts of Latin America believe "that China acts unilaterally in international affairs." As the U.S. discovered long ago, to have power is to require choice—to use it, or not. Both create friends and adversaries.

The ideology of realism: Three central ideas are prominent in Chinese thinking with regard to power in international, domestic and personal affairs. First, human beings and states are interconnected in a seamless web of mutual relations and dependency; change in one corner of the network has ramifications for the entire web. Second, the relative power of each nation in this web is reflected in the distribution of benefits and deprivations among countries. The weak get less than the strong. And finally, international life is characterized by ceaseless adjustments in power relationships, and consequently, in the distribution of gains and losses among states—these adjustments can be made through war and conflict, negotiations and discussions, or acquiescence.

This means that the "old," weak China had to put up with things that the "new" and stronger China need no longer endure. Those who have lost strength must accommodate to the new realities. The West may look at agree-

ments and arrangements of the past as nearly immutable, but international politics is much more fluid for Beijing. The PRC is not particularly predisposed to use force to overturn past arrangements, but it will use diplomatic and economic influence to push for adjustments. It will use force if other parties seek unilateral changes to old arrangements disadvantageous to China when, in Chinese eyes, the other party's strength no longer even entitles them to the old arrangement. The weakening Japan of the last decade-plus is not entitled to change the already favorable status quo it enjoyed with respect to the Diaoyu/Senkaku islands to a situation Beijing views as even more disadvantageous to itself.

■ **DRIVER TWO:** *Capabilities, expanding global interests and the action-reaction cycle:* China's capabilities are in part what Chinese people believe them to be, what others believe them to be, and what the nation objectively measures as its material and intellectual strength. No matter how viewed, PRC power—military, economic and intellectual—is growing. As one considers strength, however, do not forget weakness. Beijing's disabilities are substantial: The PRC ranks between 82nd and

Chinese "taikonaut" Zhai Zhigang emerges from a simulated Shenzhou-7 capsule waving a national flag during a parade in July 2012 for the 60th anniversary of the founding of the People's Republic of China. Zhai Zhigang performed China's first spacewalk in 2008. (FEI MAOHUA/XINHUA PRESS/CORBIS)

98th in world per capita GDP, reminding us that with an enormous population, per capita strides are harder to make than national aggregate gains; there are divisive and large regional and urban-rural inequalities, as well as widespread popular resentment of procedural injustice and endemic and large-scale corruption; and society is constantly churning as millions of formerly rural dwellers urbanize annually. The reality is that Chinese leaders are typically preoccupied with the boiling pot at home. Among their greatest fears are what China's then PLA deputy chief of staff for intelligence, Lieutenant General Qi Jianguo, asserted in early 2013: A "Western strategy of penetration and subversion" using "multiple channels, including military deployments, political transformation, economic control, and cultural penetration." A fear, in other words, that truculent foreigners will exploit internal division to weaken China.

Despite these deep-seated anxieties and inhibitions, Beijing's leaders believe their nation is rising while the West is losing dominance, and that the PRC possesses more leverage than ever before in modern times. In the words of General Qi, "The position of U.S. and Western forces is on the decline," reflecting the debilitating consequences of sustained economic slowdown in the West, the U.S.' prolonged wars in the Middle East and South Asia, and the weakening of U.S. allies, most notably Japan. (It remains to be seen what the economic reforms of Japan's Prime Minister Abe may achieve.) PRC leaders and citizens alike are encouraged by, and proud of, the fact that China's space program is making progress, new generations of cruise and other missiles, stealth aircraft and mounting cyber capabilities have appeared, and the nation is fielding ever-larger and more capable naval forces, including nuclear ballistic-missile-carrying submarines and an aircraft carrier, probably only the first of several. The U.S. Department of Defense expressed its view of growing PRC strength and its consequences in a 2013 report to the U.S. Congress concerning PRC military and security developments:

As China's interests have grown and as it has gained greater influence in the international system, its military modernization has also become increasingly focused on investments in military capabilities to conduct a wider range of missions beyond its immediate territorial concerns.... Some of these missions and capabilities can address international security challenges, while others could serve more narrowly defined PRC interests and objectives, including advancing territorial claims and building influence abroad.

On one mission in the summer of 2013, for example, elements of the Chinese Navy circumnavigated Japan for the first time, a source of pride in Beijing and concern in Tokyo.

The problem can be seen from at least one important U.S. viewpoint. PRC capabilities are growing—they could be used for global security and humanitarian missions that are widely endorsed, or they could be employed for less-welcome purposes. Often, as a nation's abilities increase, so do its ambitions and the need to protect far-flung interests. Outsiders cannot be sure how the future will unfold; hence, China's neighbors and the U.S. are inclined to hedge by increasing capabilities and drawing the wagons of treaty allies closer together, all the while seeking to reassure Beijing that it is not ill-intentioned. The Chinese are skeptical and disinclined to be as passive as when they were weaker.

This dynamic, including the ceaseless development of technology, creates an action-reaction cycle in which the new military/technological capabilities of one nation create insecurity among others. Ultimately, one nation's efforts to offset the other's new capabilities trigger an upward spiral of competitive responses—e.g., an arms race—resulting in greater cost and less security for everyone. This is why both the administrations of President Obama and Chinese leader Xi Jinping are currently promoting strategic discussions as part of the annual bilateral Strategic and Economic Dialogue (S&ED) and why both Washington and Beijing are searching for "a new type of major-power relationship" in which conflict is actively avoided and opportunities for cooperation are actively sought. It is also why both are more serious about promoting military-to-military exchanges than under the George W. Bush administration when the Chinese were inhibited by their fear of revealing weaknesses to the Americans. Despite a higher level of engagement, the upward spiral pressures will be hard to contain, a dynamic reinforced by the interests of defense sectors in both nations. U.S. efforts to strengthen anti-ballistic missile defens-

A Chinese Navy ship, the Harbin missile destroyer, arrives in Singapore in September 2013 to resupply after six months of escort missions in the Gulf of Aden. (THEN CHIH WEY/XINHUA PRESS/CORBIS)

es, for example, spur Chinese efforts to develop ways to penetrate those defenses, just as Chinese efforts to develop cyber capabilities threatening to U.S civilian and military infrastructure spur U.S. responses. Tom Donilon, former national security adviser to President Obama, said of the U.S.-China interaction in cyberspace in March 2013:

> *From the President on down, this has become a key point of concern and discussion with China at all levels of our governments. And it will continue to be. The U.S. will do all it must to protect our national networks, critical infrastructure, and our valuable public and private sector property. But, specifically with respect to the issue of cyber-enabled theft, we seek three things from the Chinese side. First, we need recognition of the urgency and scope of this problem and the risk it poses—to international trade, to the reputation of Chinese industry and to our overall relations. Second, Beijing should take serious steps to investigate and put a stop to these activities. Finally, we need China to engage with us in a constructive direct dialogue to establish acceptable norms of behavior in cyberspace.*

■ *DRIVER THREE: Interdependence.* Both economic and ecological interdependence often inject more cooperative elements into ties. Interdependence as a cohesive force was evident, for example, when in February 2009 Secretary of State Hillary Clinton urged China to work together with the U.S. and others to stabilize the world economy in the darkest days of the global financial crisis. "So by continuing to support [buying] American Treasury instruments, the Chinese are recognizing our interconnection. We are truly going to rise or fall together. We are in the same boat and thankfully we are rowing in the same direction," she said. China's own massive domestic economic stimulus of building extensive domestic infrastructure proved of global benefit, providing badly needed economic ballast to the world economy. Given that the U.S. is China's single largest national export market, Beijing had an interest in the health of the American

A Chinese woman on a bicycle waits to cross a street in Beijing in May 2013. Beijing residents often wear face masks due to extreme air pollution in the city. (ANDY WONG/AP/CORBIS)

economy, just as America had an interest in growth in its most rapidly expanding major export market—China.

In terms of the environment, the PRC will be among the hardest hit major powers by sea-level rise and temperature shifts associated with climate change. The Chinese know this. Now the world's largest carbon emitter, China must join with other major emitters, such as the U.S. and India, to make a dent in this challenge. Welcome as major reductions in China's own carbon emissions would be, even hypothetical Chinese improvements are insufficient to protect even the PRC alone, not to mention the rest of the world. This problem can only be effectively addressed through complementary and reinforcing efforts. The same general proposition holds for global health and water issues. Only cooperation among nations can change the fundamental trajectory of transnational problems. Yet the obstacles to effective cooperation are considerable, not least the unwillingness of domestic audiences to reduce their perceived economic welfare in the short run in order to address perhaps more abstract, long-run perils, against the backdrop of uncertainty as to whether others will do their share or instead free ride.

Sadly, interdependence does not invariably ameliorate conflict. Two examples include the fall 2010 Sino-Japanese tussle over the detention of a Chinese

fishing boat captain and the anti-Japan demonstrations in the PRC in 2012–13 in response to Japan's purchase of three disputed islands in the East China Sea. In the first instance, Beijing retaliated against Tokyo by disrupting the export to Japan of rare earths, a critical raw material in the manufacture of IT products, thereby upsetting the global supply chain. This use of economic leverage shocked Japan and other parts of the global supply chain that suddenly viewed the PRC as an unreliable supplier willing to harm innocent bystanders. This ill-advised act also undermined confidence in Beijing because the PRC appeared willing to damage itself by potentially impeding the production of Japanese components that used rare earths, which its own IT assembly and foreign-invested export firms in the PRC needed to import to complete assembly of its exports. It is sobering when a country acts contrary to what one had assumed were its own interests.

The second case concerned China's 2012–13 anti-Japan demonstrations in response to Japan's purchase of three islands. These disturbances damaged Japanese (including Japanese-made, but Chinese-owned) property and ignited popular efforts to boycott Japanese exports to China. This further shook confidence abroad by showing that disputes with Beijing in one domain could metastasize into isolationist and ethni-

This April 1995 aerial photo shows one of the four manned outposts equipped with a satellite dish built by China in the Philippines-claimed Mischief Reef in the disputed Spratly Islands. (ROMEO GACAD/AFP/GETTY IMAGES)

cally charged movements in the PRC. However, Beijing soon curtailed these incidents, sensing how deleterious all this could be to China's own economic interests and global image. In short, interdependence increases the cost of conflict and provides some fences around it once it has broken out, but it does not inoculate against it.

■ *DRIVER FOUR: The international environment.* The Sino-Japanese problems discussed above, along with the action-reaction cycle, are manifestations of another category of factor shaping Chinese foreign policy—the behavior of others in the international system. Often the world acts on China, and China reacts. The Chinese national narrative of being a "victim" or "bullied" for much of the 19th and 20th centuries exacerbates Beijing's tendency to justify its actions as defensive and reactive. Whether one is "assertive" or "defensive/reactive" is usually in the eye of the beholder. The political scientist Andrew Scobell calls this pattern of Chinese thinking and behavior the "Cult of Defense," explaining that it has three dimensions: the "Chinese: (1) are a peace-loving people; (2) are not aggressive or expansionist; and (3) only use force in self-defense."

This PRC narrative leaves out many of the drivers of Chinese policy discussed above, making the explanation for Beijing's behavior almost exclusively a function of what others do to China. Of course, there are many Chinese citizens and analysts who realize that the PRC, like other nations, pursues its national interests and that understanding domestic politics is central to explaining foreign policy. Nonetheless, there is a predisposition in China to see the nation as reacting to the encroachments of others rather than initiating.

In fact, China does react to the initiative of others in many instances. It reacted to: the U.S. ABM program, which could neutralize an unknown fraction of the PRC's nuclear retaliatory capacity; the Philippines' and Vietnam's moves in disputed waters of the South China Sea as Hanoi and Manila also react to Beijing's initiatives there; U.S. surveillance of military installations along the PRC's shorelines, albeit from beyond Chinese territorial waters; and European leaders' meetings with the Dalai Lama, believing that these get-togethers promote separatism in China's unsettled Tibet Autonomous Region. ■

Policy options

Given a China in the circumstances described above and playing an increasingly wide-ranging and important role in the world, and given an America that needs to both shape the global circumstance and simultaneously attend to its increasingly apparent domestic needs, what are some of the policy dilemmas and options facing America's citizens and decisionmakers as they think about the future of U.S.-China relations?

■ The story of China's modernization is the acquisition of increasing ability to project military, economic and intellectual power into domains from which it previously was absent—distant maritime and geographic areas, the global economy, air, space and now cyber-space. The example of America and Britain working out a cooperative, indeed intimate, relationship is a positive historical example of what is possible between two nations with shifting power relations. The 20th-century examples of the U.S. facing a rising Germany and Japan are far darker experiences. What Sino-American policies today could push us along a path that looks more like the former than the latter? In what specific areas is it most critical that the two nations develop shared "rules of the road"? For example, can and should the U.S. and China cooperate to a greater extent in space? Can the two nations develop some limits on their respective cyber activities, at least in the areas of commercial information and the use of cyber attack against civilian targets?

■ PRC leaders have a declining capacity to micromanage their society; domestic bureaucratic and social fragmentation is growing; and civic organizations and businesses are becoming increasingly empowered with information, human talent and money. From a human rights perspective, these developments are positive, but they also have the potential to create disorder if institutions and restraints are not built into the process. What are the most important ways in which the U.S. and others can contribute to the emergence of a humanely governed and rules-based system over the long haul? What actions by the U.S. and other like-minded nations in the world could, at the margins, contribute to strengthening China's burgeoning middle class; further developing legal, judicial, legislative and social organizations where possible; and foster sustainable economic growth in the global economy, of which China is an increasingly central part? In the wake of November 2013's third plenary meeting of China's Central Committee, Beijing's declaration that it intends to move vigorously in the direction of economic and some political reform may offer opportunities for cooperation.

■ Because interdependence is a powerful force for promoting cooperation, as well as sometimes creating conflict, how can Beijing and Washington encourage economic, ecological and energy cooperation as broadly and deeply as possible? For example, to what degree should Chinese direct investment in firms that generate local employment in the U.S. be welcomed? While considering national security concerns is appropriate, how is it possible also to assure that "national security" is not so widely invoked that it halts mutually beneficial transactions? In the same vein, should the U.S. and China proceed as rapidly as possible to reach a Bilateral Investment Treaty (a move given impetus by both sides in 2013), thereby helping ensure the security of investments each makes in the other's country and helping ensure that each does not discriminate against the firms of the other?

■ In terms of free trade and preferential economic areas, should the United States and China, the world's two largest economies, work toward free trade arrangements in which they are both members? It does not foster U.S.-PRC interdependence when China seeks to develop free trade arrangements, such as ASEAN Plus 3, that exclude the U.S., as it has done, or for the U.S. to do likewise, which the Chinese believe Washington was seeking to do with its initial announcement of the Trans-Pacific Partnership (TPP) negotiations in late 2011. Beijing's 2013 announcement that it would push ahead with a China Shanghai Free Trade Trial Zone may signal a new degree of openness in its trading policies. How should the

U.S. respond as China's policies unfold? For its part, the U.S. expression of welcome to China to eventually join the TPP under appropriate conditions is to be commended.

At the same time that military alliances create a sense of added security for members, they also can create anxiety among those who are not. History has created a legacy of five bilateral security treaties involving the U.S. with Japan, the Republic of Korea, Thailand, the Philippines and Australia. These arrangements have contributed to Asia's stability since early in the Cold War era, and they likely will persist for the indefinite future. In this context, what should be the balance between emphasizing the importance of America's alliance relationships and trying to build new security institutions that include China? One possible approach might be a security organization in Northeast Asia, a body that might eventually cover the Korean Peninsula, Japan, China, and the United States, as well as broadening the roles of multilateral forums that already exist.

■ How can the action and reaction process that drives U.S.-China security interactions and arms buildups be mitigated? What should be the mix of hard power acquired by the U.S. and

China, on the one hand, and military-to-military exchange and confidence-building efforts on the other hand? Engagement efforts could include exchanges among service academies of the two nations, crisis and humanitarian emergency cooperation exercises and cooperating in maintaining open sea-lanes as both countries are doing in the Gulf of Aden.

To what extent should each side consider more carefully actions it takes, such as close-in surveillance of the PRC coast by the U.S. and Chinese hacking into American computers, and weigh more prudently the gains and losses of such actions, including the demonstrable ill will created in both societies?

■ To what extent should the U.S. and China base their strategic relationship on the proposition that each nation faces enormous internal challenges, that excessive conflict between the two would sap the capacity of each to achieve domestic development and effective governance, and that the most effective way to be credible abroad is to be moving forward at home? Stated from an American perspective--is an important precondition for effectively dealing with China to put America's domestic house in order? ■

discussion questions

1. To what degree has the character of Chinese foreign policy changed toward more "assertiveness" pre- and post-2009-2010? If it has changed, what accounts for this? If not, what accounts for the external perception to the contrary? Do Chinese foreign policies principally reflect developments inside China or changes in the international environment to which Beijing is responding?

2. Are China and the U.S. in an arms race? What are the trends one can see in this direction and what forces tend to dampen such competition? What should the U.S. and China do to resist impulses toward military rivalry?

3. How can China's comprehensive national power (military, economic, intellectual/diplomatic) be assessed? How do Chinese leaders and citizens assess their own strength? What are the implications of these assessments?

UNKNOWN MILITARY BUDGET, CYBERCRIME, ALWAYS VOTES AGAIN U.S. @ U.N.!

4. What other countries should the U. S. rely on as it attempts to put diplomatic pressure on Iran? What role does the UN play in the Iran nuclear dispute? Is multilateral cooperation necessary? What other countries are concerned by the prospect of a nuclear Iran?

5. How important is public opinion in the formation of Chinese foreign policy? Is it genuine, coming from the PRC citizenry, or is it simply a reflection of prior regime propaganda? Is public opinion salient with respect to a few issues, or does it apply generally across the foreign policy board? What are the mechanisms by which public sentiment affects foreign policy in today's PRC? How can the U.S. or other nations affect public sentiment in China?

6. To what extent has the U.S. "pivot" or "rebalancing" toward Asia inaugurated in late-2011 been a reaction to Chinese moves, as opposed to those of North Korea or simply America's greater interests and opportunities in the region? How have the Chinese understood the "pivot" initially and how do they understand "rebalancing" now? What are the pros and cons of this policy as articulated initially and as it has been adjusted since?

suggested readings

Deborah Brautigam. **The Dragon's Gift: The Real Story of China in Africa**. Oxford: Oxford University Press, 2009. 397 pp. $21.95 (paper). Brautigam provides a balanced answer to the questions of why and how China's presence in Africa is dramatically expanding (albeit from a low base) and what this means for Africa. Part of the author's answer is that Africa needs viable businesses and effective businesspeople and China's involvement in Africa generally contributes to this. Another observation concerns the limited effectiveness of western conditional development assistance and the merits of the Chinese approach of less conditionality. China is in Africa to do business and in so doing has brought net benefit to the continent.

M. Taylor Fravel. **Strong Borders, Secure Nation: Cooperation and Conflict in China's Territorial Disputes**. Princeton, NJ: Princeton University Press, 2008. 376 pp. $37.50 (paper). A detailed account of, and explanation for, China's behavior with respect to maritime and land boundary disputes. Among its core findings are: China generally has not used force in territorial disputes and is more accommodating to rival claimants when it is worried about the PRC's own internal security. Finally, Beijing is more likely to use muscle when it feels that the legitimacy of its claims is being eroded.

David M. Lampton. **Following the Leader: Ruling China, from Deng Xiaoping to Xi Jinping**. Berkeley: University of California Press, 2014. 385 pp. $31.95 (hardcover). A look at Chinese governance and foreign policy through the eyes of Chinese leaders at all levels. Based on 558 leadership interviews since the early 1970s, among other things the volume addresses: Chinese views of the world, governance and leadership, the "nightmares" of leaders, negotiating strategies, and how domestic politics and the policy-making process shape Beijing's foreign policy.

Bobo Lo. **Axis of Convenience: Moscow, Beijing, and the New Geopolitics**. Washington, DC: Brookings Institution Press, 2008. 277 pp. $32.95 (cloth). From the mid-1980s on, Moscow and Beijing have gradually improved relations. This book examines the strengths and limitations of evolving Russia-China ties. Currently Moscow and Beijing seek to use each other to offset American strength, while at the same time each has anxieties about the other. The bottom line is: "Russia and China's chief preoccupations and interests are with the West, not each other."

James Reilly. **Strong Society, Smart State: The Rise of Public Opinion in China's Japan Policy**. New York: Columbia University Press, 2012. 331 pp. $55.00 (cloth). The author describes and explains the careful tightrope that Chinese leaders have thus far navigated in policy toward Japan. Reilly argues that public opinion in China matters and generally has been anti-Japan in character; anti-Japan nationalism is a force that the Chinese party-state seeks to harness to boost legitimacy by providing limited opportunities for political participation to its citizens; and nationalist fervor could run out of control, thereby threatening the Communist Party's grip on power and China's standing abroad.

David Shambaugh. **China Goes Global: The Partial Power**. Oxford: Oxford University Press, 2013. 409 pp. $ 29.95 (cloth). This volume's central points are: China's comprehensive national strength and global reach have grown dramatically in the reform era, but China's actual global influence remains more limited than many think. China has pools of excellence but oceans of problems. In the author's view, it is essential not to overlook China's many remaining disabilities, none greater than Beijing's still anemic soft power. The past strategy of integrating Beijing into the international system has had important successes, but as China gets stronger more effort needs to be expended in working with Beijing to adopt global norms to an ever-larger extent.

TO LEARN MORE ABOUT THIS TOPIC AND TO ACCESS WEB LINKS TO RESOURCES GO TO www.greatdecisions.org

U.S. trade policy
by Michael O. Moore and Robert Maxim

A sailor on the Bahia Castillo, a Hamburg-based refrigerated cargo ship carrying fresh Chilean fruit and other goods signals as it docks at Packer Avenue Marine Terminal, in Philadelphia, PA, in May 2013. (AP PHOTO/MATT ROURKE)

In the wake of World War II, the U.S. played the leading role in establishing a consensus among the world's major democratic powers that greater international cooperation would help prevent future war. A centerpiece of this effort was trade liberalization. Over the next six decades, presidents from both parties supported a commitment to relaxing restrictions on the international flow of goods, services and investment.

The support for trade liberalization has reflected broad agreement among trade policy analysts that economic globalization has been beneficial to the both the U.S. and the world. A wide consensus among economists has held that trade liberalization leads to greater economic prosperity. Foreign policy specialists have believed that greater economic integration reduces the chances for conflict.

However, many in the U.S. public have a starkly different view towards trade policy. U.S. citizens have become increasingly anxious about the future of the American economy. Many fear that a rapidly globalizing economy has diminished the U.S.' position as the world's leading economic power. These skeptics fear that increased integration has hurt average citizens, especially by undercutting millions of U.S. manufacturing jobs and the middle-class existence long associated with them.

This general unease is evident in public surveys about

MICHAEL O. MOORE *is Professor of Economics and International Affairs at George Washington University. Moore's research and teaching focuses on U.S. trade policy, especially adherence to WTO rules and commitments. He was founding director of George Washington University's Institute for International Economic Policy and the masters program in International Trade and Investment Policy. Moore served as a Senior Economist at the White House Council of Economic Advisers in 2002–03.*

ROBERT MAXIM *is a competitiveness and foreign policy research associate at the Council on Foreign Relations in Washington, DC. He holds a BA in international affairs and economics, and an MA in international trade and investment policy, both from the George Washington University. His research interests include international trade, U.S. economic policy, and Internet policy and governance.*

trade policies. For example, many U.S. citizens and advocacy groups continue to voice strong opposition to the North American Free Trade Agreement (NAFTA), a trade pact among the U.S., Canada and Mexico, 20 years after its implementation. Additionally, a broad swath of Americans express growing nervousness about the rise of China as an international competitor. These worries have been exacerbated by the economic convulsions surrounding the "Great Recession" of 2008–09 and its aftermath.

A public opinion poll compiled in November 2010 by NBC and The Wall Street Journal reflects this skepticism: only 23% of the 1,000 adults polled agreed that "free trade" with foreign countries has helped the U.S., while 47% believed that it has hurt the U.S. (NBC/Wall Street Journal). But many citizens do not view trade with every nation identically. A Pew Research Center poll of 1,255 adults, also conducted in November 2010, found that significant majorities supported increased trade with Canada (76%) and the European Union (58%), while only 45% supported increased trade with China. This last result is especially notable; many U.S. citizens fear increased trade with China will result in job losses arising out of "unfair" Chinese practices, including low wages, currency policies, and lax domestic regulations. Moreover, the results suggest that recent trade skepticism is focused especially on competition from lower-income countries rather than richer countries.

The ambivalent attitude about trade evident in the Pew Poll also cuts across demographic lines. Only a minority of Republicans (28%) and Democrats (40%) agreed that that "free trade agreements like NAFTA and policies of the WTO were good for the U.S." Only in families whose incomes were over $100,000 did a larger proportion believe that free trade agreements benefited their own personal finances.

Politicians in both major U.S. political parties regularly offer statements that acknowledge this anxiety, especially during electoral campaigns. Democratic candidate (and later President) Barack Obama promised repeatedly in 2007 and 2008 that upon his election he would "renegotiate" NAFTA since the agreement "on balance" had not been good for America. Mitt Romney, the 2012 Republican candidate for president, argued repeatedly during his campaign that trade with China was "cheating" on its trade commitments and unfairly harming U.S. workers and companies.

However, these sentiments did not first arise with recent economic tumult. A Republican former governor and later president encapsulated such views:

This country will not and can not prosper under any system that does not recognize the difference of conditions [abroad] and in America. Open competition between high-paid American labor and poorly paid [foreign] labor will either drive out of existence American industry or lower American wages.

The speaker? William McKinley, elected president of the U.S. in 1896, who was discussing competition with European workers. While President McKinley may have been worried about the onslaught of "low wage" European workers, today the focus is on China and other developing countries. Nonetheless, the basic concerns are remarkably consistent.

In stark contrast, many in the academic and policy communities have a positive view of international economic integration. They will argue that globalization has led to increased choice and lower prices for American consumers and businesses, even if some face significant dislocation and lower incomes from increased foreign competition. They also claim that integration offers important opportunities for economic growth and high-wage jobs in export-oriented sectors. Secondly, trade policy experts argue that globalization is only partly to blame for stagnant wages and job prospects for some Americans. Massive technological changes, which have occurred simultaneously with increased globalization, have been even more important than international competition in reducing the demand for low-skilled workers and contributing to stagnant middle class wages. Advocates for open markets frequently contend that the U.S. government can do little to thwart the intense pressures from continued globalization, since much of these changes are a result of policy decisions in other countries, rather than recent trade liberalization in the U.S. Moreover, these analysts maintain that global economic integration is a reality, whatever one might think of its costs or benefits.

In short, the divergence between the opinion of "elites" and the broader public on the effects of economic globalization are striking. Candidates from both parties will make statements that nod in the direction of skeptics' worries about trade, but policies have remained notably consistent across the decades. At the same time, public dissatisfaction on U.S. trade policy remains high. This dichotomy reflects a common aspect of policy discussion in the U.S. today: advocates of particular policies often ignore some of the truths in the positions of those that disagree. As will be made clear below, free trade is neither a panacea that brings prosperity and happiness to all nor the source of only disruption and pain to average Americans.

The U.S. open economy

Despite long-standing political pressures from globalization's skeptics, the U.S. economy remains remarkably open to foreign products. Average U.S. tariffs (taxes that importers must pay before bringing goods into the American economy) were around 60% in 1930, but fell to 4% in 1989. By 2011, the average tax on foreign goods was only 1.6%. These changes reflect a critical fact about U.S. trade policy: the vast majority of the United States' increase in openness to foreign goods was largely completed over 35 years ago.

Commercial realities also continue to integrate the U.S. into world markets. U.S. households stretch budgets by purchasing goods made abroad. Cheaper clothing that arrives from garment factories across the world allows lower income Americans to buy needed items such as shirts for work, shoes for children, and winter coats. Inexpensive imported electronic goods such as mobile phones and more advanced "smartphones" not only allow family members to stay in touch with relatives and summon emergency help in remote locations, but have also spawned countless new business ventures that take advantage of an interconnected world. But it is not just final consumers heading to the shopping mall who benefit from high quality and inexpensive foreign goods. U.S. manufacturing firms increasingly rely on imported inputs to compete in international markets. For example, U.S. automobile firms, which struggled with the industry's near complete collapse in 2008 and 2009, depend on imported auto parts to stay competitive with foreign automakers. Imported steel, a critical input in manufacturing processes, finds its way into construction projects that create jobs for carpenters, welders and plumbers or into automobiles assembled in the U.S. Exotic metals such as titanium, sourced from abroad, help Boeing build the most advanced civilian aircraft in the world. Low-cost computers, assembled in other countries, have revolutionized workplaces and homes across the U.S.

Despite these clear benefits, global competition causes enormous disruptions to individual workers, companies and communities. During its heyday in the 1960s, the U.S. automobile industry, dominated by the Big Three (GM, Ford and Chrysler), directly employed tens of thousands of well-compensated workers and supported hundreds of thousands of other jobs in related industries. From the 1980s forward, many of these jobs were lost, with the rise of intense new competition from Japanese and European automakers. Similar international pressures occurred in other manufacturing industries such as steel, footwear, textile and apparel.

The reduction in employment in these sectors is key to understanding the anxiety that many Americans feel toward globalization. In many Americans' minds manufacturing jobs are synonymous with middle-class opportunity. Indeed, the industrial expansion of the U.S. economy from the mid-19th century to the mid-20th century resulted in high paying jobs for multiple gen-

erations of American workers, many of whom only had modest specialized skills.

In recent decades, millions of such manufacturing jobs have disappeared. In 1970, 31% of private sector employment was in manufacturing. By 2008 (just prior to the Great Recession) manufacturing jobs were only 11.7% of private sector employment. As recently as 2000, 17.3 million U.S. workers were employed in manufacturing. By 2012, this had fallen to 11.9 million employees. Much of this contraction has occurred as the U.S. economy has become more globalized. As a result, many citizens point to imports and job "outsourcing" to low-wage countries such as Mexico and China, facilitated by trade agreements, as the principal reasons for this drop in manufacturing sector opportunities.

The focus on job losses in import-competing sectors often ignores a critical fact: technological change has resulted in turmoil in the labor market as well, often as a direct result of dramatically increased productivity. One reflection of this is the increased use of

advanced technology in manufacturing: many jobs once performed by Americans workers are now performed by robots. Today manufacturing output is over two and a half times its 1972 level in constant dollars, even though manufacturing employment has dropped by 33%. In fact, during the wave of outsourcing from 1997 to 2008, the value of U.S. manufacturing output actually increased by one third, to $1.65 trillion, thanks to the strongest productivity growth in the industrial world.

Critics also point to U.S. trade deficits as another piece of evidence that the free trade policies are hurting the American economy. In 2012, American consumers and businesses imported $2.3 trillion worth of foreign manufactured goods, compared to $1.5 trillion of U.S. goods exports. Moreover, this trade deficit has persisted for decades.

The pressures to act to mitigate import competition have sometimes led political leaders to "do something" to limit the pressures. However, one critical aspect for readers to recall is that the U.S. increased its openness to international competition many decades

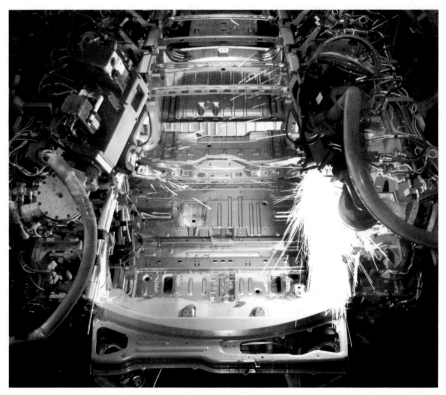

A crossover SUV vehicle is welded by robot arms as it goes through the assembly line at the General Motors Lansing Delta Township Assembly Plant in Lansing, Michigan in March 2010. (BILL PUGLIANO/GETTY IMAGES)

ago. Most of the change in the last 35 years has come from changes in other countries' domestic policies toward integration into the global economy. For example, Mexico maintained very high barriers to foreign goods and had significant policy restraints on U.S. and other foreign investment prior to 1986, which was part of a policy of "import substitution" that focused on growing Mexican firms at the exclusion of multinational corporations. After 1986, Mexican policies dramatically opened the country to foreign investment, which in turn allowed U.S. firms to consider channeling investment to Mexico. In short, most of the opportunities for U.S. firms to move to Mexico have not been because the U.S. government changed policies, but instead because Mexico adopted a more open attitude toward integrating their economy into the world. This pattern has been repeated across the developing world. This is a critical point since it means that it may be

difficult for U.S. politicians to fundamentally change the opportunities for offshoring and the intensity of foreign competition.

Concrete examples help illustrate some of the economics surrounding globalization. Conventional wisdom about trade can often be summed in the following: imports are bad because they result in a loss of jobs, while exports are good because they create jobs. This view, which goes by the moniker of "mercantilism," would suggest that restricting foreign imports would help the U.S., and increasing U.S. exports should result in unambiguous benefits. Under this interpretation, a trade deficit (when the value of imports exceeds the value of exports) is a measure that a country is "losing" in its trade relations while a trade surplus means that a country is "winning." This notion is further promoted because the word "deficit" has a naturally negative connotation.

However, realities are more nu-

anced than this. Consider one way in which a trade deficit can fall. During a recession, a worker who has lost his job (or who fears that he will lose it) will buy fewer goods, including fewer imports. This can result in a falling trade deficit. The more severe the recession, the more likely it is that the deficit will fall. For example, the U.S. merchandising trade deficit fell from $816 billion in 2008 to $503 billion in 2009 as the financial crisis hit. For the same period, goods imports fell 35%. Few would argue that these "improvements" in the trade deficit and falling imports reflected well on the state of the U.S. economy.

Additionally, the U.S. remains the world's top exporter of services. In 2012, the U.S. exported $649 billion worth of services, and had a positive trade-in-services balance of nearly $207 billion. Simply put, a country's balance of trade, particularly looking at goods alone, is not enough to ascertain its economic health. ∎

U.S. leadership and the multilateral trade system

The U.S. took the lead in designing the international trade system in the aftermath of World War II. The establishment of the General Agreement on Tariffs and Trade (GATT) in 1948 enshrined a core set of principles governing multilateral trade in goods that focused on a rules-based system of non-discrimination among GATT members. This basic approach reflected U.S. values and leadership—signatories to the GATT would negotiate binding, and transparent, commitments to a set of trade policies that would apply to all participants.

The primary commitment was that the U.S. (and all other GATT members) would agree to a maximum tariff rate for individual products that were imported from other adherents to the GATT system. In return, these other GATT partners would make similar commitments and agree not to discriminate against U.S. exports. This policy

of non-discrimination toward others is known as the "most favored nation" (MFN) principle, i.e. no member is treated more favorably than any others (and no worse). The GATT system, in short, was an attempt to encourage member nations to liberalize trade and replace special bilateral arrangements (such as trade preferences for former colonies) with equal treatment across member states.

Note that this principle of non-discrimination does not mean that, for example, the U.S. tariff on automobiles will be the same as Japanese tariffs on imported cars. Instead, it means that Japan should treat all imported autos from all exporting countries in the same fashion. In addition, this GATT system did allow countries to impose further import restrictions under certain limited exemptions. These exceptions were codified in language agreed upon by all countries in the GATT.

The World Trade Organization succeeded the GATT in 1995 at the conclusion of the Uruguay Round of multilateral trade talks. The WTO expanded this tradition of non-discrimination to the areas such as services and intellectual property rights, in addition to the traditional focus on manufactured and agricultural goods. The establishment of the WTO coincided with a large influx of membership into the new organization, which has 159 members as of 2013, including every major global economy. High-income countries of North America, Europe and Japan were already long-standing and fully engaged GATT members. The new participants in the multilateral trade system came primarily from the developing world.

A critical aspect of decisionmaking at the WTO is the requirement of consensus for any changes in underlying commitments or membership. For example, when China undertook to join the WTO in the late 1990s, every WTO member had to agree. This need for consensus gives current members significant leverage over a country attempting to join the WTO. The U.S. negotiated a host of internal Chinese commitments to improve market access, intellectual property protections, and investment rules before agreeing to Chinese WTO membership. Moreover, new members are required to accept the terms that were negotiated by existing members in previous talks. However, once a country becomes a member, it has veto power over changes in the existing terms. This need for consensus has been a major contributor to the impasse in the current round of trade talks (the Doha Round) that was launched in 2002.

The WTO is also the venue for countries that have disputes about living up to multilateral trade commitments. The WTO "Dispute Settlement Body" (DSB) was set up with a very American approach that focuses on rules and legal procedure. Parties make arguments before an impartial body of experts (a "DSB Panel") that rules whether a country's policies are consistent with WTO commitments. The decision by the Panel can be challenged in the "Appellate Body," which makes a final assessment. However, it is important to note that these rulings are not binding on a country. For example, if the U.S. loses a case, the government can change the policy to come into compliance, enter into negotiations with the petitioning government for some sort of compensation (for example, lowering trade restrictions in another sector that will satisfy the other nation), or face WTO-approved retaliation, typically raising barriers against the "offending" country's exports. The existence of these various options are critical: the WTO cannot violate a member country's sovereignty to force its government to change any policy. In essence, the WTO dispute system is a kind of public shaming for a country not living up to its obligations.

As noted above, the U.S. and other WTO members have the right to deviate

Teamsters hold signs reading, "NAFTA kills," during a news conference by congressmen and union leaders against the cross-border trucking program, Oct. 19, 2011, in San Diego, CA. The first Mexican carrier is set to roll into the U.S. interior within days under a new agreement, which had been stalled for years by safety concerns and political wrangling. (AP PHOTO/GREGORY BULL)

from the principle of non-discrimination in certain situations. For example, the WTO agreements recognize the right of the U.S. government to impose trade restrictions on imports that have been subsidized by foreign governments, on imported products that pose a health hazard (as long as those hazards are based on scientific evidence), or on goods deemed to constitute a national security risk (for example, banning the export of certain computer technologies as part of economic sanctions against Iran). But these deviations are based on established rules, an approach very much consistent with U.S. notions of the rule of law and due process.

Another exception allowed from the WTO principle of non-discrimination is the establishment of a "free trade agreement" (FTA). A group of WTO members can agree to eliminate all barriers among each other without having to remove all restrictions in place on other countries. For example, member states of the European Union have access to each other's markets that far exceeds what non-EU countries might receive. The U.S., Canada, and Mexico formed NAFTA in a similar way. These agreements can integrate member economies far beyond what is possible under general globalization. Such agreements have become more attractive to coun-

tries as the Doha Round negotiations have stalled (see below for discussion of TPP and TTIP, two regional trade agreements that the U.S. is currently negotiating). For the U.S., such agreements primarily result in partner countries lowering barriers to U.S. exports, since the American economy is already very open to foreign products.

The emergence of a parallel set of trade preferences among a subgroup of WTO members undercuts the system that the U.S. played the lead role in establishing after the end of World War II. Some of the bilateral and regional agreements that have been negotiated are far reaching, and include reduced barriers for goods, services, and investments. However, others are narrower, and exempt large swaths of the member countries' economies from liberalization. The resulting patchwork of rules and barriers complicate business decisions about how to organize global operations, and may lead to political tensions as some nations get better treatment than others.

Trade misconceptions

Trade policy discussion is rife with misunderstanding, both among those who support continued liberalization and those that oppose it. Below are five common misconceptions about trade.

■ U.S. manufactured goods are not competitive in the world market.

The U.S. has had a multi-billion dollar "trade deficit" (where imports of goods exceed exports of goods) for decades. In addition, many products that consumers buy in stores can easily be identified as "made in China" or "made in Mexico." These facts lead many people to assume that the U.S. "doesn't make anything anymore" or cannot compete in international markets under current rules.

The data tells a more complicated story. It is true that goods imported into the U.S. now far exceed exports to other countries. But U.S. exports have continued to grow over time, doubling from $781 billion in 2000 to $1,546 billion in 2012, an all-time record for U.S. exports. Some believe that many of U.S. exports are agricultural goods like corn or wheat. But the vast majority (87%) of U.S. exports are manufactured goods. Major categories of U.S. exports include civilian aircraft, petrochemical products, automobiles and automobile parts, and pharmaceuticals.

U.S. exports have also been robust to some of its free trade agreement partners. U.S. sales of manufacturing goods to our NAFTA-partner Mexico have increased from $101 billion in 2000 to $197 billion in 2012. Critics will respond that the U.S. had a $1.3 billion goods trade surplus the year NAFTA was signed and in 2012 has a trade deficit of $61.6 billion. However, about 60% of that deficit results from petroleum imports, which has not been the focus of critics' arguments about NAFTA's impact on U.S. manufacturing.

Of course, the growing trade deficit makes clear that U.S. imports of goods have grown even faster than the increase in exports. But the fact remains that U.S. firms, farmers, and workers can, and do, compete successfully in many international markets.

■ Free trade always lowers prices to consumers

Free trade proponents frequently argue that international trade results in lower prices and greater variety to consumers. But this is only half of the story. Economic theory also suggests that increased exports can raise prices to consumers. Domestic firms will go to the trouble to sell goods abroad (e.g. identifying foreign customers, establishing distribution networks, and dealing with customs procedures) only if the price they can receive is higher than domestic sales. In addition, goods sold internationally reduce the supply in the domestic market, which will tend to bid up the prices within the U.S. If the exported good is an input into a production process, increased foreign sales can reduce employment in downstream industries.

A recent example illustrates this phenomenon. The U.S. government has considered approving expanded exports of liquefied natural gas, which is now possible because of a revolution in new extraction techniques (so-called "fracking"). Some firms in the U.S. chemical industry have lobbied against this proposal by arguing that access to cheap natural gas has helped manufacturing jobs in the U.S. Potential exporting firms argue that exporting the good will help create well-paying jobs in the natural gas industry.

This debate reflects the fact that increased exports of a good will not make everyone better off, since it can result in higher prices in the exporting country. In addition, this example reflects the reality that trade policy choices can pit large companies and different industries against each other.

■ U.S. multinational corporations invest in low-wage countries at the expense of American workers.

Discussions about trade policy include a myriad of stories about U.S. factories shutting down and moving operations to developing countries to take advantage of low wages and lax environmental standards. There are certainly many high-profile examples that are consistent with these stories. For example, the stock of U.S. multinational manufacturing investment in China rose from $7.1 billion in 2000 to $31.5 billion in 2012. The comparable figures in Mexico were $19.5 billion (2000) to $35.6 billion (2012).

However, the vast majority of U.S. "foreign direct investment" (FDI) abroad, where a U.S. multinational either purchases an existing company or establishes a new affiliate abroad, occurs in high-wage countries with environmental and labor regulations similar to, or even more strict, than the U.S. For example, Canada had a stock of over $75.4 billion of investment by U.S. multinational corporations in the manufacturing sector in 2012 compared to $53.4 billion in 2000. This means that the $22 billion increase in the value of U.S. manufacturing investment in

Workers assemble a Boeing Co. 737 airplane on line 2 at the company's factory in Renton, WA, on May 30, 2013. Boeing Co., rebounding from the 787 Dreamliners three-month grounding, is moving closer to a further production increase. (MIKE KANE/BLOOMBERG VIA GETTY IMAGES)

Canada alone from over these twelve years almost matched the increase in China, though the percentage change was greater in China.

The focus of U.S. manufacturing investment in high-wage countries is even clearer with the inclusion of Europe. The stock of U.S. manufacturing investment in the "EU-15" (the 15 EU members) was $152 billion in 2000 and rose to $265 billion in 2012. This means that the increase in U.S. manufacturing investment in these high-wage EU countries over this period ($113 billion) was almost five times as large as the increase in China. Indeed, U.S. manufacturing investment in the Netherlands alone exceeded that of China in 2012.

■ International trade agreements can force the U.S. government to change domestic law.

Critics often express grave concerns about how international trade agreements may force the U.S. government to gut policies, like those protecting the environment, that come into conflict with free trade principles. One frequently cited example was a 1995 WTO dispute between the U.S. and Venezuela concerning the U.S. Clean Air Act.

These fears are entirely misguided. International trade agreements such as those embodied in the WTO do not undercut the sovereignty of a government. Instead, WTO dispute settlement procedures allow a neutral third party to make a public judgment about whether a nation is living up to its international commitments. The U.S. government would retain all rights to continue to pursue a policy judged inconsistent with WTO rules by a dispute panel. Ignoring a panel's judgment results in possible retaliation by the complaining government. But if the WTO did not exist, a country disapproving of another country's policies would still have the right to impose retaliation.

The U.S.-Venezuela case instead marks a victory for non-discriminatory treatment of foreigners. The U.S. government had regulations under the Clean Air Act that treated domestic gasoline refiners more favorably than foreign refiners. The WTO merely ruled that this

A worker checks new tires at a plant in Nantong city, China, in May 2010, shortly after the WTO rejected China's appeal of a ruling that backed the U.S. duties on Chinese tire imports. (XU CONGJUN NT/IMAGINECHINA/CORBIS)

was discriminatory but did not rule what particular standards were appropriate. In the end, the U.S. decided to remove the discriminatory treatment, but was under no obligation to do so. The U.S. could have demurred and Venezuela could have retaliated in response.

■ Restricting imports will increase U.S. employment

Worries about international competition can result in strong pressures for restricting imports as a way to increase jobs. These pressures are especially intense in periods of high unemployment.

Broadly speaking, U.S. presidents from both parties have resisted these calls for protection. One reason is that the U.S. has signed international agreements that it will not increase tariffs beyond certain specific levels. Ignoring these obligations can result in retaliation against U.S. exporting firms thereby destroying jobs in other sectors. In addition, import restrictions can increase prices inside the U.S. and hurting other Americans.

Two recent examples illustrate these downsides.

President George W. Bush imposed 30% tariffs on essentially all sources of imported steel in 2002, with the stated intension of helping U.S. steel firms and workers facing international competi-

tion. But the increase in tariffs helped lead to a short-run increase in the domestic price of steel, which in turn reduced employment in steel-using firms, thereby eliminating jobs in those sectors even as steelworkers retained theirs. In 2009, President Barack Obama imposed similar tariffs on Chinese tires to help U.S. workers. This resulted in an increase in the price of low-end tires (which was the area in which Chinese firms operated); these higher prices hurt poor Americans, since they were the most likely to purchase these types of tires. In the end, other countries quickly replaced China as a source of imported tires, so that the impact on U.S. employment was minimal. Ultimately, the tariffs produced an estimated increase of only 1,000 U.S. workers, a miniscule amount in the broader U.S. economic context. Neither President Bush nor President Obama was trying to hurt American firms that consume steel, or low-income Americans buying cheap tires. But import restrictions often have real, if unintended, negative consequences.

U.S. trade with China

Trade with China is likely the single most controversial aspect of U.S. international economic relations. Criticism of China's trade policy was a critical aspect of both the Obama and

..SPENDING IS GOOD FOR THE ECONOMY..!   ..WHICH ONE..??..

Romney 2012 presidential campaigns.

Public opinion polls reflect this concern. In the November 2010 Pew poll, 76% of respondents thought that increased trade with Canada would be beneficial for the U.S. compared to only 45% for increased trade with China. The skepticism about China crossed political parties: 42% of Republicans polled were supportive compared to 49% of Democrats. There were however interesting differences based on age and education. While 56% of respondents aged 18–29 years supported increased U.S.-China trade, only 37% of those over 65 years did so. Fifty percent of those with college or advanced degrees thought that increased China trade was good for the U.S. while only 39% of those with a high school degree or less thought so.

The increased concern about China probably reflects broader concerns about the consequences of globalization, especially for relatively unskilled workers. But this nervousness also reflects the sudden ascendance of China in trade with the U.S. Imports from China to the U.S. were $62.6 billion in 1997 and increased to $425.6 billion by 2012; China has been the single largest source of imports into the U.S. since 2009, when it overtook Canada. U.S. exports to China have increased as well (from $12.8 billion in 1997 to $110.4 billion in 2012) but have been significantly smaller than imports. As a result, the U.S. has a massive bilateral trade deficit with the People's Republic of China (PRC).

Many Americans see this bilateral deficit as a clear indication that U.S. trade agreements have opened America to a flood of Chinese products. Many argue as well that U.S. trade policies have allowed American multinational corporations to close U.S. factories and reopen them in China. Another argument is that China must be cheating on its trade commitments (including "undervaluing" the Chinese currency in foreign exchange markets). Many who make these points argue further that the U.S. could and should raise trade restrictions on imports from China.

The reality is far subtler than these sentiments would suggest.

The first complication is that this dramatic increase in Chinese exports to the U.S. has taken place during a period of stability in American policies toward products made in the PRC. In particular, the U.S. has imposed the same tariffs on Chinese imports as it has on other international partners (such as Germany, Japan, Brazil and the United Kingdom) since the 1980s. However, since China was not a member of the multilateral trade system "club," the U.S. could have raised import restrictions on Chinese goods unilaterally and without limit. When the U.S. agreed (along with all other members) to allow China to join the WTO, these tariff rates were "permanent," i.e. the U.S. could not increase tariffs on Chinese goods beyond the "normal" tariffs on other WTO members. But the U.S. did not lower tariff restrictions on China after its WTO "accession." The major change instead was that the Chinese government reformed its own domestic policies. China, which was largely closed to the world economy prior to the 1980s, began to open up dramatically to foreign investment, especially in the late 1990s and early 2000s. The decreased risk for foreign firms operating within China was far more important than any change in U.S. policies.

A second serious complication with the trade deficit figures with China is that traditional statistics do not take into account the reality that many products in China are only assembled there from imported components and services, some of which may come from the U.S. Thus, "made in China" may only mean that the final stages of an import's production actually take place inside the PRC. A recent WTO report estimated that the 2008 U.S.-China trade deficit would be about 41% lower if statistics properly accounted for these effects.

Fast track

One controversial aspect of U.S. trade policy is "fast-track" authority, which allows the president to submit a completed trade agreement to Congress for an up-or-down vote without the possibility for amendment and only limited debate. This procedure, now referred to as "Trade Promotion Authority" (or TPA), has raised concerns about presidential usurpation of congressional prerogatives on both the political left and right. It is important to note that this procedure is a consequence of congressionally approved legislation: the president cannot assert this authority unilaterally.

Congress has granted fast-track authority to every president from Gerald Ford to George W. Bush. TPA lapsed in 2007 and President Obama did not ask for the authority during his first term. However, in late 2013 he started the process of requesting its renewal for the Trans-Pacific Partnership and the Trans-atlantic Trade and Investment Partner-

An Odd Way to Discredit DeVos

Chile's education success story.

BY **DARÍO PAYA**

Off to class in Punta Arenas, Chile

The opponents of Donald Trump's pick to be secretary of education, Betsy DeVos, are animated in large part by anger at her support for school voucher programs. And in their efforts to undermine vouchers, they've gone far afield—to Chile, to be exact, where an expansive school choice system was begun in 1980. To discredit DeVos, her opponents have set out to discredit Chile's voucher program, a parent-driven, choice-based, quality-improving education reform that has been a decades-long success.

The week of DeVos's confirmation hearing, the *Washington Post* published an article by associate political science professors Jennifer Pribble and Jennifer L. Erkulwater labeling the Chilean voucher system a "cautionary tale."

How so? Before the voucher system

Darío Paya is the former Chilean ambassador to the Organization of American States.

was put in place, Chile tended toward the bottom of educational achievement rankings in Latin America; now it is at the top, as consistently shown by international tests such as the PISA (Program for International Student Assessment). The reason for the change has not been spending: Argentina and Uruguay no longer lead the regional rankings, but still generally outspend Chile on education.

Then there are the criticisms that are in fact endorsements of the system: The *Washington Post* article presents as problematic the fact that "since vouchers were introduced, public school enrollment has continued to decline." You bet. Given a choice and a voucher, people left the public system and stayed away.

The article offers a puzzling indictment of school choice in Chile, that "the voucher system has not improved education opportunities for many poor or rural children." I say

"puzzling" because the article itself describes the very poor and rural children as those with no access to private options. If the problem is that the rural poor do not have enough choices, is the solution to do away with choices altogether or to find ways to provide to the poor the full extent of choice enjoyed by other students?

Chile recognized that some kids—primarily the very poor and rural—were being "left behind." But the way to fix that problem was not to get rid of vouchers, but to expand the system. That expansion, now the better part of a decade old, has had amazing results that Pribble and Erkulwater somehow forgot to mention.

The revision to the voucher system was led by socialist Michelle Bachelet, who, when Chile's "experiment" with school choice began in 1980, was living in exile in East Germany. To her credit, 30 years later as president, she led the most significant reform towards expanding a system based on parental choice.

With massive bipartisan support, a "preferential" school voucher was created—that is, one worth more, sometimes almost twice the value of regular vouchers—to provide more options for very poor and rural families. The results have been significant.

Economist Christopher Neilson noted in a 2013 working paper that "this reform raised the test scores of poor children significantly and closed the gap between these students and the rest of the population by one third." Neilson said the "policy changed the nature of competition among schools" and that "the observed policy effect is due mostly to the increase in the quality of schools in poor neighborhoods and not to a resorting of students to better schools or the entry of new higher-quality schools. The introduction of targeted vouchers is shown to have effectively raised competition in poor neighborhoods, pushing schools to improve their academic quality."

The performance gap between the country as a whole and the poorest 40 percent was cut by one-third in just five years.

Back when the base voucher wasn't

which would subject executive actions on trade to congressional approval.

When asked why placing tariffs on companies that move factories overseas is such a bad idea, Lee recalls that his grandfather, a "T-Man" or federal agent employed by the Treasury Department in the 1930s,

used to bemoan the fact that he as a T-Man was involved in the enforcement of the Smoot-Hawley Tariff Act, which he blamed—and many economists have blamed—for creating the set of conditions that led to the Great Depression. The minute we start to look at job losses that occur here in the United States as something that requires action that would kick off a trade war, we have to take into account those risks.

Lee insists his bill isn't targeting Trump. "We've made clear that this is part of a much broader effort, one that I've undertaken for the last few years to try to restore power to Congress that properly belongs to Congress. It has nothing to do with this particular president," Lee says. "We started this effort long before we had any idea who was going to be in the White House or what their position might be on trade." Lee points out that Trump has expressed support for the REINS Act, a bill that requires congressional approval of major executive regulations, and the senator hopes that Trump will see his trade bill in a similar light.

It's hard to imagine Trump relinquishing power on an issue he cares so much about, and Lee's effort is just getting off the ground. It doesn't have any cosponsors yet. "It's not the kind of thing that's exciting immediately to everyone," Lee says. "Most senators I know don't stay up late at night worrying about section 338A of the Tariff Act."

Right now in Washington, trade policy matters are wrapped up in a broader effort to reform the tax code. The House GOP proposal calls for switching from a corporate income tax rate of 35 percent to a business consumption tax of 20 percent. The plan would allow full and immediate expensing of investments—making the tax on investment effectively zero—and would eliminate the deduction for interest, thus favoring equity over debt. The tax is "border adjustable," meaning that it applies to imports but not exports.

That last piece of the reform, "border adjustment," has been the subject of some controversy since Trump was quoted in the *Wall Street Jour-*

Lee: Really, it's about trade—not Trump.

nal January 16 calling the idea "too complicated." The president quickly walked that comment back and told the news website *Axios* on January 18 that his comments in the *Journal* "didn't totally reflect [his views] accurately" and said that the idea is "certainly something that is going to be discussed."

Senior GOP sources say that Trump's top White House advisers are united behind the proposal. On January 19, *Breitbart News*, a reliable barometer of populist sentiment in the White House, reported that Paul Ryan had called border adjustment "responsible nationalism." The headline blared: "'Responsible Nationalism': Paul Ryan Warning to Donald Trump's Ideology with 'Border Adjustment Tax.'" *Breitbart* did not note that Ryan's Roadmap for America's Future Act called for a "border-adjustable business consumption tax" as far back as 2008, but it did report, "Sources close to the Trump transition team described the coming fight for a border adjustment tax as one of the key policy battles the president-elect and his team will aim to tackle early on in his administration."

It certainly fueled some overblown headlines Trump's first week in office. Because the United States imports far more than it exports, the border-adjustment part of tax reform would generate $1 trillion in revenue over a decade, according to the Tax Foundation. White House press secretary Sean Spicer suggested that therefore the portion of revenue collected on Mexican imports could be used to cover the cost of a border wall. The media erupted with reports the administration was ready to slap a 20 percent tariff on Mexico, though the corporate tax replacement would apply to all goods, of domestic or foreign origin, consumed in the United States. Spicer's suggestion was something of an accounting fiction anyway. Kyle Pomerleau and Stephen J. Entin of the Tax Foundation write that "the plan also lowers the corporate tax rate and enacts full expensing, so on net the tax changes will likely reduce overall business tax revenue." In other words, the revenue from border adjustment can't both finance a tax reform and pay for a wall.

Of course, even if tax reform passes and spurs high growth among American businesses, Trump could still pursue a protectionist policy of raising tariffs. If Trump's actions on trade go beyond penny-ante squabbling with air-conditioning companies, Mike Lee's bill could become very exciting, very quickly. Overriding a presidential veto with bipartisan support would be difficult but it isn't unthinkable. Democratic senator Jon Tester of Montana told THE WEEKLY STANDARD last week that Congress should "absolutely" have the final say over raising tariffs. The politics of trade isn't easy for members of Congress, but the politics—and consequences—of a trade war could be far worse. ◆

and Linda Sarsour, a hijab-wearing Palestinian-rights agitator whose résumé includes organizing a group called Muslims for Ferguson and persuading New York City schools to close on Islamic holidays. Mallory, Perez, and Sarsour had earlier teamed up to co-chair another Ferguson-themed event, the 2015 March2Justice from New York to Washington in a protest against alleged police brutality.

More image trouble arose for the march in mid-January when it ejected one of its "partners," an anti-abortion group called New Wave Feminists—because you can't exactly extend the hand of sisterhood to abortion opponents when your chief sponsor is Planned Parenthood. A few white women expressed distress at what they perceived as the march organizers' growing hostility to them. Bland had posted an admonition for white women to "understand their privilege" and pay more attention to "intersectionality": the idea that minority women accumulate more points in the victim game than white women because of their twofer status as objects of discrimination. A blogger finger-wagged the whites: "Now is the time for you to be listening more, talking less."

Then there was the matter of the bright pink "pussyhats." The cat-eared caps and the patterns for knitting them were the Instagram-friendly brainchild of several L.A. women, including a knit-shop owner, distressed by the impending Trump presidency. The idea was to play on a vulgar remark involving the word "pussy" that Trump had uttered in 2005 and also, as one Southern California knitter put it, to be "reappropriating the word 'pussy' in a positive way." As knitters clicked out tens of thousands of the hats with their needles, and ads for commercially produced versions pullulated on Etsy and elsewhere, *Washington Post* columnist Petula Dvorak worried that the feline headgear would make wearers look silly instead of serious: "an unruly river of Pepto-Bismol roiling through the streets of the capital rather than a long overdue civil rights march." Citing such issues as equal pay and equal representation in corporate corner

offices, Dvorak begged the marchers to leave the pussyhats at home.

Her words went unheeded, as I discovered at the march's official start on the south side of the National Mall, where it was more like a lake of Pepto-Bismol. There were not only thousands of bright pink hats but thousands of bright pink jackets, shirts, scarves, sneakers, socks, and shoelaces. A mother posed for a photo with her small daughter who sported a junior-size pussyhat and a poster reading "I Vote in 8 Years."

Marchers were marching—or at least some of them were marching as they chanted "Not my president!" and other anti-Trump mantras. A great deal more of the protesters simply milled about or stood in line at an agglomeration of food trucks whose operators were among the dozens of entrepreneurs on the sidewalks ignoring a "Peace Over Profit" poster held by one of the demonstrators and putting capitalism to work peddling water bottles, rainbow flags, candy bars, and "Thank You Obama" T-shirts.

What the march seemed mostly to be about was self-expression via posters—but a peculiar sort of self-expression, oblivious to the impression that the marchers might be making on onlookers who didn't share their ethos. The well-funded Planned Parenthood had printed up its own posters that said, not surprisingly, "I Stand With Planned Parenthood." NARAL's signs, also professionally designed, featured a cat emoji preceded by the words "Keep Your Laws Off My."

But relatively few demonstrators seemed to want to carry the canned and relatively sedate slogans that the advocacy groups had prepared. They preferred to write and draw their own, with no holds barred. The word "nasty" appeared in many of the homemade signs: "Nasty Woman," "You Haven't Seen Nasty Yet," "Stay Nasty," and (on a poster held by a man) "I Like Women Extra Nasty." The word "pussy" also got play: "I Grab My Own Pussy," "This Pussy Has Claws." Other demonstrators drew elaborate renderings of uteruses and fallopian

tubes. "Why RU So Obsessed With My Uterus?" a sign asked. There were several pinkish, purplish hats, neckrings, and paintings that apparently represented vaginas. "My Gender Is a Dynamic, Not a Disorder," a sign read.

The other thematic focus of the posters was the president himself: "No Trump-Pence." "Trump Is Hitler." "No Trump—No KKK." "Putin's Bitch." And most colorfully: "Good Cheeto, Bad Cheeto," with cutout photos of the cheese snack and Trump's face.

Furthermore, it seemed that for all the efforts of the Mallory-Perez-Sarsour diversity troika and all the online rhetoric about intersectionality and privilege-checking, the demographics of the march were exactly what its critics of color had complained about: overwhelmingly white. There were a few African-American, Latina, and East Asian women to be sure, but not many. And after three hours' worth of trudging through the crowds and looking at thousands of demonstrators, I spotted exactly four hijabs. Perhaps socially conservative Muslim women don't really want to associate with double-entendre hats and "I Grab My Own Pussy" posters.

There was another demographic not much in evidence: men. The march's organizers had begged "all defenders of human rights" to get themselves to the Mall and show the flag. *New York* magazine writer Jonathan Chait wrung his hands: "For men misinformed by its poorly-chosen name, the Women's March is for ALL anti-Trump Americans. Please attend!" Yet the female-male ratio on Jan. 21 stagnated at an overwhelming 30-1: the occasional guy in a T-shirt reading "Ask Me About My Feminist Agenda." I asked one of the men, Joe Newton, who hailed from Brooklyn and looked as though he could be Bob Bland's next-door neighbor with his earring and skinny pants, what had happened to the rest of his sex. "I don't know," Newton answered. "I wish there were more men here. It wasn't intended to be exclusive."

The most telling aspect of the march was its sad-sack aura, of which the relative absence of male participants was only one part. Ultra-saturated pink is a color that doesn't flatter most complexions and hair hues, and it especially doesn't flatter women who believe that attention to one's looks is internalized sexism and would rather stay up all night painting uteruses on posters. When the most glamorous female at a gathering is the 82-year-old Gloria Steinem (who was distinctly not wearing one of the cat caps but, rather, a perfectly tailored parka and a perfectly styled blowout), something is off.

The vast crowds and the general chaos prevented me (and many of the marchers) from getting anywhere near the central and most sensationalized portions of the event. I missed Madonna's various bombs: F- and blowing-up-the-White-House. (She later clarified that she'd had no serious thoughts of anti-presidential violence.) I missed Ashley Judd's recitation of a poem about Trump's supposed sexual yearnings for his daughter Ivanka.

But what I didn't miss was the feeling that the march wasn't really about an opportunity to "make history," as the website put it. None of the "serious" issues that the *Washington Post*'s Petula Dvorak alluded to in her column—the glass ceiling, the 78 cents that women are said to earn for every man's dollar—found its way onto any of the handmade posters I saw. Only a handful of the demonstrators' signs mentioned, say, immigration, climate change, and restrictions on Muslims, favorite progressive causes all. The march instead seemed to be a form of grief work: Hillary Clinton was supposed to win the election, but she didn't. The hated Trump won instead, and the huge gathering of the likeminded who had voted for her was therapy.

"I came for my daughters," said Bonnie Rae of South Bethany, Delaware, who had risen in the middle of the night to ride in a caravan of five busloads of women. "I want something better for the future than what we have now."

Late that night on a D.C. Metro train a woman sitting five rows behind me who had attended the march announced loudly, "I felt comforted. All around me it's all red. I'm from western Michigan where it's all red." ♦

Chilly Trade Winds

Sen. Mike Lee's quest for a congressional say on tariffs. BY JOHN McCORMACK

Shortly after noon on January 20, America's newly installed president issued a declaration of war against global free trade. "We must protect our borders from the ravages of other countries making our products, stealing our companies, and destroying our jobs. Protection will lead to great prosperity and strength," Donald Trump said in his inaugural address. "We will follow two simple rules: Buy American and hire American."

One of the big questions surrounding the Trump presidency is just how aggressively he'll advance protectionism. The new Republican president, who has changed his party affiliation five times as an adult, is famous for his bluster and shifting political views. But his mercantilist position that international trade is a zero-sum game is perhaps the most consistent political belief he's ever held. Back in the 1980s he warned that Japan was ripping us off. Now China and Mexico are the two biggest threats. "I'd love to have a trade war with China," Trump said in a 2010 interview on Fox Business. "If we did no business with China, frankly, we'll save a lot of money."

During the election, Trump advocated a 45 percent tariff on Chinese imports and vowed to slap a 35 percent tariff on any company that leaves the United States or builds a new factory outside of the United States. Three days after taking office, Trump fulfilled one protectionist campaign promise by signing an executive order withdrawing the United States from the Trans-Pacific Partnership (a trade deal that President Obama negotiated but Congress never held a vote to ratify). Right now, the markets

John McCormack is a senior writer at THE WEEKLY STANDARD.

seem confident that Trump won't spark a global trade war: The Dow Jones industrial average hummed right along to a record 20,000 points on January 25 (up nearly 2,000 points since Election Day).

But it's possible that the markets are either underestimating Trump's willingness to follow through on his more aggressive promises or overestimating Congress's ability to block the president from doing anything disastrous. Senator Mike Lee argues that Congress has ceded too much power to the executive to raise tariffs. The Utah Republican points to a 1974 law that allows the president to enact temporary tariffs of 15 percent and a 1930 law that might have transfered to the president even broader authority.

"The Tariff Act of 1930 in section 338A allows the president, when he finds that the public interest will be served, to declare new or additional duties for as long as he sees fit," Lee tells THE WEEKLY STANDARD. So President Trump could unilaterally enact a 35 percent tariff on a particular company's imports under the Smoot-Hawley Tariff, as the act is better known? "That is a concern," Lee says. "One could read this provision in a way that would suggest a president could take an action like that. I'm not certain there isn't another limit in the law that might complicate that." World Trade Organization agreements, for example, could theoretically block some executive actions, but it's not clear to Lee that any private party could successfully challenge the administration.

In Lee's view, it's too dangerous for Congress to leave any chance of a trade war up to the whims of any president, and just before the close of business on January 20, Lee's office announced that he had introduced the Global Trade Accountability Act,

ship. The primary argument for TPA is negotiating credibility: in its absence, Congress would be able to change the terms of a trade agreement that had been completed with other nations. But critics argue that "fast-track" undermines the ability of Congress to uphold its constitutional responsibilities.

Article I, Section 8 of the U.S. Constitution lays out the powers of the Congress. The first one noted vests Congress with the "power to lay and collect taxes, duties, imposts and excises…[and] regulate commerce with foreign nations." This clear constitutional prerogative stands in sharp contrast with other areas of foreign policy: the president is commander-in-chief, but only Congress can declare war; the president can negotiate treaties, but only the Senate can approve them (with a two-thirds majority). In contrast, the Congress has clear and exclusive constitutional power to determine trade policy (though the president could sign or veto any trade legislation). Trade agreements are not treaties but instead must be passed through the regular legislative process in both the House and the Senate. Congress may grant temporary powers to the president to act on its behalf but the constitutional prerogatives remain unchanged.

Congress took the lead in setting specific tariff rates for much of early U.S. history. Starting in 1934 (after the disastrous results of sharply increased trade restrictions in the Smoot-Hawley Tariff Act of 1930), Congress has delegated authority to the president to negotiate reciprocal trade liberalization with partner countries. A continuing complication arising out of this constitutional arrangement is that a foreign country cannot be sure that Congress will fully implement any deal negotiated with the president using standard legislative processes. Starting in 1974, Congress agreed to consider trade agreements negotiated by the president as an up-or-down vote and with limited debate, as long as the president met certain conditions. The president was required to consult with the relevant congressional committees before and during trade negotiations, and no-

tify Congress at least 90 days before beginning formal negotiations or entering into any new trade agreements.

Fast-track authority was instrumental in a series of successful U.S. trade agreements, including the completion of various multilateral trade agreements such as the Tokyo Round (1979) and the Uruguay Round (1994), as well as bilateral trade agreements, including NAFTA (1994) and the U.S.-Korea FTA (2011). While the process smoothed negotiating efforts because of the resulting U.S. credibility, critics have become more and more concerned that the procedure led to a limited ability for Congress to play its constitutional role in trade policy in an effective manner. This skepticism about delegating this authority to the president mirrored the overall growth in nervousness about trade liberalization more generally. This criticism led to cosmetic as well as substantive changes in the procedure in 2002, the last time that Congress granted this authority. For example, President Bush's administration renamed the procedure "Trade Promotion Authority" or TPA, which sounded more benign than the informal name of "fast-track," with its hint of minimal congressional deliberation and "railroaded" outcomes. In addition, the 2002 bill required even more ex-

tensive congressional consultation and more detailed negotiating goals than in previous versions. Nonetheless, the bill only narrowly passed the Republican-controlled House by a vote of 215 to 212 in July 2002, but with a larger Senate majority (64 to 34).

Recent battles about extending TPA have focused increasingly on how much input Congress should have in the midst of negotiations. Many in Congress would like to set out clear limits on how far the president can compromise on congressional priorities and, at the very least, would argue for more detailed consultations throughout the negotiations. For example, some Democratic legislators have called for TPA legislation to specify exactly how the president would include labor and environmental standards commitments in any future U.S. free trade agreement. Any future TPA legislation will require a complex balancing act between negotiating flexibility and adherence to congressional concerns.

TAA

Most economists argue that increased trade is beneficial for a nation as a whole. However, economic theory and practical experience suggests that these benefits are not distributed equally within a nation. Some sectors "win" and

Mike Partridge, Tom Nolty and Kerry Role leave the Rock County Job Center in Wisconsin in January 2009 after attending a math class partly funded by TAA. All three were laid off when their employer, United Industries, closed. (SHANA WITTENWYLER/REDUX)

8

some "lose." Within import-competing sectors, thousands of lives can be disrupted. When people lose their jobs because of international competition, they often may not be able to move easily into a new job with similar pay. Some will need to be retrained to enter into a new industry, others have to accept a pay cut as they accept another job, and still others may remain unemployed.

Congress established Trade Adjustment Assistance (TAA) to help employees and companies injured by trade deal with some of these negative consequences. TAA, established originally in 1962 during the Kennedy administration, provides workers with extended unemployment insurance if increased import competition results in job losses. TAA has been extended and expanded by subsequent Congresses to deal with the disruption associated with international competition.

TAA currently is divided into three distinct programs, covering workers, firms and farmers. Employees who qualify for trade adjustment assistance receive retraining, a relocation allowance and extended unemployment benefits. Companies that qualify receive loans, loan guarantees, technical assistance, and tax benefits. TAA for farmers provides free technical assistance and cash benefits to producers of certain agricultural commodities and to fishermen.

TAA supporters claim that it increases economic efficiency by reallocating labor resources. By helping workers move from import-competing jobs and sectors into positions that are more competitive, TAA helps improve the U.S. economy. Proponents also claim that trade adjustment assistance helps spread the benefits of trade more equitably throughout society and build support for continued openness to the world economy.

Opponents argue that trade adjustment assistance generates economic inefficiency by reducing workers' incentives to find new employment. They also argue that it is arbitrary to provide additional support to those negatively affected by trade but not those who are negatively hurt by other forms of

economic change. They are also skeptical how effective associated retraining programs are.

Trade adjustment assistance has often been used as a "sweetener" to trade promotion authority legislation or other trade bills. TAA was included as a provision to gather bipartisan support for presidential trade negotiation authority in 1972 and 2002. TAA was passed as a standalone bill in 2011 but was an implicit part of the implementation of the Colombia and Korea free trade agreements.

Historically, "TAA for workers" benefits were only applicable for manufacturing sector employees. However, beginning in 2009, service sector and public sector workers who lost their jobs due to import competition became eligible for trade adjustment assistance. In the 2011 program reauthorization, service sector workers remained eligible, although public sector workers were not.

In fiscal year 2012, 81,510 workers received $575 million in assistance: 67% of TAA for workers recipients in fiscal year 2012 were in the manufacturing sector, while 33% were in the services sector.

Emerging agreements

The Doha Round of multilateral trade negotiations, which was launched in 2002, is at a standstill. This reflects a profound difficulty in reaching consensus among 159 WTO member countries. The lack of progress has led the U.S. to pursue other plurilateral agreements in the Pacific and with Europe. These efforts allow for continued trade and investment liberalization with critical U.S. trading partners. They may also allow for the U.S. to help establish a baseline for economic integration that mirrors American priorities and approaches.

President Obama has promoted trade liberalization within the context of "21st-century trade agreements." These agreements would go beyond eliminating traditional barriers to trade, and would "build up" core standards among parties to the agreement in a wide variety of different policies. Agreements would cover areas such

as labor and environmental policies, government procurement, measures for food safety, standards for plant and animal health and intellectual property rights, among many others.

In the fall of 2011 President Obama announced that his administration would intensify its focus and involvement in Asia and the Pacific Rim nations. One of the key pillars of this "pivot to Asia," consists of deepening already strong economic ties with the region.

The economic centerpiece of this effort is the ongoing negotiations on the Trans-Pacific Partnership (TPP). The TPP began in 2003 as a trade deal among Singapore, New Zealand and Chile. In 2005 Brunei joined negotiations and in 2006 the Trans-Pacific Economic Partnership was created. President Bush notified Congress of his intention to begin negotiations with existing TPP members in late September 2008. Nine months into his first term President Obama announced that the U.S. would remain committed to TPP, provided that the agreement would expand into new areas of cooperation, including commitments to labor, governance, and environmental standards consistent with U.S. interests.

Australia, Peru, Vietnam, Malaysia, Mexico, Canada and Japan have also become TPP negotiating parties since 2008. The U.S. already has comprehensive free trade agreements with several TPP nations, including Australia, Canada, Mexico, Singapore, and Chile. The TPP could therefore result in the U.S. binding together an even greater array of trade partners in the vibrant Pacific economy. A notable country not included in the TPP negotiations is China. Some view TPP as an attempt to provide a counterweight to growing Chinese economic influence in the region.

The Trans-Pacific Partnership would be one of the most comprehensive plurilateral trade agreements ever negotiated, both because of the number of countries involved and its emphasis on new areas of commitments. The agreement reportedly will have 29 chapters on topics ranging from labor and environmental standards to rules governing e-commerce and investors' rights. Due to this complexity, one challenge that the U.S. has faced has been finding ways to apply appropriate standards across the different countries involved. This process is even more complicated given the wide divergence in economic development among TPP member countries. This has sparked debate within both the TPP negotiations and the U.S. Congress about how much variation in labor, environmental, and regulatory standards should be allowed between the developing and developed countries in the agreement.

The Obama Administration has also launched an important initiative between the U.S. and the European Union. The Transatlantic Trade and Investment Partnership (TTIP) would further integrate what is already the world's largest bilateral trading relationship. The two parties account for 40% of the world's GDP and one third of global trade. In the first round of negotiations in July of 2013 the two negotiating sides established as many as 20 areas that the agreement would cover. Among these topics were government procurement, investment, energy and raw materials, sustainable development, small- and medium-sized enterprises, and state-owned enterprises.

Policy options

In the heat of an electoral battle, politicians may argue that their economic initiatives have only benefits and no costs. However, economic theory and practical experience suggest that such promises can rarely be kept. Policymakers invariably face tradeoffs when pursuing any particular policy.

Trade policy is a classic example of the juggling act between "winners" and "losers. Open trade creates opportunities for those in exporting sectors. But competition from imports can disrupt the lives of workers and communities producing a similar product. However, allowing cheaper goods to enter the country improves the spending power of millions of U.S. families and can increase the competitiveness of U.S. firms that use imported inputs.

These conflicting interests raise the following question: Is it in the broad

U.S. Secretary of State John Kerry, left, speaks with U.S. Trade Representative Michael Froman at the Trans-Pacific Partnership meet in Bali, Indonesia, Tuesday, Oct. 8, 2013. Leaders of the dozen countries involved in the U.S.-led Trans-Pacific Partnership met in Bali after the Asia-Pacific Economic Cooperation (APEC) summit to work on plans for a free trade area they hope will eventually encompass the entire region. (AP PHOTO/WONG MAYE-E)

U.S. interest to utilize restrictive trade policies on imports? For example, should the U.S. curb Chinese imports, even if it increases prices to U.S. consumers and businses? Should the U.S still do so if the policy simply results in imports shifting to other low-cost suppliers (such as India, Indonesia or Mexico), rather than increasing U.S. jobs?

Balancing openness with protection has a long history in U.S. trade policy. However, with the rise of comprehensive 21st-century trade agreements, the definition of "trade policy" has been expanded to include not only tariffs and quotas, but also an array of new policy areas. Among these areas, environmental and labor policies have received significant focus by American policymakers. Should the U.S. insist that strict environmental and labor provisions be included in the Trans-Pacific Partnership? If so, how should they be structured to account for differences in levels of development among TPP member countries? What should be the U.S. response if other countries reject tying internal domestic policies to trade commitments?

Another topic for consideration is

whether U.S. law should continue to provide special help (through Trade Adjustment Assistance) to those who lose their job to international competition. Proponents argue that TAA increases economic efficiency by helping to reallocate labor resources more quickly, and spreads the benefits of trade more equitably. However, opponents claim that it unfairly benefits certain workers by providing support to those who lose their jobs to international competition, but not to those displaced by domestic competition or technological change.

Finally, the current round of WTO negotiation, the Doha Round, has seen almost no progress in recent years. In its absence, a variety of new bilateral and regional agreements have been passed. Should the U.S. apply greater effort in reviving the multilateral Doha Round trade negotiations at the WTO, which is predicated on non-discriminatory treatment of members and originally inspired by U.S. leadership? Or are U.S. resources better spent focusing on bilateral and regional agreements? Does the U.S. stand to lose if other countries also focus on such agreements at the exclusion of the WTO? ∎

✔ Don't forget to vote! www.greatdecisions.org/ballot

discussion questions

1. Should the U.S. restrict Chinese imports, even if it increases prices to U.S. consumers and workers? Should the U.S do so even if the policy only results in shifting imports to other low-cost suppliers (e.g., India, Indonesia or Mexico) rather than increasing U.S. jobs?

2. Should the U.S. insist that strict environmental and labor provisions be included in the Trans-Pacific Partnership? If so, how should they be structured to account for differences in levels of development among TPP member countries? What should be the U.S. response if other countries reject tying internal domestic policies to trade commitments?

3. Programs such as Trade Adjustment Assistance provide special help to those who lose their job to international competition, but not to those displaced by domestic competition and technological changes. Should U.S. law continue such programs?

4. Should the United States apply greater effort in reviving the multilateral Doha Round trade negotiations at the WTO, which is predicated on non-discriminatory treatment of members and originally inspired by U.S. leadership? Or are U.S. resources better spent focusing on bilateral and regional agreements? Does the U.S. stand to lose if other countries also focus on such agreements at the exclusion of the WTO?

5. In what ways are multilateral trade agreements more effective than bilateral trade agreements? In what ways are they more constricted?

6. A common criticism of trade negotiations is that there is not enough transparency or public input. At the same time, trade negotiators need freedom to discuss positions or compromises that might hurt domestic interests groups. What is a good balance between the two? How can negotiations be more transparent without limiting negotitators' freedom?

---

suggested readings

Card, Andrew H., Thomas A. Daschle, Edward Alden, and Matthew J. Slaughter. **U.S. Trade and Investment Policy.** Washington: Council on Foreign Relations, 2011. 128 pp. Available free online: <http://www.cfr.org/trade/us-trade-investment-policy/p25737>. This study provides an overview of current U.S. trade policy but focuses on concrete policy recommendations for new trade initiatives and approaches.

Destler, I.M. **American Trade Politics.** Washington: Peterson Institute for International Economics, 2005. 337 pp. $25.00 (paper). A classic book about the politics and history of U.S. trade policy.

Drezner, Daniel. **U.S. Trade Strategy: Free Versus Fair**. Washington: Council on Foreign Relations, 2006. 130 pp. Available free online: <http://www.cfr.org/trade/us-trade-strategy-free-versus-fair/p11184>. This study by a prominent political scientist examines the differences between the U.S. pursuing a strategy of "free trade" as opposed to "fair trade."

Fergusson, Ian F., William H. Cooper, Remy Jurenas, and Brock R. Williams. "The Trans-Pacific Partnership: Negotiations and Issues for Congress." **Congressional Research Service**, August 2013. Available free online: <http://www.fas.org/sgp/crs/row/R42694.pdf>. This short paper provides an overview of the negotiations between the U.S. and eleven other Pacific Rim nations.

Rivola, Pietra. **The Travels of a T-Shirt in the Global Economy: An Economist Examines the Markets, Power, and Politics of Free Trade**. Hoboken, NJ: Wiley, 2005. 336 pp. $18.95 (paper). The author examines the complex system by which a simple t-shirt is produced, distributed and sold in the modern global economy.

Schrim, Stefan A. **New Rules for Global Markets: Public and Private Governance in the World Economy**. New York: Palgrave MacMillan, 2004. 288pp. $130.00 (hardcover). A collection of scholarly essays that makes the case that new rules are needed to guide further globalization, especially while attitudes about global economic governance continue to diverge.

World Trade Organization. "Trade Policy Review: United States of America." December 2012. Available free online: <http://www.wto.org/english/tratop_e/tpr_e/tp375_e.htm>. The WTO publishes periodic critical external reviews of how the U.S. is living up to its obligations under multilateral trade agreements.

TO LEARN MORE ABOUT THIS TOPIC AND TO ACCESS WEB LINKS TO RESOURCES GO TO www.greatdecisions.org

Global Discussion Questions

No decision in foreign policy is made in a vacuum, and the repercussions of any single decision have far-reaching effects across the range of strategic interests on the U.S. policy agenda. This GREAT DECISIONS feature is intended to facilitate the discussion of this year's topics in a global context, to discuss the linkages between the topics and to encourage consideration of the broader impact of decisionmaking.

---

1. Consider "U.S. trade policy" in the context of "Climate change and food security." What role can trade negotiations and agreements within organizations such as the WTO have on climate change? For example, to what extent could "green tariffs" on countries that are slow to reduce their carbon emissions interfere with free trade policies that WTO tribunals stand for? How does a country's stance on climate change compare to its trade commitments and interests?

2. Consider "Defense technology" in the context of "China's foreign policy." To what extent should U.S. defense priorities be directly targeted at maintaining incontestable technological superiority? Is maintaining technological superiority possible without provoking an arms race?

3. Consider "Defense technology" in the context of "Islamic Awakening." As more and more information comes out on the U.S.' covert drone attacks against Islamic militants, how will it affect perceptions of the U.S. in among Islamist regimes? Can the U.S. continue its covert war on terror without losing face in the Middle East and North Africa? How?

4. Consider "Energy Independence" in the context of "China." As the U.S. grows increasingly energy independent, China's growing consumer class is making increasingly energy dependent. What challenges do these simultaneous developments pose, and how can the two countries work together to resolve them?

5. In "Israel," close U.S.-Israeli relations have produced some resentment and strained U.S. ties with other Middle Eastern countries. How can the U.S. simultaneously secure its diplomatic relations with countries such as "Turkey" or Islamist regimes in the Maghreb while retaining its strong diplomatic ties to Israel? How can the U.S. help improve relations between Israel and other countries in the region?

6. Consider "Energy Independence" in the context of "U.S. Trade Policy." Russia, for instance, plans to increase its crude oil exports to China by about 400,000 barrels a day in the next decade. Yet Russia's oil production remains relatively stagnant, while U.S. oil production is rising rapidly. What foreign policy considerations must be made by a country dependent on oil exports? How does the possibility of energy independence change these considerations, specifically what countries the U.S. is willing to establish trade relationships with?

7. Consider "Turkey" in the context of "Israel," particularly how Turkish-Israeli relations evolved after the 2010 Israeli raid on a Turkish flotilla. Is there any room for reconciliation between Turkey and Israel? If so, what diplomatic talking points would be best suited for revived cooperation between the two countries? Could Turkey's energy concerns and attempts to diversify its energy trading partners ultimately lead to deals with Israel?

8. Consider "Energy Independence" in the context of "Climate change and food security." Should the U.S. government favor funding sustainable energy over domestic "traditional" energy extraction and production? How should policymakers balance the challenges posed by climate change with those posed by energy dependence?

For glossaries, additional readings and more, visit
www.GreatDecisions.org

TOPIC 1: FUTURE OF THE EURO

ISSUE A. To what extent do you agree or disagree with the following two statements?

U.S. banking regulators should scruntinize European banks that operate in the U.S. more closely.

Strongly agree	53%
Agree	36%
Disagree	6%
Strongly disagree	3%
Not sure	3%

U.S. banking regulators should discourage American financial institutions from investing in Europe

Strongly agree	64%
Somewhat agree	11%
Somewhat disagree	34%
Strongly disagree	46%
Not sure	6%

ISSUE B. To what extent do you support or oppose the creation of Eurobonds by the European Union?

Strongly support	28%
Somewhat support	40%
Somewhat opposed	6%
Strongly oppose	4%
Not sure	22%

ISSUE C. Suppose European countries need a bailout to avoid defaulting on their debt. To what extent do you support or oppose the U.S. providing funding to help bailout European countries?

Strongly support	4%
Somewhat support	27%
Somewhat opposed	29%
Strongly oppose	33%
Not sure	7%

TOPIC 2: EGYPT

ISSUE A. Which of the following should be the highest priority for the U.S. in Egypt?

	1	2	3	4	5
Building relationships with Islamist politicians	17%	33%	27%	18%	5%
Building relationships with the Egyptian military	6%	19%	33%	33%	10%
Providing economic aid	14%	27%	23%	30%	6%
Preserving regional stability and security	65%	15%	11%	8%	1%
Other	9%	8%	5%	8%	71%

ISSUE B. To what extent do you support or oppose the U.S. establishing a free trade agreement with Egypt?

Strongly support	20%
Somewhat support	50%
Somewhat opposed	13%
Strongly opposed	5%
Not sure	13%

ISSUE C. How much pressure should the U.S. government put on Egypt's new regime to uphold the Camp David accords and maintain good relations with Israel?

A great deal of pressure	48%
Some pressure	38%
Not too much pressure	9
No pressure at all	3%
Not sure	2%

ISSUE D. How convincing do you find each of the four arguments below about how the U.S. should reassess its economic aid to Egypt?

The U.S. should continue to provide aidto Egypt because it helps Egypt's emerging democracy as it goes through a transition.

Very	56%
Not very	44%

The U.S. should continue to provide aid because it helps provide stability and is a continuing way for the U.S. to influence events.

Very	69%
Not very	31%

The U.S. should stop giving aid to the Egyptian government because it has been slow to criticize, and has failed to effectively confront, those who have perpetrated attacks against Americans and the U.S. Embassy in Cairo.

Very	20%
Not very	80%

Given the difficult economic times the U.S. is going through, it is unwise for the U.S. to give large amounts of aid to Egypt.

Very	44%
Not very	56%

So now, do you think U.S. foreign aid to Egypt should be:

Increased	5%
Kept the same	46%
Decreased	36%
Not sure	14%

TOPIC 3: NATO

ISSUE A. To what extent do you agree or disagree with the following statement? NATO faces a crisis in purpose and direction.

Strongly agree	26%
Somewhat agree	47%
Somewhat disagree	19%
Strongly disagree	6%
Not sure	2%

ISSUE B. To what extent do you agree or disagree with the following statement? The U.S. government should shift its priorities away from NATO and Europe toward other regions and security concerns.

Strongly agree	12%
Somewhat agree	46%
Somewhat disagree	25%
Strongly disagree	13%
Not sure	4%

ISSUE C. Which of the following should be the highest priority for the U.S. in Afghanistan?

	1	2	3	4	5	6
Preventing the country from becoming a sanctuary for terrorists	57%	15%	13%	10%	4%	1%
Building a viable democratic state	12%	16%	19%	23%	26%	4%
Eradicating the Taliban	6%	20%	11%	21%	36%	6%
Increasing economic development	12%	24%	28%	23%	12%	1%
The protection of human and women's rights	15%	25%	27%	16%	15%	2%
Other	7%	3%	2%	4%	6%	80%

ISSUE D. Do you support or oppose a reduction in U.S. government defense spending, even if doing so significantly reduces NATO's military capacity?

Strongly support	36%
Somewhat support	39%
Somewhat opposed	14%
Strongly oppose	9%
Not sure	3%

TOPIC 4: MYANMAR

ISSUE A. Regarding international economic sanctions in Myanmar, to what extent do you agree with the following two statements?

The U.S. should not roll back sanctions further until Myanmar has made more reforms for democratization.

Strongly agree	11%
Agree	33%
Somewhat disagree	34%
Strongly disagree	18%
Not sure	4%

The democratic reforms undertaken by Myanmar's leadership demonstrate that international sanctions were a successful strategy.

Strongly agree	8%
Somewhat agree	33%
Somewhat disagree	34%
Strongly disagree	18%
Not sure	4%

ISSUE B. Which of the following should be the top priority in U.S. relations with Myanmar?

	1	2	3	4	5
Fair and free elections	25%	36%	23%	14%	1%
Human rights issues, incl-uding ethnic minority rights	40%	27%	20%	11%	1%
Economic investment	20%	21%	35%	21%	3%
The "pivot to Asisa" in national security strategy	19%	12%	18%	47%	5%
Other	5%	3%	3%	5%	85%

ISSUE C. To what extent do you support or oppose the U.S. government encouraging private-sector investment and engagement of American firms in Myanmar?

Strongly support	31%
Somewhat agree	52%
Somewhat disagree	9%
Strongly disagree	3%
Not sure	5%

Copies of the **National Opinion Ballot Report** *are available upon request. The* **NOBR** *is also available at* www.fpa.org *as a PDF.*

TOPIC 5 INTERVENTION

Issue A. To what extent do you agree or disagree with the following statements about the responsibility to protect doctrine? A U.S. military intervention in Syria is justified under the R2P doctrine.

Strongly agree	9%
Somewhat agree	30%
Somewhat disagree	22%
Strongly disagree	32%
Not sure	8%

Issue B. The international intervention in Libya in 2011 was an example of the R2P doctrine well-applied.

Strongly agree	30%
Somewhat agree	48%
Somewhat disagree	11%
Strongly disagree	6%
Not sure	6%

Issue C. In addition to being a moral responsibility, R2P is in the national security interests of the U.S.

Strongly agree	23%
Somewhat agree	49%
Somewhat disagree	15%
Strongly disagree	7%
Not sure	7%

Issue D. The U.S. should channel its R2P efforts through the newly created Atrocities Prevention Board.

Strongly agree	21%
Somewhat agree	40%
Somewhat disagree	11%
Strongly disagree	10%
Not sure	19%

TOPIC 6: IRAN

Issue A. To what extent do you agree or disagree with the following statement regarding U.S. sanctions against Iran? The economic sanctions against Iran to keep it from building nuclear weapons are working.

Strongly agree	6%
Somewhat agree	29%
Somewhat disagree	29%
Strongly disagree	30%
Not sure	16%

Issue B. When should the U.S. begin to roll back sanctions on Iran?

Right now	17%
After it reopens nuclear talks	36%
After it stops its nuclear program	31%
After it holds fair and free elections	9%
Other	7%

Issue C. To what extent do you support or oppose U.S. military cooperation with Israel if Israel launches a preemptive strike against Iran's nuclear program?

Strongly support	15%
Somewhat support	20%
Somewhat opposed	21%
Strongly oppose	39%
Not sure	5%

Issue D. Which of the following represents the best U.S. policy regarding Iran? (Rank in order from 1 to 4, with 1 being the best policy.)

	1	2	3	4
Military action	2%	6%	8%	84%
Diplomatic dialogue	73%	15%	9%	4%
Covert actions, e.g., cyberattacks	10%	26%	59%	5%
Sanctions	19%	53%	22%	6%

TOPIC 7 CHINA IN AFRICA

Issue A. What is the most important concern facing the U.S. regarding China in Africa? (Rank from 1 to 6, with 1 most important.)

	1	2	3	4	5	6
China as a supplier of small arms and light weapons to African countries	23%	22%	22%	20%	12%	1%
China's military operations in Africa	9%	18%	23%	22%	24%	4%
China's Communist economic system serving as a possible economic model for Africa	17%	20%	19%	22%	18%	4%
China's increasing economic cooperation with Africa	30%	14%	13%	15%	25%	4%
China's support for undemocratic forms of government	25%	25%	19%	14%	15%	2%
Other	7%	3%	3%	4%	4%	79%

Issue B. What should be the top U.S. priority in Africa? (Rank from 1 to 8, with 1 most important.)

	1	2	3	4	5	6	7	8
Peacekeeping	11%	10%	16%	17%	15%	16%	14%	2%
Democracy building	8%	7%	11%	15%	16%	18%	24%	2%
Humanitarian assistance	28%	20%	15%	16%	11%	7%	3%	0.2%
Human rights	14%	19%	16%	18%	15%	11%	8%	1%
Economic investment	1%	10%	16%	17%	15%	16%	14%	2%
Natural resources	7%	13%	14%	12%	13%	22%	19%	1%
Trade	11%	14%	16%	10%	13%	17%	19%	1%
Other	4%	1%	1%	0.3%	0.3%	1%	3%	90%

TOPIC 8 THREAT ASSESSMENT

Issue A. Which of the following represents the greatest threat to the U.S. today? (Rank from 1 to 6, with 1 being the greatest threat.)

	1	2	3	4	5	6
China	5%	9%	14%	23%	38%	11%
Global health crisis	9%	18%	15%	28%	27%	5%
Economic crisis	46%	20%	19%	10%	4%	1%
Radical Islamist government	15%	26%	25%	20%	12%	2%
Rogue nuclear states	19%	25%	23%	17%	14%	3%
Other	16%	4%	4%	3%	4%	69%

Issue B. Which of the following do you think will represent the greatest threat to the U.S. two decades from now? (Rank from 1 to 6, with 1 being the greatest threat.)

	1	2	3	4	5	6
China	17%	15%	15%	15%	29%	10%
Global health crisis	16%	19%	19%	20%	22%	4%
Economic crisis	23%	21%	22%	25%	15%	4%
Radical Islamist governments	13%	21%	22%	25%	16%	4%
Rogue nuclear states	21%	23%	19%	18%	16%	4%
Other	22%	5%	3%	3%	3%	64%

Issue C. To what extent do you agree or disagree with the following statement? The U.S. Senate should pass legislation to regulate national infrastructure in private hands?

Strongly agree	23%
Somewhat agree	32%
Somewhat disagree	16%
Strongly disagree	18%
Not sure	11%

Issue D. To what extent do you agree or disagree with the following statements regarding U.S. policy toward North Korea?

1. The U.S. should continue using economic sanctions to address the threat of a nuclear North Korea.

Strongly agree	52%
Somewhat agree	29%
Somewhat disagree	10%
Strongly disagree	4%
Not sure	5%

2. The U.S. should continue using multilateral talks to address the threat of a nuclear North Korea.

Strongly agree	78%
Somewhat agree	16%
Somewhat disagree	3%
Strongly disagree	1%
Not sure	2%

Become a member

FOREIGN POLICY ASSOCIATION 1918

For nearly a century, members of the Association have played key roles in government, think tanks, academia and the private sector.

As an active participant in the FPA's Great Decisions program, we encourage you to join the community today's foreign policy thought leaders.

Associate—$250
Benefits:
Free admission to all Associate events (includes member's family)
Discounted admission for all other guests to Associate events
Complimentary GREAT DECISIONS briefing book
Complimentary issue of FPA's annual *National Opinion Ballot Report*

Visit us online at **www.fpa.org/membership**

Make a donation
Your support helps the **FOREIGN POLICY ASSOCIATION's** *programs dedicated to global affairs education.*

Make a fully tax-deductible contribution to FPA's Annual Fund 2013.

To contribute to the Annual Fund 2013, visit us online at **www.fpa.org** or call the Membership Department at **(800) 628-5754 ext. 232**.

The generosity of donors who contribute $500 or more is acknowledged in FPA's *Annual Report*.

All financial contributions are tax-deductible to the fullest extent of the law under section 501 (c)(3) of the IRS code.

FPA also offers membership at the SPONSOR ASSOCIATE and PATRON ASSOCIATE levels. To learn more, visit us online at www.fpa.org/membership or call (800) 628-5754 ext. 232.

- -

Return this form by mail to: Foreign Policy Association, 470 Park Avenue South, New York, N.Y. 10016.
Or fax to: (212) 481-9275.

ORDER ONLINE: WWW.GREATDECISIONS.ORG

OR CALL (800) 477-5836

FOR MEMBERSHIP: WWW.FPA.ORG/MEMBERSHIP

❏ MR.   ❏ MRS.   ❏ MS.   ❏ DR.   ❏ PROF.

NAME _____

ADDRESS _____

_____**APT/FLOOR** _____

CITY _____ **STATE** _____ **ZIP** _____

TEL _____

E-MAIL _____

❏ AMEX   ❏ VISA   ❏ MC   ❏ DISCOVER
❏ CHECK (ENCLOSED)

CHECKS SHOULD BE PAYABLE TO FOREIGN POLICY ASSOCIATION.

CARD NO.

[ ][ ][ ][ ][ ][ ][ ][ ][ ][ ][ ][ ][ ][ ][ ][ ]

SIGNATURE OF CARDHOLDER

EXP. DATE (MM/YY)

PRODUCT	QTY	PRICE	COST
GREAT DECISIONS 2014 TEACHER'S PACKET (1 Briefing Book, 1 Teacher's Guide & 1 DVD) E-MAIL: (REQUIRED) _____		$65	
GREAT DECISIONS 2014 CLASSROOM PACKET (1 Teacher's Packet & 30 Briefing Books) E-MAIL: (REQUIRED) _____		$460	
GREAT DECISIONS 2014 DVD		$40	
Headline Series Nos. 333-334, THE PERSIAN GULF: TRADITION AND TRANSFORMATION (Double issue)		$14.99	
ASSOCIATE MEMBERSHIP		$250	
ANNUAL FUND 2014 (ANY AMOUNT)			

For details and shipping charges, call FPA's Sales Department at (800) 477-5836.

Orders mailed to FPA without the shipping charge will be held.

SUBTOTAL $ [   ]

plus S & H* $ [   ]

TOTAL $ [   ]